The Story of Shoreham

Old Houses formerly in High Street Stockton (On site of "Green Dragon" &c.)

A.B.P.
From an old drawing

The Story of Shoreham

By
Henry Cheal
Hon. Curator and Librarian to the Sussex
Archaeological Society

Illustrated by Arthur B. Packham

COUNTRY BOOKS

Published Country Books
Courtyard Cottage, Little Longstone, Bakewell, Derbyshire DE45 1NN
Tel/Fax: 01629 640670
e-mail: dickrichardson@country-books.co.uk

ISBN 1 898941 96 3

© 2005 Country Books
First published 1921 Combridges, Hove

This is a facsimile of the first edition of 1921.
This should be borne in mind when considering
the chronological context of the subject matter

Printed and bound by:
Antony Rowe Ltd.
Eastbourne

To all those my Fellow-townsmen who fared forth to the Greatest War known to History.

And to the memory of those Gallant Heroes who fell, nobly fighting in the Cause of Freedom and Justice, this Story of Shoreham is dedicated.

PREFACE

To very many people the study of the past seems to be a valley of dry bones which they are more than content to leave unexplored. Indeed, it is said to be one of the peculiarities of the average Englishman that he knows little or nothing of the history of his own town or village, or even of his own country, although it is the most interesting in the world.

"To keep the past alive for us is the pious duty of the historian." So says a well-known writer, and in so far as this small corner of England is concerned, my aim has been to clothe again the dry bones of history with life.

Recent researches at the Record Office and elsewhere have added not a little to our knowledge of the earlier history of this ancient Sussex sea-port. The Patent Rolls, Close Rolls and Assize Rolls have been carefully examined and Shoreham cases copied from them.

The Assize Rolls for the reigns of Henry III. and the first three Edwards contain many references to our subject, but are, on the whole, somewhat disappointing. Most of them relate to disseisin of lands, but beyond the names of the parties concerned in the disputes and that the property was in Old or New Shoreham—as the case may have been—we learn nothing of its precise situation. To give all such cases in detail would mean a monotonous repetition which it is well to avoid, and therefore, they have been used somewhat sparingly. On the other hand full use has been made of those cases dealing with the privilege of Sanctuary, and those of assault and robbery, which are of considerable interest.

Extracts will be found from Wills at Somerset House, the State Papers and other sources of historical information preserved at the Record Office, the British Museum and elsewhere.

PREFACE

Among numerous published works, to which reference has been made and from which I have freely quoted, are the Sussex Archaeological Collections, the Victoria History of Sussex, Social England, History of the Blaker Family (W. C. Renshaw), Science Arcady (Grant Allen), the Dictionary of National Biography, tc. Also certain MSS. relating to the history of the family of Poole of Old and New Shoreham, to which, by the courtesy of Capt. Herbert Ross Hooper, I have been allowed free access.

For many biographical details of the Shoreham M.P.'s and notes on the Parliamentary History of the town I am indebted to Mr. John Patching, of Lewes. My thanks are also due to Mr. Burton Green, Mr. A. F. W. Eade and Mr. E. F. Salmon.

The Story of Shoreham has been written during the somewhat scanty leisure of the past few years. I am conscious that, whatever measure of success it may meet with, will be due in no small degree to the clever pen-work of Mr. Arthur B. Packham, whose pictures illustrate its pages, and to whom I am indebted for many practical suggestions and much valuable assistance.

HENRY CHEAL.

CONTENTS

	PAGE.
PREFACE	vii.
CHAPTER I.	1

The Adur Valley and its Ancient People—A Stone-age "Sheffield"—A British Prince—Traces of the Roman Occupation—The Saxons—Steyning a Port—Bramber Castle—Sele Priory—Ancient Bridges.

CHAPTER II. 18

The Town and Harbour in the Middle Ages—Changes in Coastline—The Origin of New Shoreham—Havoc Wrought by the Sea—Situation of the Mediaeval Harbour — Decline of the Town — Excused from Taxation—Revival of its Industry—Old Roads into the Town.

CHAPTER III. 35

Old Shoreham—A Royal Manor—Held by Princes of Wales—Shoreham Marsh—The Ferry—The Timber Bridge—Picturesque Cottages—Former Water-mills and Windmills—Ancient Litigation.

CHAPTER IV. 50

Old Erringham—Held of King Edward the Confessor—Early Records—Will of John Cobye—Bellingham Family—The Old Manor House—The Chapel—A Restless Spirit—New Erringham House—An Old Coach-road.

CHAPTER V. 63

Old Shoreham *alias* "Ruspar"—Buckingham Family in Early Deeds—Blaker, Monk, and Bridger Families—Buckingham House.

CHAPTER VI. 69

New Shoreham—The Manor and the Town—De Braose and De Mowbray families—Former and Present Government of the Town—Fairs and Markets—Market Houses — Suspension Bridge — Inns — Old Houses — Place-names—Bungalow Town.

CHAPTER VII. 82

Grants to Ancient Religious Houses — Knights Hospitallers and Templars—Carmelite Priory—Its Gradual Ruin by the Sea—Hospitals of St. Catherine, St. Saviour, and St. James.

CHAPTER VIII. 91

The Ancient Ferry at New Shoreham—The "Marlipins" — Forgotten Street-names — Old-time Traders—Custody of the "Cocket"—Wool-trade—"Owlers."

CONTENTS

CHAPTER IX. ... 102
Scenes in the Market Place—Assault and Robbery—Murder—The Church as a City of Refuge—Revenge for Piracy.

CHAPTER X. ... 114
A Gateway to the Sea—King John's Visits to the Town—Maritime Traffic—Thirteenth Century "Ship-carpenters"—Piracy—Ships for the Wars of Edward III.—A "Pilgrim" Ship—An Action Fought off Shoreham—Recommendations for "Defence"—The Royal Fugitive—The King and the Quaker.

CHAPTER XI. ... 136
Privateering—Prize Ships—Loyal Privateers—Smuggling—Custom Houses.

CHAPTER XII. ... 147
Ships of Shoreham—Revival of Industry in Elizabeth's Reign—Ships for East India Company—A Relic of the Shipwrights' Art—A Seventeenth Century Builder and his Ships—Men-of-War—Later Builders—The Last of Her Kind—Concrete Ships and "Mystery" Towers—The Harbour in Modern Times—Oyster Industry—Steam Packets—War's Effect on Harbour Trade.

CHAPTER XIII. ... 164
The Churches of Shoreham—Scanty Documentary History—St. Nicholas, Old Shoreham—Saints in a Window—An Elizabethan Captain and his Family—"Rizpah"—The Parish Clerk and the Sailor King—The Church of St. Mary de Haura—The "Atonement" of William de Braose—The Ruined Nave—Chantry Property—Memorial Inscriptions—Vicars of Old and New Shoreham—Lancing College—The Free Churches—The Church of St. Peter (R.C.).

CHAPTER XIV. ... 207
Parliamentary History—Payment to Members in Early Times—Eighteenth Century Bribery and Corruption—Extravagance at Elections—List of the Members for New Shoreham—Biographical Notes.

CHAPTER XV. ... 245
Coaching Days—The Carrier and his Cart—Opening of the Railway—Shoreham in the 'Fifties—The Swiss Gardens—Some Old Customs.

CHAPTER XVI. ... 258
Aviation—The Military Camp—Memorials to the Fallen.

INDEX ... 265

LIST OF ILLUSTRATIONS

	PAGE
OLD HOUSES FORMERLY IN HIGH STREET ... ... *Frontispiece*	
ON THE RIVER ADUR	3
SOMPTING CHURCH	8
HIGH STREET, STEYNING	11
BRAMBER	13
BEEDING CHURCH AND SITE OF SELE PRIORY FROM THE RIVER	14
SHOREHAM	18
COAST-LINE MAPS—13TH TO 19TH CENTURY	20-21
LANCING	24
KINGSTON PARISH CHURCH	33
COTTAGE BACKS, OLD SHOREHAM	36
COTTAGE AT OLD SHOREHAM	37
COTTAGES IN MALTHOUSE LANE, OLD SHOREHAM	40
CHURCH AND BRIDGE, OLD SHOREHAM	41
OLD COURT CUPBOARD AT OLD SHOREHAM	43
HOUSE AT LITTLE BUCKINGHAM	45
AT LITTLE BUCKINGHAM	46
OLD ERRINGHAM, WEST SIDE	51
ARMS OF BELLINGHAM	52
OLD ERRINGHAM, SOUTH END	54
REMAINS OF MEDIÆVAL BUILDING AT OLD ERRINGHAM	57
EXTERIOR AND INTERIOR OF OLD BUILDING AT OLD ERRINGHAM	58
PLAN AND ELEVATION OF OLD BUILDING	59
NEW ERRINGHAM	61
ARMS OF BLAKER	64
ARMS OF MONK	65
BUCKINGHAM PARK IN 1782	66
ARMS OF BRIDGER	67
AT SHOREHAM	73
THE SHOREHAM SHILLING	75
THE SADDLER'S SHOP, EAST STREET	77
OLD COTTAGES, FORMERLY ON SITE OF CATHOLIC SCHOOL	79

LIST OF ILLUSTRATIONS

	PAGE
THE FERRY	80
SEAL OF THE HOSPITAL OF ST. SAVIOUR	89
"ROGER DEMANDED FREIGHTAGE FOR THE FERRY"	92
HIGH STREET, SHOREHAM	93
THE COCKET	99
"BEAT, AND KNOCKED HIM TO THE GROUND"	104
THE ASSAULT ON SIR RICHARD DE PESHALE'S HOUSE	107
ISABEL CLAIMS THE PRIVILEGE OF SANCTUARY	109
"THEY WERE THROWN OUT OF THE BOAT"	112
THE KING'S RETINUE ACCOMPLISHED THE LONG JOURNEY FROM LINCOLN TO SHOREHAM IN SAFETY	115
KING CHARLES' COTTAGE, SOUTHWICK	132
"FELL DOWN UPON HIS KNEES AND KIST MY HANDS"	134
"THE FISH PRIZE LIES AT WASTE AND SAVOURETH"	139
"THEY OFTEN DRINK THEIR MAJESTIES' HEALTH"	140
YE OLDE "SUSSEX PAD" INN	142
THE CUSTOM HOUSE AT NEW SHOREHAM (IN 1830)	145
OLD CHIMNEY-PIECE, SHOREHAM	148
THE BARQUE "BRITANNIA" ON THE STOCKS AT THE OLD SHIPYARD	157
OLD SHOREHAM CHURCH	166
IN OLD SHOREHAM CHURCH	168
MEMORIAL BRASS IN OLD SHOREHAM CHURCH	172
ARMS OF CAPTAIN RICHARD POOLE, THE YOUNGER	173
CHURCH OF ST. MARY DE HAURA (EXTERIOR)	180
INTERIOR OF THE CHURCH	184
MEMORIAL BRASS IN THE CHURCH OF ST. MARY DE HAURA	188
IN SHOREHAM CHURCH (THE TOWER ARCHES)	190
LANCING COLLEGE FROM THE RIVER	204
"THE CRIER WENT THROUGH THE TOWN"	208
HIGH STREET, SHOREHAM, EAST END	246
THE CARRIER	248
BALL ROOM AND LODGE, SWISS GARDENS	253
MAP OF SHOREHAM, CIRCA 1350	*End of volume*

CHAPTER I.

THE ADUR VALLEY AND ITS ANCIENT PEOPLE—A STONE-AGE "SHEFFIELD"—A BRITISH PRINCE—TRACES OF THE ROMAN OCCUPATION—THE SAXONS—STEYNING A PORT—BRAMBER CASTLE—SELE PRIORY—ANCIENT BRIDGES.

Although you will doubtless find many people who will tell you that any attempt to re-construct the period prior to Caesar's arrival in these islands is quite hopeless and mere foolish guesswork, it will be necessary for our purpose to say something concerning it. The Adur Valley was the centre of a primitive civilization and the Story of Shoreham begins far back in that distant past usually termed Pre-historic.

It is true—as one writer remarks—" we have still much to learn about the race on whose shores the Roman conqueror planted his eagles, but enough is known to tell us that Caesar descended upon a country which had already been the scene of repeated invasions and successive conquests, so that in the men who resisted the Romans we now see something more than a mere horde of naked woad-bedaubed savages."

The Neolithic (later stone age) population of Britain—a darkwhite race—are said to have come from the deserts of the east, from Arabia and Egypt, and to have followed the shores of the Mediterranean in journeying hitherward. Any attempt to fix a date for this immigration is quite hopeless. It was far back in the distant ages, but this ancient people had settlements in this part of the country which we now call Sussex, in the coast district between the Downs and the sea and in the river valleys.

On the alluvial lowlands of the Adur estuary they grew in abundance those cereals upon which they largely depended for their daily bread. At Cissbury Hill they obtained in abundance the flints for the manufacture of their stone hatchets and other implements.

These flints they obtained by mining in the chalk in a most expert manner, though their mining tools consisted solely of deerhorn picks and wedges and shovels made from the shoulderblades of oxen.

THE STORY OF SHOREHAM

With these tools shafts were sunk and the whole hillside honeycombed with tunnels in the work of excavating the copious material found in the chalk. Some of the actual tools used in these mining operations are now in the British Museum, while flint implements from Cissbury are to be seen in the Museums of Brighton and Lewes.

No one can tell us the duration of this industry at Cissbury, but the large number of implements found point to long and continued operations and its occupation as a factory. Some say that it must have lasted several thousand years. It was the Sheffield of the flint industry in Neolithic times.

Another race threw up the great hill-fort and in so doing cut the imposing ditch of their citadel through the filled-in shafts of the older mines.

If you have not already visited Cissbury, do so. You may follow the track over Lancing Downs and beyond, and will tread much the same path by which the primitive yet cunning artizan made his way up from the river of "running waters" to the flint factory on the hill-top. The place cannot fail to impress you. It was once teeming with a busy industry, the evidence of which is to be found in the countless flint chips and flakes scattered broadcast over the whole hill-side. When the Romans came stone weapons had long been superseded by bronze and iron, and still to-day this monument, sublime in its solitary grandeur, remains to speak to us of a people and a period so remote from our own time, as to make the Roman invasion of Britain appear in comparison as an event of yesterday.

At the time that this flint factory was in full swing we may reasonably conclude that the coast district from the Chichester marshland to Pevensey was not consolidated under a single rule, but that there existed chieftainships over several villages, confined for the most part to single river valleys. Such a principality in the fertile valley of the Adur and the coast strip from Worthing to Brighton would roughly correspond to the modern Rape of Bramber, possessing its own boundary of forest and its own camp of refuge on the hill-top.

Now the flint-workers of Cissbury knew nothing of metals; the iron ore in the almost inaccessible Weald was of no use to them. If aware of its existence they were totally ignorant of its possibilities. Copper and tin were alike unknown to them and therefore they could not manufacture bronze.

A STONE-AGE "SHEFFIELD"

The secret of the manufacture of bronze was probably first discovered in Asia, where tin and copper were most workable, and thence spread to Europe, where it was quickly adopted by the Aryan Celts. Having learnt the use of bronze certain great improvements followed, notably amongst others an immense advance in the art of boat-building. The men of the Bronze Age soon constructed vessels which enabled them to cross the narrow seas and invade Britain. Their superior weapons gave them an enormous advantage over the natives, armed only with their polished flint hatchets, and in a very short time they over-

ran nearly the whole island. This great invasion is said to have taken place some 1,000 or 1,500 years before the Christian era.

Thus the people of Britain came in two great waves. First the short dark Iberian (who mined for flints at Cissbury) and then the mighty Celt who conquered him. Thence forward the two peoples existed side by side, for the Celts did not exterminate those whom they had conquered, but made slaves of them, and these slaves learned the tongue of their masters.

At the date of the first Roman invasion these two distinct

THE STORY OF SHOREHAM

types of people were to be found in Sussex—a Celtic aristocracy of Aryan type, round-headed, fair-haired and blue-eyed, together with Celticised Euskarian or half-cast serfs, the latter retaining the long skulls and dark complexion of their aboriginal ancestors.

Under the bronze-weaponed Celts a more advanced type of civilization became possible, and a more extended chieftainship resulted from the improved weapons and consequent military power, and much of Britain became amalgamated into considerable kingdoms, some of which seem to have spread over several modern shires.

But while this was generally so, Sussex, enclosed by its barrier of forest, seems to have remained a single little principality of itself, held at least in later times by a tribe known to the Romans as the Regni, whose prince or king had his seat of government at Regnum (Chichester).

The Celts occupied the fertile valleys and alluvial slopes, cut down the woods by the river-sides and built their more regular camps of refuge upon the Downs for protection from the neighbouring tribes, so that we find the traces of their occupation mainly confined to the Downs and the seaward slopes.

In the polished Stone Age the district had been self-supporting because of its possession of flint. In the Bronze Age it was dependent on other places through its non-possession of copper and tin. During the former period it may have exported weapons from Cissbury ; during the latter it must certainly have imported the material of weapons from Cornwall and Gaul.

Before the Romans came iron as well as tin was found and manufactured in Britain and bronze axes had been discarded in favour of iron swords and spears. There seems to have been a considerable intercourse with the continent and among the agricultural exports were cattle and hides, wheat and barley.

An important personage at the period of Julius Caesar's invasion, reigning over part of Britain, was Commius. This prince appears to have had three sons : Tincommius, who was king of the Regni (practically answering to the present county of Sussex) ; Verica, whose sway was over the eastern part of the Atrebates (Berkshire and the north part of Wilts), and Eppilos, who ruled over Kent.

Tincommius was king of the Regni when Caesar came and his coins have been found at various places, both in East and West Sussex, in our own immediate neighbourhood, at Bramber

TRACES OF THE ROMAN OCCUPATION

and Steyning, and on Lancing Downs. Coins of Verica have been found at several places in Sussex, including Shoreham and Steyning and on Lancing Downs. By this we may infer that the Regni and the Atrebates traded one with the other and that by the time the two brothers, Tincommius and Verica, ruled over their respective principalities some sort of overland communication—probably by track-ways through the dense forests—existed.

It is only reasonable to suppose that when the Romans came they found considerable village settlements on the shores of the Adur—at Shoreham, Botolphs, Bramber, and Steyning—although these names were then unknown. It was then less a river and more an arm of the sea, which ran inland as far as Steyning, and its great importance must very early have been appreciated by them.

If the site of the Roman Portus Adurni is to be found in these waters it may have embraced the whole of this estuary. Some place the actual Roman station in the neighbourhood of Aldrington and tell us that, like the lost " Atlantis," it long since sank beneath the waves. Others favour Bramber, and some say that its site was at Shoreham—Old Shoreham. On the analogy of other Roman ports in Britain the latter would seem to be the most likely place. It was but a short distance up the fair-way, but so far from the open sea as to give complete security to the vessels of the period. The name New Shoreham sufficiently proves that the first wharfing must have been higher up the river, and although the first opportunity for fortification was at Bramber, where it is quite likely that the Roman military governor of the district had his seat, we have the analogy of every port upon the Sussex rivers of *a harbour forward of the first fortification.*

But there are some who tell us that we must seek elsewhere than in this neighbourhood for Portus Adurni and that the river name " Adur " was first applied to these waters by Drayton in his poem " Polyolbion " (A.D. 1612). Up to that time, they say, it was usually known as the " Sore " (as in Holinshed's Chronicle, A.D. 1577). It is referred to in documents of the reign of Henry VIII. merely as " a certain river " and has been named at various times Bramber Water, Beeding River, Alder and Shoreham River. From this evidence it is argued that no Roman soldier ever set foot within miles of the Adur Valley and no Roman galley was ever seen upon its restless waves.

THE STORY OF SHOREHAM

Alternative names for rivers, and especially for particular reaches of rivers, are of course quite common but they do not exclude one general name. The word Adur is of Celtic origin, "Dwyr" = running or flowing waters, and sufficiently describes the river as a whole, for it is seldom at rest. We may reasonably conclude that even before the Romans came and made it their Portus Adurni it was known as the Dwyr, the running waters, "hurrying down to the live sea" as one has so aptly written of it.

We know that the Roman engineers, nearly two thousand years ago, made that great military highway from the east gate of Regnum (Chichester) to London Bridge. We call it the "Stane Street" and much of it is still in use. From this road, in the neighbourhood of Croydon, there was apparently a junction which led directly to the Adur mouth. Of this highway two short sections have been discovered and they are in direct alignment towards Shoreham. Apparently the way was across St. John's Common (Burgess Hill) to the Hassocks sand pits, where many fine specimens of Romano-British pottery and Samian ware have recently been found. These are now exhibited in the Sussex Archaeological Museum at Lewes. The road ascended the South Downs by way of the old track up the Saddlescombe side of the Devil's Dyke and made for Portslade (Portus ladus = the way to the port) and so to the Adur mouth, joining or crossing a highway which ran from east to west through the county—from Anderida (Pevensey) to Regnum (Chichester). The latter highway probably crossed the Ouse at Lewes, which has been claimed as the site of the small Roman town of Mutuantonis.

Several specimens of Romano-British Pottery now in the Brighton Museum were found during the erection of the soldiers' huts north-east of Buckingham Park.

Mention may be made of several important Roman finds in the neighbourhood. Just across the river where the Downs rise towards Lancing Clump the foundations of a Roman villa, a bath and interments, were discovered in the year 1828. Numerous coins were also turned up at the same time, and these, ranging from the date of the Emperor Claudius (A.D. 41-54) to Gallienus (A.D. 260), seem to indicate a long possession of the spot by the Romans. Only a few years ago the foundations of a Roman temple were discovered amidst the trees at Chancton-

THE SAXONS

bury Ring. In the course of the excavation of these remains coins were again found and these cover a period from the reign of Nero (A.D. 54-68) to Gratian (A.D. 375-383). Roman remains have also been discovered at Botolphs. In the year 1800 about one hundred Roman urns were found on Beeding Hill, near the confines of Edburton and Old Shoreham parishes. Roman coins innumerable have been and are continually found in Shoreham. Worthing has yielded important finds of pottery and a notable incised stone now in Lewes Castle Museum. The discovery of a Roman villa at Preston (Brighton) and another at West Blatchington, near Hove, seems to suggest that the highway from east to west before mentioned ran through those places.

From the foregoing we may infer that Roman civilisation influenced this part of the country to a considerable extent. Doubtless the native population were for the most part engaged in agriculture and other useful arts and as the centuries passed they almost forgot the use of arms.

So it was that after four hundred and fifty years, when Imperial Rome was distressed by troubles nearer home and was compelled to withdraw her legions from these shores, the Britons were left without military protection and became an easy prey to their enemies. In a few years horde after horde of Saxon pirates swooped down upon the unprotected shores of Britain. Very soon their keels were swarming into the creeks and penetrating up the rivers of this county.

In the year A.D. 477 the Saxon warrior, Ella, and his three sons, Cymen, Wenceling, and Cissa, "came to the land of Britain" and landed at Cymensora, the modern name of which is Kynor, near West Wittering. Another and somewhat later landing is said to have been at Shoreham. Tradition tells us that one of those sanguinary but fruitless struggles between the Romanized Britons and the Saxon invaders took place on Slonk Hill, north-east of Shoreham, and that the origin of the word "slonk" is to be found in the Saxon "slaught." The term "slonk-butcher" is still used in some parts of the country. It would appear that the hill-name has therefore some connection with slaughter North-east of the Slonk is another hill known as "Thunder's Barrow," possibly derived from Thor, the God of Thunder, to whom the Saxons offered sacrifices—it may be on this hill—before they accepted Christianity as their religion.

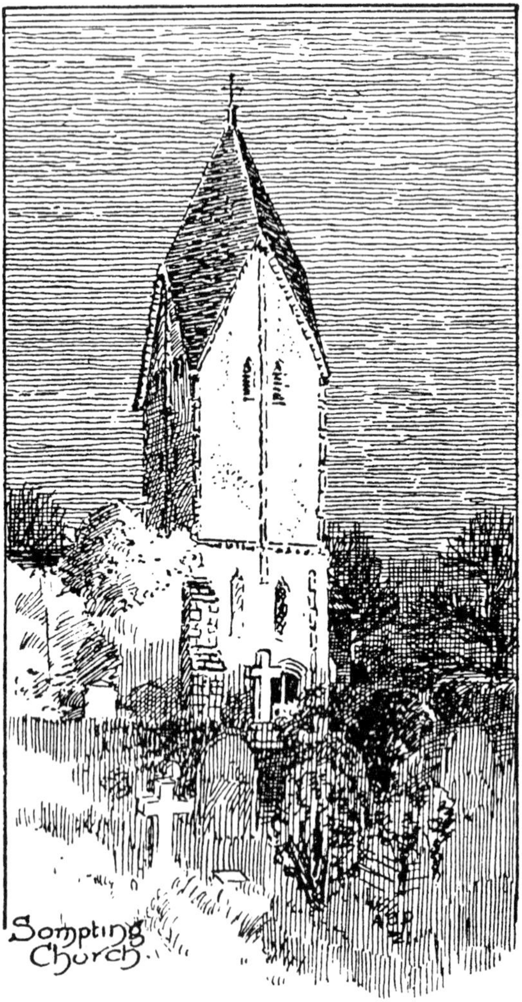
Sompting Church.

THE SAXONS

Having been successful in establishing himself in the possession of the district comprised in the modern counties of Sussex and Surrey, Ella formed his newly acquired province into a kingdom, of which he became the first king. Cissa succeeding him in the government of this province, to which the part of Hampshire bordering on Sussex was afterwards added, made Regnum his chief place of residence. From this circumstance the name of the city was, out of compliment to him, shortly afterwards changed to Cissa-ceaster, from whence it derived its present name of Chichester.

In the valley of the Adur Saxon settlements soon began to appear, most of them doubtless on the sites of earlier villages whose inhabitants had been driven out or slaughtered by the invaders. In addition to establishing themselves on the old hill-forts on the high points of the Downs we find them settling at and naming many places in the neighbourhood and elsewhere. The Saxon terminations "ham," "ing" and "ton," common in the Adur Valley, indicate the abode of Saxon communities.

After the introduction of Christianity by St. Wilfrid, the exiled Bishop of York (A.D. 680) and its spread all through the South Saxon kingdom came the building of churches. These, of course, were at first of wood, but as the centuries passed they were replaced by more worthy buildings. The work of Saxon masons may still be seen at many places in Sussex and near at hand—Old Shoreham, St. Botolphs, further up the Adur, and at Sompting.

During the eighth century a somewhat remarkable man appeared in the Adur Valley, a Saxon saint named Cuthman. As a youth, before his coming thither, he dwelt in the West Saxon Kingdom and there tended his father's sheep. It was his daily custom to perform a miracle. On the approach of mid-day the shepherd boy would describe with his crook a circle round the flock, bidding the sheep in the name of the Lord not to stray beyond it during his absence at dinner.

After his father's death Cuthman and his mother were left in great poverty and were forced to leave their home. They set forth travelling eastward but the aged mother was too infirm to journey in any other way than by means of a wheelbarrow-couch, which her dutiful son constructed for her comfort and which he partially supported by means of a cord over his shoulders.

As they were thus passing through a certain hayfield the cord broke and Cuthman replaced it with elder twigs and thereupon was greatly ridiculed by the haymakers. This ill-timed levity was at once severely punished. A heavy storm forthwith broke over the field and destroyed the crop. Ever after, says the legend, a rain-storm visited that field at haymaking time.

Cuthman and his mother journeyed on and came to Steyning. Again the cord broke and, as one writer says, "let down the old lady." This second mishap was supposed by the monkish chronicler to have been a divine intimation to the saint that his journey should now end, and possibly charmed with the delightful surroundings, he decided to settle there.

In due time St. Cuthman began to erect a church, but while the work was in progress a beam shifted and much of the building collapsed. Whilst he ruefully contemplated this disaster and thought on the vast amount of labour necessary to make it good, a stranger suddenly appeared and pointed out how the damage might be speedily repaired. Cuthman and his labourers followed the advice of the stranger, who also worked with them, until at length the sacred edifice was finished and beautified.

When all was complete the saint fell at the feet of this great artizan and asked his name. "I am He in Whose honour thou hast raised this temple," he replied, and then vanished.

In the fulness of time Cuthman, with filial piety, laid his aged mother to rest, and later was himself buried in the church which he had built. Over his bones a shrine was erected and here pilgrims from far and near paid their devotions, and many wonderful cures were claimed to have been vouchsafed to the crippled and sick. The Saint's anniversary was anciently kept at Steyning on February 8th. In the church porch may be seen what is most probably Cuthman's grave-slab. It bears a rude double cross in low relief and is certainly of pre-Conquest date. A second slab, probably as old, may have covered the grave of the Saint's mother.

So great was Cuthman's influence on the fortunes of the charming little town of Steyning that for several hundred years after his death, and certainly as late as the beginning of the 12th century, it was known as St. Cuthman's Port.

Here in the year 858 King Ethelwulph, the father of Alfred the Great, was buried, but the body was afterwards taken up and re-buried at Winchester.

King Alfred had estates at Steyning and Beeding and bequeathed them to two of his nephews. The Steyning property

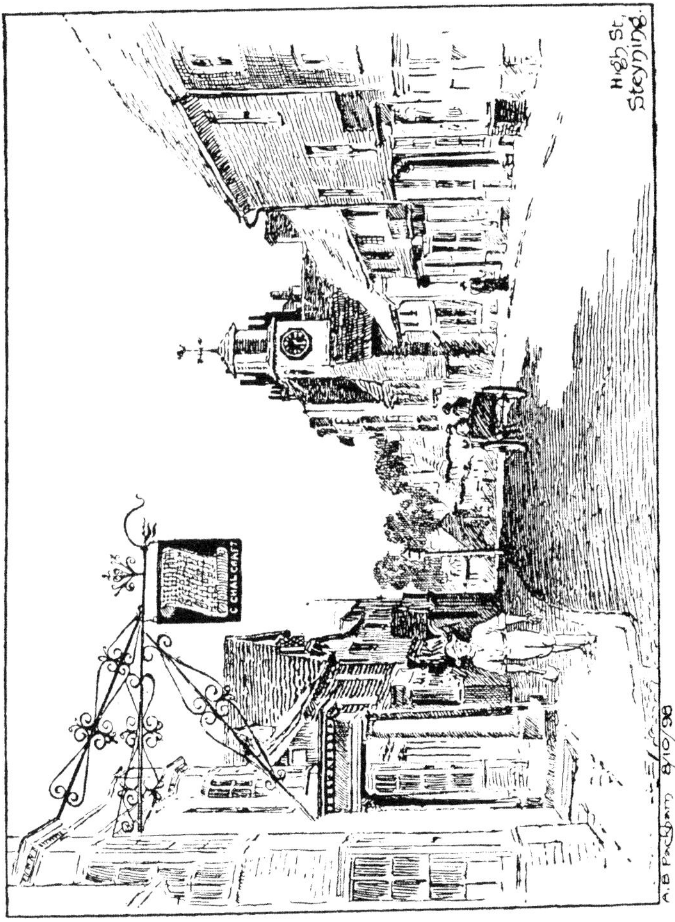
High St,
Steyning.
A.B Packham 8/10/98

THE STORY OF SHOREHAM

afterwards reverted to the Crown and Edward the Confessor granted it to the Abbey of Fécamp, but afterwards revoked the grant at the instance of Earl Godwin, whose son, King Harold, held Steyning until his death at the Battle of Hastings. The Conqueror restored the estates to the monks of Fécamp, who thereupon sent over some of their number to form a priory or cell at Steyning. In process of time the church built by St. Cuthman gave place to one of nobler proportions erected by these monks and its beautiful arcades and lofty chancel arch remain to-day, a very fine example of Norman style. The Abbot of Fécamp had remarkable privileges in Steyning, among which may be noted that of punishing felons, hanging murderers, and disposing of their property. The town was important and in those days actually had more houses than Southampton or Bath. In the days of Edward the Confessor money was minted at Steyning.

The Saxon kings had a stronghold at Bramber and at King's Barns near at hand a farmstead. Now but a picturesque village the former place possesses nothing of its ancient importance, yet this must have been considerable. The arm of the sea running up to Steyning was here of great breadth and washed the castle mound, whereon after the Conquest William de Braose, a kinsman of the Conqueror, to whom had been granted the territory known as the Rape of Bramber, erected his feudal stronghold. The area covered by this fortress was considerable, and its grim towers frowned upon the waters of the Adur for centuries, but to-day a few ivy-clad fragments are all that remain to tell us of its former grandeur. Of the little Norman church outside the castle walls, nave and tower are all that is preserved of a former cruciform building.

To the position of this stronghold at Bramber and to the influence of its powerful lords, many of whom figure in the early annals of English History as eminent barons, statesmen, and crusaders, the town of New Shoreham owes much of its early development and prosperity. It became and remained for some centuries one of the great highways to the Continent and one of the most flourishing sea ports.

William de Braose, viewing with jealous eye the power wielded at Steyning by the Abbot of Fécamp, where he also held some lands, determined to set up a religious establishment of his own. He founded, almost beneath his castle walls but on the opposite

BRAMBER

side of the river and, therefore, in Beeding, a Priory to be dependent upon the Benedictine Abbey of St. Florent, near Saumur in Anjou. The foundation charter of this Priory of Beeding, or Sele, as it was more generally called, was dated 1075, and therein are mentioned the churches of St. Peter "of the old bridge" (de Veteriponte), St. Peter at Sele, St. Nicholas

Bramber Feb. 1896

at Bramber, and St. Nicholas, Old Shoreham, which were granted to the monks of St. Florent to enable them to establish the Priory.

The situation of "the old bridge" mentioned in the charter is a matter of much uncertainty. While some maintain that it was at Bramber, many are disposed to believe that it carried the road across the river at Botolphs and that the church of St. Peter

Beeding Church & Site of Sele Priory, from the River. A. B. Packham

SELE PRIORY

de Veteriponte stood upon it. Some believe that it was at this point that the Roman highway from east to west crossed over, and that if "the old bridge" was not the actual Roman bridge it was its successor. The designation "old" leads to the conclusion that the bridge was ancient in 1075.

The first mention of a bridge actually at Bramber appears in an agreement of the year 1103, between the Abbot of Fécamp and Philip de Braose. Apparently then but recently erected it proved a great hindrance to the passage of ships up to the port of St. Cuthman. It was agreed that the bridge should be altered in such a manner "that ships shall freely pass at the bridge, going up and down according to such custom and quiet as they enjoyed at the time of King Edward" (the Confessor).

Returning once more to the "old bridge." If this was in existence in 1075, and to go much further back, in Saxon times—and it is only reasonable to believe that somewhere between Shoreham and Steyning the river was crossed by a bridge during that period, otherwise why was it referred to as "old" only nine years after Edward the Confessor's death?—if this was in existence in Saxon times, surely, like the later bridge at Bramber, it must also have offered no small impediment to shipping unless there existed some means of opening or raising part of it to let the ships pass through, and there seems little reason to doubt that such would have been the case. The "old bridge" may have been constructed wholly of timber, much in the same manner as the present Old Shoreham Bridge, or again, its piers may have been of masonry and its spans of timber. The engineers who could construct a drawbridge over the moat of a castle, you may be sure, would not be at fault in devising some means of raising part of a bridge to let ships pass through.

In the year 1220 we find a reference to two bridges. John de Braose granted to the monks of Sele, among other possessions, "both the bridges of Bramber, three vassals with their lands situated on the east side of the little bridge, and five messuages next the greater bridge of Bramber to the west."

In the year 1348, John, Duke of Norfolk, Earl Marshal of England, confirmed to the Prior and monks of Sele, belonging to the Abbey of St. Florent, a grant made by his ancestor, John de Braose, of the Churches of St. Peter, Sele; St. Nicholas, Bramber; St. Nicholas, Old Shoreham; St. Peter de Veteriponte, and St. Mary, Shoreham, tithes in various parishes and "all the grantor's bridges, etc., of Bramber, and timber for repairing the bridges." Also mills and fisheries in Bramber Water, five houses at the Port of Shoreham, and the third part of markets held in that town. The limits of the fisheries in the Water of Bramber are defined in the deed as "from the Church of Old Shoreham to a place called Bedenye."

Three years later Bishop Praty of Chichester held an enquiry into certain charges against the Prior of Sele. This took place in the Chapel of the Blessed Virgin Mary, "upon the bridge at Bramber."

In 1468 John Arundel, Bishop of Chichester, granted an Indulgence of forty days to all persons in his Diocese who contributed to the repair of Bramber Bridge and the causeway of the common road "leading from Bramber towards the eastern parts of England, and from the east to the west, which are now in so bad a condition that they cannot easily be repaired without the alms of the faithful."

Five years after this a charge was brought against Prior Alleyne of Sele that, through his neglect, "the chapel of St. Mary, belonging to the Priory (of Sele) on a certain great bridge of stone in the highway between Bramber and Sele, is, with the bridge, falling to ruin and cannot be sufficiently repaired for forty pounds," a considerable sum in those days.

Four years later, when the Priory of Sele and all its property had been surrendered to Magdalene College, Oxford, there was an agreement between Bishop Waynflete, the founder of the College, and John Cowper of Winchester, mason. The latter was to "stapul and hew" one hundred loads of stone at a quarry in the Isle of Wight, and therewith repair the pillars of Bramber Bridge in Sussex, for which work the Bishop was to pay £19 and provide the carriage of stone and lime and sand, and timber for the scaffolds. As much of the old stone as possible was to be re-used and if more than one hundred loads of new stone was required, then the Bishop was to pay 3s. 4d. for each additional load. It would appear that these repairs were duly carried out, as in January, 1479-80, John Cowper acknowledged the receipt of certain moneys for work already done on the "peris, ventis, archis and wallis" of the bridge, and there was a further agreement to "stapul and hew" sufficient stone for the further repair of the bridge, paid for "at a quarry in the county of Sussex and at a quarry in the Isle of Wight." These repairs were to be fully completed before the following Michaelmas and John Cowper was to receive in payment twenty marks " and a gown !"

This " great bridge of stone " is known to have consisted of several arches, and its foundations were discovered many years ago in making up the causeway which leads from Bramber to the insignificant modern Beeding Bridge, which is now sufficient to carry the road over the river at this point.

CHAPTER II

THE TOWN AND HARBOUR IN THE MIDDLE AGES—CHANGES IN COASTLINE—THE ORIGIN OF NEW SHOREHAM—HAVOC WROUGHT BY THE SEA—SITUATION OF THE MEDIAEVAL HARBOUR—DECLINE OF THE TOWN—EXCUSED FROM TAXATION—REVIVAL OF ITS INDUSTRY—OLD ROADS INTO THE TOWN.

Documents of early date present several variants of the name of our town. Domesday Book (1086) gives Soresham and later we find Soreham, Scoreham, Schorham, Sorham, Shoram and Shorham, but not until late in the 13th century is either "Old" or "New" used as a prefix to distinguish the one place from the other.

In an Assize Roll of 1263 the situation of certain property is described as in "Great Schorham" and a few years later there is a reference to a messuage in "parva Schorham" (Little Schorham).

Shoreham.

These terms doubtless refer to acreage and not to the relative importance of the two places. The area of New Shoreham—even at that time a considerable town—was decidedly "little" in comparison with that of Old Shoreham, of which, indeed, it was formerly part.*

In the 7th year of Edward I. and again in the 15th of Edward II. we find the more ancient place described as "Eldesorham."

* Old Shoreham Parish has an area of 1,923 acres, but New Shoreham has only 135 acres.—("Victoria History of Sussex.")

18

IN THE MIDDLE AGES

The new town usually appears as "Nova Shorham," but we find it written "Neushorham" for the first time in an Assize Roll dated 16th Edward I. (1288).

In 1324 Roger de Stratton was summoned by writ to answer the charge of having unjustly disseised Isabel, daughter of Walter Randolph of Horsham, of her free tenement "in Shorham." Roger de Stratton appeared and actually contended that " the writ need not be responded to, because," said he," the tenement named is in New Shorham and there is no town in this county called Shorham without an adjunct." The same individual, with a desire for accuracy of spelling not usually associated with those early times, says that " he is called Roger de Stretton and not de Stratton as it is put in the writ."

The jurors in the above case said on oath that the tenement in question was in New Shorham, " there being in the county towns called Old and New Shorham and no town called Shorham without one or other of these adjuncts." They also declared that Isabel was seised of the said tenement until Roger unjustly disseised her, to her damage 40 shillings.

While the obverse of the ancient borough seal informs us that the town is " Nova Shorham Brewes " (New Shorham, Braose) a free translation of the legend on the reverse tells us that " this sign of a hulk is worthy of my name, for I am called Hulkesmouth." And so it appears in a deed of 1302 relating to the ferry " across the water of Hulkesmouth with appurtenances in New Shorham," and again in 1457, when John Wody and Robert Oxenbrigge, executors of the will of Richard Wakehurst, and the Prior and Convent of Lewes answer for the profits of 60 acres of land " in the port of Hulkesmouth *alias* Shorham."

The maps showing the outline of the coast and the plan showing the probable arrangement of the town itself during the Middle Ages should perhaps be accompanied by a few words of explanation. At first sight it may appear that there can be very little data to go upon in attempting to re-construct the mediaeval town or in forming an idea of the coast outline in that far-off time. More closely considered, however, certain documentary evidence, combined with existing appearances, seems likely to enable us to form conjectures which may not be far from the truth.

With reference to the maps showing the coast-line. It will be noticed that two lines are drawn through and cross each other

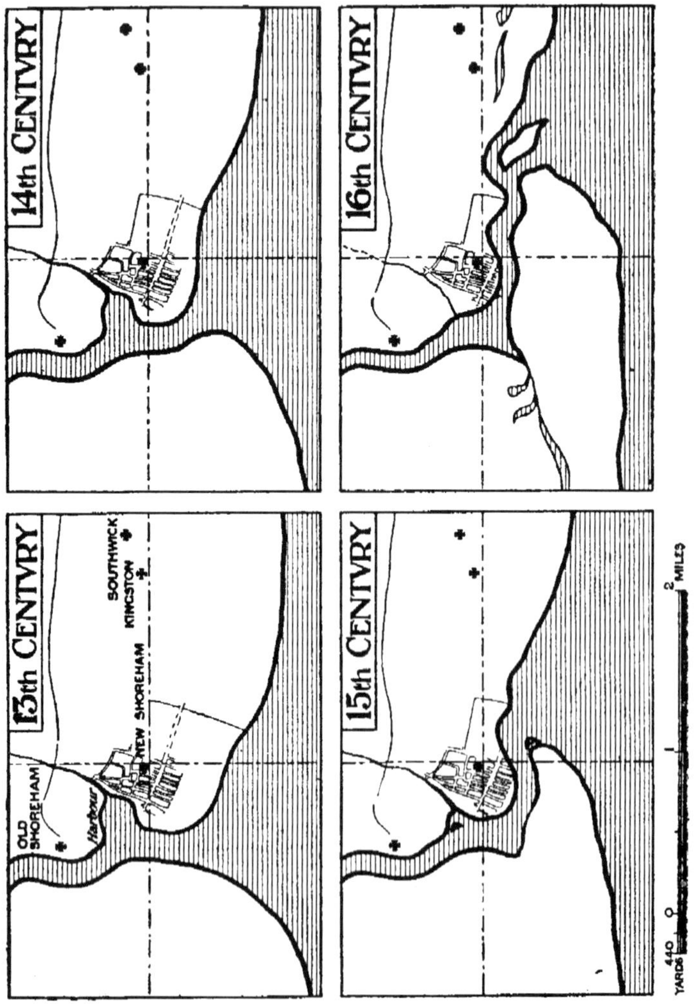
13th CENTVRY
OLD SHOREHAM
Harbour
NEW SHOREHAM
KINGSTON
SOUTHWICK
14th CENTVRY
15th CENTVRY
16th CENTVRY
440 YARDS
0
1
2 MILES

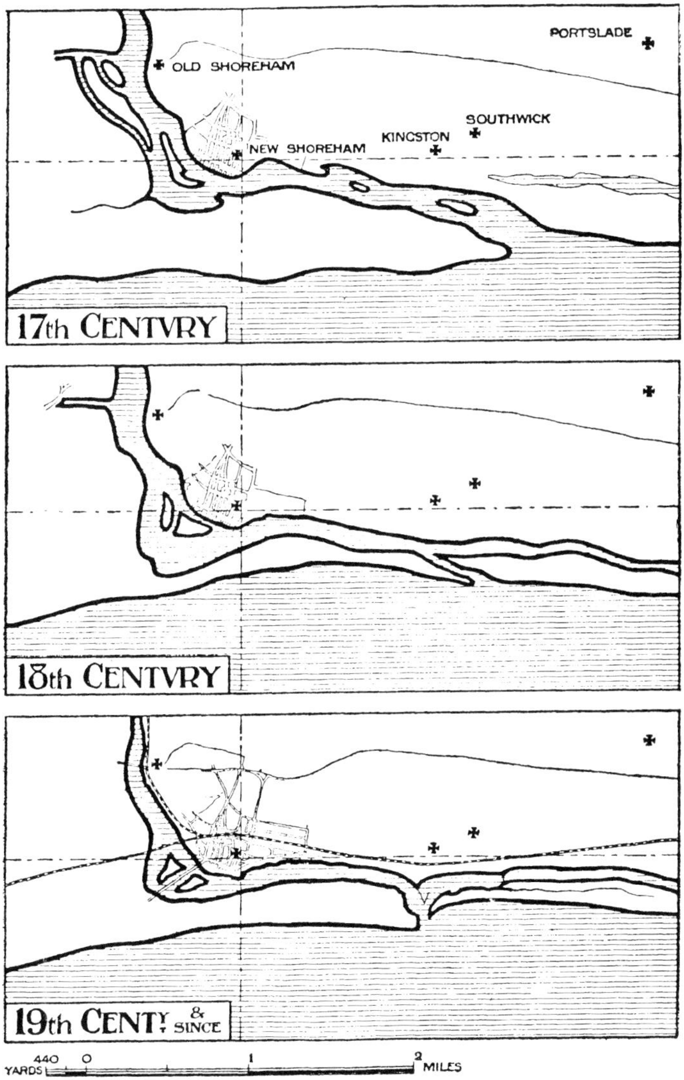
PORTSLADE
OLD SHOREHAM
SOUTHWICK
KINGSTON
NEW SHOREHAM
17th CENTVRY
18th CENTVRY
19th CENTY. & SINCE
440
YARDS
0
1
2
MILES

THE STORY OF SHOREHAM

in the churchyard of New Shoreham ; one runs north and south, the other west and east, and the latter continues slightly south of Kingston Church.

These are intended as datum lines from which the amount of coast alteration may be estimated, being drawn in identically the same places on all the maps. It is not contended, of course, that these maps show all the fluctuations that have taken place, nor do they exhaust the number of different river-mouths that have been formed from time to time. Indeed, almost every few hundred yards between Shoreham and Portslade seems to have provided the site for a mouth at one time or another, and once more at least (in 1760) the river again found its way straight out to sea at Shoreham for a while. The most easterly mouth ever formed seems to have been very nearly three-quarters of the entire distance east from old Aldrington Church to old Hove Church.

The earlier maps of this series are founded on documentary and inferential evidence. The 16th century one is based on the Armada map of that period, while the later ones are based on 17th and 18th century maps, one of the former being a very rare map in the Admiralty Library.*

During the Middle Ages it is likely that a road (now for the most part buried beneath the waves) followed the coast-line from the east, roughly parallel to it, at no great distance inland. The western end of this road is represented in this district by Shoreham High Street, and from a point at the west end of the latter, near the site of the present Norfolk Bridge, probably went the ferry which figures so largely in the early records. This ferry, in all likelihood, crossed the water in the direction of the upper Lancing road rather than further south, although doubtless it also gave access to a by-road leading to the place called Pende, which was in all probability situated south-west of Shoreham. However, the upper Lancing road would be the main objective because it had the advantage of being sufficiently far inland to avoid the "broad-water"—an inlet of the sea which furnished the origin of the name of the parish of Broadwater.

There can be little doubt that in quite early times, and while "Old" Shoreham was still flourishing and much more important than "New," some sort of settlement had sprung up at the river-end of the coast-road mentioned just now. Waiting for

* From Plan kindly lent by Mr. Rocksborough Smith.

HAVOC WROUGHT BY THE SEA

the ferry-boats, for instance, would lead to a shelter of some kind appearing in due course and this would, we can imagine, prove a nucleus for further erections. It would seem that both north and south of the ferry-road the land was laid out in the long narrow acres characteristic of the period for purposes of cultivation. Each acre was 40 perches long by four perches wide (220 yards by 22 yards) and their greatest length lay north and south at right angles to the main road to the ferry. The length was a furlong (a furrow-long), this being the greatest convenient length for ploughing. The existing streets running into the High Street from the north are all approximately a furlong in length and it does not seem at all unlikely that this arrangement was repeated on the south side, for opposite each of the streets is an opening down towards the water as though in continuation of the plan of the north side. This "cultivation basis" may well have originated the plan of the entire town, for probably the first houses to be built would be the farm buildings along the main road, such as we often see in villages to-day where very old buildings still exist.

The long "acres," through continuous ploughing, often took on a gentle curve throughout their whole length. The origin of this is said to have been the pulling round of the team at the end of the furrow and has been noticed in ancient cultivations in other places. It can surely hardly be fanciful to discern in the slight curve of most of Shoreham's ancient streets the surviving result of the same original cause. It was a long S-like curve.

It is probable that to the south of the south group of streets there was still more ground, this being more or less vacant and unbuilt upon. South of this open land would lie the beach and the open waters of the Channel.

You will understand that you are being asked to dismiss from your mind altogether the present aspect of the town south of the High Street and to put in its place something very different and of much greater extent. There is ample warrant for this.

Camden, writing in the 16th century, referring to New Shoreham, says :—"*The greater part also being drowned and made even with the sea is no more to be seen,*" while further evidence, to be quoted presently, shows what a large amount of land has gone, leaving only the broken-off remnant.

What led to this devastation ? The answer to this question

Lancing

HAVOC WROUGHT BY THE SEA

is that the land on part of which Shoreham lay was directly exposed to the waves. At the period of which we are treating no intervening shingle-bank existed to break up the waves of the Atlantic in their progress up the English Channel as now.

With regard to the general coast-line hereabouts in early times there is, of course, no really reliable information. There is among authorities a general agreement that in Roman times the land along the Sussex and Hampshire sea-board extended for some distance (some say a mile) further out than now. There is also documentary evidence—in the Nonae Rolls for instance—of considerable tracts of land having been overwhelmed and lost in early mediaeval times; but many circumstances combine to render such information vague even at its best.

With regard to the sea-frontage of the land about Shoreham, however, there is one very important piece of evidence which helps us to understand what has occurred. From it we may infer that the law of the "eastward drift," which, quite early in the Middle Ages, closed the port of Hastings and pushed the mouth of the Ouse as far east as Seaford, did not affect very much the mouth of the Adur till a much later period. It is likely that this immunity was shared by the Arun as well and was due to the fact that neither the Arun nor the Adur possessed, on its western bank, any strong and steep promontory which could form a base or anchorage for the huge masses of shingle coming up channel to accumulate against, and from which such masses could afterwards work round and operate to stop the river-mouths. The low-lying coastal plain was probably fretted and washed away to a fairly equal extent all along these western shores. Perhaps, too, the "broad water" inlet before mentioned, which gave name to the parish north of Worthing and which converted the site of the latter into a peninsula, took a fairly long time to fill up and may thus have helped to preserve, in the case of Shoreham, the Adur's direct access to the sea for some centuries. However this may be it seems fairly certain that the land, which included the site of the town, lay all through the early Middle Ages immediately upon the sea-shore with no protruding peninsula of beach like the site of Bungalow Town to preserve it from the direct assaults of the sea.

How do we know this ? In the 14th century Sir John de Mowbray, Lord of Bramber, gave to the Carmelite Priory in Shoreham an acre and a half of land south of the High Street to enable them to enlarge their house. In the enquiry held to ascertain whether this grant would be to the prejudice of the King it was elicited that the Priory was situated on the sea-coast on the east side of the town and that it was in imminent danger of being washed away, the ground on which it stood being specially subject to inundations from the sea. Probably the land which was given to the Carmelites comprised one of the long narrow acres lying south of the High Street and at right angles to it, and a half acre alongside of the acre. Indeed, an earlier grant, which had been made to the Knights Hospitallers—of whom later—expressly mentions a "selion" of land extending to the sea ; this term signifying a long narrow strip between other plots. Sir John Mowbray's grant shows that the north side of the property, till then owned by the Carmelites, lay at least a furlong south of the High Street. Now it is hardly reasonable to suppose that the Priory, as at first built, was right upon the shore—in fact other grants to it make it quite clear that there were houses to the south of it, and probably there was vacant land as well before reaching the beach. By the middle of the 14th century, however, everything to the south of the Priory had been washed away and the buildings themselves were threatened.

Now it is practically certain that no such devastation could have been wrought by the ocean unless it had possessed direct and unimpeded access to the town, unhampered by any great projecting spit of land and beach such as exists to-day. It is practically certain, moreover, that this direct access must have been from the south-west, and the damage wrought by the incoming tides on their way up channel. Winds and waves from the opposite quarter, powerful enough for such results, are extremely rare. This, then, is the chief proof that the river ran in a fairly straight course out to sea, with little or no diversion to the east. Possibly the beginnings of a spit of land and beach may have made their appearance by the period in question because the *east* part of the town is spoken of as being the part specially liable to floods. This may indicate that the tides dashed themselves more against the eastern end because the western bank was beginning to form a protection to the west end of the town. Evidently it did not do much in this way, nearly the whole of the place south of the High Street having eventually disappeared.

HAVOC WROUGHT BY THE SEA

As time passed on and the pressure on the east end of the town continued the Priory vanished in the waves; then the land north of it, then part of the High Street, and finally some ground even north of the latter, till the washing away by the sea had formed the low cliff on which the modern houses in New Road are built. There can be little doubt that before this cliff was formed "Tar-mount" sloped gradually southward to the sea. Looking at the town from the summit of the church tower it is evident that what was originally a fairly regular and right-angled arrangement of streets has been obliquely cut into at the east end. The line of the High Street, if continued eastward now, would run out into the water in spite of the fact that some of the land lost here has been regained in more modern times. Moreover, it is quite apparent that the inconvenient "off-set" which connects East Street with the High Street proper can have had no place in the original "plan," it simply owes its existence to the fact that the sea, having eaten back so much of the town, forced the inhabitants to make this irregular little street at a much later date. Hence the property on the south side of this "off-set" stops off, so to say, the main thoroughfare, while foundation walls of ancient buildings have been discovered in excavating in the road at this point, proving that the building line has been set back.

By the time that all this had happened, however (the latter half of the 16th century), Neptune's assaults had begun to work their own cure. A spit of land from the west side of the river-mouth had formed and had been receiving thousands of tons of beach annually. It stretched itself further and further east till at length it masked the whole of the front of the town and protected it from further inroads. The river-mouth then lay opposite a point midway between Shoreham and Kingston Churches, and an eastern arm was forming out of lagoons where the sea had percolated through the beach in the same manner as at Lancing in our own day. A considerable "hump" of beach had collected west and south of the mouth by this time, as may be seen from the map of the coast prepared in connection with the expected swoop of the Spanish Armada. Anon, it seemed as though the sea were anxious to take this protection away from the town again. The outer water's edge began to be driven further and further in till the shingle bank became very narrow from north to south. Had not the system of groyning been introduced

THE STORY OF SHOREHAM

there might have been eventually an entire removal of the shingle spit again and a general break through of sea to river once more. As a matter of fact, at a much later period (the 18th century) the outlet from river to sea was once more almost direct, but as a whole the shingle spit has remained—to receive Bungalow Town.

Meanwhile, to go back to the Middle Ages, what was the effect of all these changes on the fortunes of the town ? It may be described in one word—disastrous ! The prosperity of Shoreham began seriously to suffer, for there was involved in all this the very core of the economic position of the place—the haven. And this brings in the very important question—where was the mediaeval harbour situated ?

The evidence for placing it where shown on the map may be thus given. It is certain that no shelter for ships can have existed along the outer coast-line, and while the river still had almost a straight course out to sea there was clearly nothing that could be called a haven merely in the river itself. The dashing in of the tides from the Channel on the one hand and the powerful current outwards, when the tide turned, on the other would, together, have the effect of making the river-mouth useless for such a purpose. In the absence of strong piers jutting out to sea—and it may well be doubted whether the engineering science available would have been capable of the construction of these—the chief necessity would be a " pocket " of water lying off the main course of the river. Where was such a pocket or back-water to be found ?

Here, where present appearances baffle and the records are silent, tradition and the " old inhabitant " step in. The former asserts that " the river was once at the back of the town," the latter recalls the fact that fragments of a ship were once unearthed in the direction of the cemetery. A further clue comes from the fact that all that part of the town has been found (during drainage excavations, etc.) to lie over a stratum of sea beach. With these indications as a starting point some levels have been taken for the special purpose of this enquiry. These levels disclose the fact that if existing banks were removed the high tides would flow over much of the land on the town-side of the cemetery known as the " Meads " and the former site of the Swiss Gardens. Further investigation shows that a stream (without doubt that referred to as the " Northbourne " in the

28

SITUATION OF THE MEDIAEVAL HARBOUR

list of property belonging to the Chantry in New Shoreham Church) must have come from Old Shoreham Parish, down in this direction. Ancient records mention two water mills in the Parish of Old Shoreham and more particular reference to these will be found elsewhere in these pages. For our present purpose it is sufficient to say that unless they were tidal-mills situated right on the side of the main river—which there is no evidence to show could have been the case—their position in Old Shoreham can have been nowhere else but at Little Buckingham. Here the Northbourne stream (rising still further north up the valley) would supply the ponds, afterwards flowing downwards and outwards in a westerly direction to join the main river over the site of the Meads, the Swiss Gardens, and the area whereon in modern times the adjacent streets were built.

It is possible that, after entering New Shoreham Parish, the same stream supplied yet another water mill, which may have been the main town mill, before emptying itself into the upper end of the broad estuary off the main river, which the levels indicate to have existed hereabouts. All this ground has evidently and inevitably received deposits, which have raised it as the centuries passed considerably above its original level.

Here, then, it is surely no extravagant speculation to infer, was situated the harbour of mediaeval Shoreham. In size it would not have compared badly with some modern ones in constant use for it probably had an area of some nine or ten acres. The ships of the Middle Ages were small compared with modern vessels and, above all, they were (especially in the earlier periods) of very shallow draught. A harbour situated here would have been possessed of all the essential conditions : it would be out of the storms and strong currents of the main river and would always have been able to provide sufficient depth of water. The Northbourne, as a feeder, would have contributed materially to this. It was, no doubt, a considerable stream, flowing down from a valley more thickly wooded than now, though trees are plentiful even at present. In former times, and not so many years back either, the trees are said to have closely approached the town of Shoreham.

Finally it may be remarked that the road leading down beside the track of the Northbourne stream was known formerly as Green Lane. This seems to suggest a connection with "Green Street," the designation of so many old roads, and it leads to

THE STORY OF SHOREHAM

ground known as Stone Gate. This may not imply the former existence of an actual gateway but may well indicate a metalled road forming a " gate " (*i.e.*, an entrance) into the town from this direction. A strip of land accompanying the Green Lane and dividing it from the site of the stream was known as the Green Dam. A "dam" of any sort can scarcely have been required to restrain a small and insignificant stream—and in the direction of its length, too—and seems clear proof that what existed there was a very large volume of water which had to be kept within bounds. This would be the broadening mouth of the Northbourne, above where it emptied into the estuary, and the upper end of the harbour itself.

It is possible that the harbour, in this position, may have served Old Shoreham first. In that case, of course, the theory that " New " Shoreham succeeded " Old " Shoreham, on account of increasing difficulty of access to the harbour, would have to be abandoned.

There had doubtless been some early trouble at the river-mouth—the conflict between the tides would have led to a certain amount of deposit in the river-bed and to a consequent difficulty in entering and leaving the haven at times. In the absence of methods of prevention, familiar to us moderns, a sort of " harbour bar " would have been always in danger of forming.

Some indication of these early troubles may be discerned in the agreement between Philip de Braose and the Abbot of Fécamp before mentioned. The latter had property at Steyning (the " Port of St. Cuthman ") and ships on their way to that place were impeded by a bridge maintained at Bramber by de Braose. The agreement records an arrangement by which the bridge was evidently to be prevented from being an obstruction in the future. Apparently its shape was to be modified (probably by a drawbridge, which could be raised) to let the ships through. What is evident, however, is that in spite of this plan *some obstruction was still anticipated,* and this may have been due to a decrease at times in the amount of water in the river. This was in 1103. Whether tidal difficulties were the cause or not it seems apparent that the trouble did not become really acute till the 14th century. By that time the changes in the coast-line were probably beginning to affect the haven. The gradual formation at last of a spit of land on the west side of the river-mouth, from which the accumulation of beach could extend eastward, no doubt led,

EXCUSED FROM TAXATION

by the time the 15th century was reached, to an "overlap" of the mouth that diverted the latter, about its own width, further east. Probably by then, too, the sand-banks, subsequently known as the Mardyke Bank and the Scurvy Bank, were forming and presently blocked the approach to the haven within the river.

Meanwhile, the destruction of that part of the town situated south of the High Street proceeded apace, being doubtless assisted by the efforts of the partially blocked river to get past the sandbanks now beginning to choke its outlet. Before the latter half of the 15th century Shoreham was, for the time being, ruined.

Indeed, there is an entry in Bishop Robert Read's Register, dated January 16th, 1404, which tells us that the collectors of the 10th were inhibited at that early date from exacting tax from Shoreham, which was one of the benefices described as "destroyed by the sea." In 1432 the inhabitants of the town, shrunk from about 2,500 to a poor 200 or less, petitioned Parliament for a reduction of the assessment of 12s. for the 10th due to the Crown, "as by the encroachment of the sea and other causes they are not able to pay the same," and between the years 1472 and 1496 it is on record that the town was exempted from contributing to the 10ths and 15ths nine times. In 1489 the town was excused from contributing to the tax for raising "an armee of 10,000 archers for the defence of the realme against its auncyen enemies." The petition from Parliament to King Henry VII. anent this matter expressly stated that "the Borough of Newe Shoreham in the Shire of Sussex" was "now greatly wasted by the sea and the inhabitants much impoverished thereby." The towns of Lincoln, Great Yarmouth, and Cambridge were also exempted from the tax on account of their poverty.

The type of vessel coming into use at this time required more depth of water than former ships had done and the haven must have become incapable of accommodating its former number. In the early part of the 15th century some attempt seems to have been made to give a much-needed stimulus to the fortunes of the town. Permission was given to pilgrims to embark from it as well as from Dover. But measures of this kind were valueless in face of the fact that the forces of nature seemed arrayed against the place. The torpor which followed the

THE STORY OF SHOREHAM

destruction of the haven would seem to have lasted throughout most of the 16th century.

But a better state of things was at hand. In the early years of the 17th century the inhabitants seemed to have awakened to the fact that, although the original haven was now quite useless, the projecting shingle-bank along outside the coast-line proper had made the river itself available as a harbour. Advantage was taken of the new formation to transfer the ship-building and harbour works to the south of the town and this step inaugurated a new era of prosperity, the "river at the back of the town " being finally abandoned.

The ship-building principally carried out well on into the 17th century was by Robert Tranckmore, whose yards were near the west end of the High Street on the south side. Hereabouts stood the "Fountain Inn."[*] The carved oak chimney-piece, removed from this house and now fixed in the Town Hall, has upon it a carving of the Arms of the Shipwrights' Company and it is not unlikely that Tranckmore was a member of that body and that he had the Arms carved and placed in what was possibly his own residence. The Arms were granted to the Company in 1605 and this approximately fixes the date of the carving—or rather corresponds with the probable date of it and with Tranckmore's occupancy of the house.

One or two other points in the plan of mediaeval Shoreham may be touched upon. The two Hospitals are shown on roads forming entrances into the town from the east. Institutions of this character were generally so placed and although there may be no definite historical reference to the actual sites the voice of tradition is not silent.

As to the question of roads leading to the town, it would appear that, in addition to the highway already alluded to as nearer the coast and conducting to the ferry, there was probably another road leading from Brighton past Aldrington, Southwick, and Kingston Churches to Shoreham. Reaching the latter it divided, the branch on the right or upper side ascending to Old Shoreham and the hills, the other turning down into New Shoreham on the left. The first-named branch would have

[*] The reader is referred to the Map of the Town at the end of book. It is not claimed that the 14th century existence of all the Inns shown can be guaranteed, or that the names of the various plots of land in the Town can be proved mediaeval. At the same time there is nothing improbable in the theory—place-names usually go back a surprising way.

OLD ROADS INTO THE TOWN

gone along Mill Lane. Though this way is associated, to our modern ears, with a windmill which stood there and has been removed only in recent years, it is probable that the name is much older and originally referred to the water-mill in New Shoreham Parish, over the weir of which it would pass on its way to the hills and Old Shoreham. A reason for thinking that

Kingston Parish Church.

a mediaeval road ran past the three churches named is that at two of them—Aldrington and Kingston—there were anchorites' cells. Now the occupants of such places were built into their domiciles and being unable to get out to procure for themselves the necessaries of subsistence, were dependent on the charity of passers-by. As a consequence the Bishops of those times would not licence an "anchorage" unless it happened to be in such a

THE STORY OF SHOREHAM

situation that support for the occupant could be relied on from the travellers to and fro. It follows then that a line of anchorages implies a well-frequented road at the period at which they existed. The road in question from Kingston doubtless took much the same direction as the present Middle Road, crossed the Ham Field, and came out into the Buckingham Lane about opposite Mill Lane.

The third road from the east was, of course, the main Old Shoreham Road from Brighton and Lewes. It is likely that this was a Roman road. Its Shoreham end has been diverted in modern times further south to make a more direct approach to Old Shoreham Bridge, the original alignment having lain across the lower slope of Slonk Hill and Buckingham Park, through Little Buckingham Farm to Cockeroost, with a turn down at Old Shoreham.

This is, no doubt, the road to which reference is made in two Assize Rolls of the reigns of Henry III. and Edward I. The former records that, on the day of the Exaltation of the Holy Cross, 1265, Alexander de Pevense and Alan the Blowere, with arms and strength, assaulted Robert Oter of Lewes, pulled him from his horse, wounded and maltreated him, broke his left leg and robbed him. This took place "in the King's way between Shoreham and Lewes."

The latter Roll records that in 1280 a murder had been committed and the body, that of an unknown man, was found in the neighbourhood of Hangleton "in the King's way between Shoreham and Lewes."

Having given this short sketch of the varying fortunes of the place, you are invited to review the History and Antiquities of Old and New Shoreham in a more detailed manner.

CHAPTER III.

OLD SHOREHAM—A ROYAL MANOR—HELD BY PRINCES OF WALES — SHOREHAM MARSH — THE FERRY — THE TIMBER BRIDGE — PICTURESQUE COTTAGES—FORMER WATER-MILLS AND WIND-MILLS—ANCIENT LITIGATION.

THE homesteads of the Saxon community at Shoreham on the left bank of the Adur mainly centred near the Church of St. Nicholas (patron saint of mariners) in much the same position as the cottages of to-day. In the time of King Edward the Confessor, Azor was the great man of the place and "held Soresham of the King," while Fredri held the neighbouring Manor of Erringham. If any habitations were then in existence further southward (the nucleus of the later town) they were all included in "Soresham," the home or dwelling place on the shore.

William the Conqueror's Great Survey, Domesday Book, completed in 1086, informs us that in the time of Edward the Confessor "Soresham was assessed for 12 hides," but when the survey was made, "for five hides and half a virgate." There was land for 15 ploughs. On the demesne were three ploughs and 26 villeins (persons in absolute servitude) and 49 bordars (cottagers) with 12 ploughs. There was a church, six acres of meadow, and woodland yielding (support for) 40 swine. In the time of King Edward the manor was worth 25 pounds, and afterwards 16 pounds. At the time the survey was made the value was stated to be 35 pounds, "and yet," says Domesday Book, "it was (formerly) farmed for 50 pounds, but that could not be borne."

"William (de Braose) himself holds Soresham" we are informed by the same ancient chronicle quoted above. It was part of that great baron's share of the spoils of conquest and included in his grant of the Rape of Bramber. His descendants continued to hold it until the reign of King John, but the then Lord of Bramber, another William de Braose (of whom more will be related in future pages) falling into disfavour with the King, John seized his estates, and although the greater part was afterwards restored to the family on the payment of 9,000 marks, the Manor of Old Shoreham remained in possession of the Crown for many generations.

THE STORY OF SHOREHAM

King John gave it to his second son, Richard, Earl of Cornwall, who as King of the Romans, many years later, cut such a sorry figure at the Battle of Lewes when de Montfort's soldiers dragged him forth white with flour from the windmill where he had taken refuge.

Richard's son, Edmund, Earl of Cornwall, also held the manor. He died 1st October, 1300, and leaving no issue, the Earldom of Cornwall became extinct.   His widow, Margaret, daughter of Richard de Clare, 8th Earl of Clare and 7th of Gloucester, survived him.

Cottage Backs, Old Shoreham. Arthur D. Packham 1918.

Shortly after his death an Inquisition was taken at "Schorham" before Walter de Gloucester, the King's Escheator, concerning the lands and tenements "whereof Edmund, Earl of Cornwall, died seised in his demesne as of fee in county Sussex."   The jurors said on oath that the said Edmund held 14 virgates of land in Old Schorham "belonging to his castle of Berkhampstead" by what service was unknown to the jurors.   The land was in the hands of 35 bondmen and rendered yearly £8 6s. 7d.   There was a windmill for which they paid their lord 50s. a year.

Master Thomas de Ambberbye held of the Earl in Old Shoreham one messuage and one carucate of land and rendered therefore

OLD SHOREHAM

at Michaelmas 12d. for all services. The total value of all the tenements was stated to be £10 18s. 7d. and they "(the jurors) say that Edward, King of England, is next heir of Edmund, Earl of Cornwall, and is of full age."

King Edward ordered that the yearly rents from certain

Cottage at Old Shoreham.
Arthur B. Packham
1918.

tenements in Old Shoreham should be delivered to Margaret, Countess of Cornwall, as part of her dower; but in the year 1318 "lands in Old Shoreham which the King lately assigned to Margaret" were to be delivered to Hugh de Audele, whom she had married.

Richard de Abberbury held in fee the Manor of Old Shoreham,

THE STORY OF SHOREHAM

with appurtenances, of Hugh de Audele and Margaret, his wife, as of the Honour of St. Waleric, by the service of 12d. or a sparrowhawk at Michaelmas. After his death in 1335 it was stated that there was at Old Shoreham "a court built with houses" (a manor house and cottages) and that "there are in the manor 228 acres of arable land worth yearly £8 4s., and five acres of several pasture for sheep."

John, son of Richard de Abberbury, "held in dower as of fee the day he died (26th September, 1347) a tenement in Schorham of the Prince of Wales, and 200 acres of land worth 100s. yearly, and rents of assize of one free tenant 3s. 4d. yearly at Christmas and the Nativity of St. John the Baptist."

The Manor of Old Shoreham formed part of the dower of Joan, Princess of Wales, widow of the Black Prince and mother of Richard II., but in 1380 this Princess, "in consideration of services rendered to herself and to her daughter, de Courteney," made a grant of all her rents in Old Shoreham to Henry Norton, who enjoyed the income for life. In 1396 the manor was granted to Adam atte Wode, yeoman of the chamber. It was then of the yearly value of £10.

In 1397 there was a grant "without rent" to the King's brother, John de Holand, Earl of Huntyngdon, of the reversion expectant upon the death of Walter Dalingrygg of the Manor of Old Shoreham during the minority of the heir of John de Arundel, knt.

In June, 1400, a commission was appointed to enquire into "certain trespasses, extortions and injuries committed on the tenants of Henry, Prince of Wales, in the towns of Old and New Shoreham." The nature of these grievances has not transpired. Twelve years later this Prince is mentioned as holding the Manor of Old Shoreham, "worth £10 a year."

On the 6th June, in the 9th year of his reign, King Henry V. granted for life to Elizabeth, wife of William Ryman, the Manor of Old Shoreham. This was just after the birth of the Prince who was shortly to become the luckless Henry VI. It appears that this grant was in recognition of the services rendered to the Royal family by Elizabeth Ryman. She had been summoned by King Henry V. "to come to him in his realm of France to do service about the person of the Queen" and "came to the King at Paris and attended the Queen—Katherine, the "Fair Kate" of Shakespeare's play—until the young Prince was born, at which

A ROYAL MANOR

time the King charged Elizabeth to watch and attend on the Prince."

Henry VI., in 1424, "by advice of his council," confirmed this grant. The King was then but an infant of about two years of age. He made his nurse a further grant of £20 a year and confirmed another of £20, which had been made to her by his grandfather, Henry IV.

After Elizabeth Ryman's death her husband held the manor, and in September, 1441—probably after his decease—there was a grant for life to William Dawtre of the keeping of the King's Manor of Old Shoreham.

In the reign of Elizabeth the tenants of the manor inned and recovered some twenty-seven acres known as "Shoreham Marsh," which had formerly been "overflown" by the sea. This area is that portion of the parish stretching northward of Old Shoreham Church and bounded by the old river-bank and the foot of the Downs. Having recovered these acres at their own expense, the inhabitants made division amongst themselves, "apportioning every man according to his hold and in recompense of the charges he had been at in the inning."

A foot-path turning in at the top of Old Shoreham Street and crossing the field opposite Adur Lodge, leads down to the marsh and marks the road by which the tenants of the manor drove their cattle down to pasture. This could have been the only way of access to it in those days as the sea waters then washed the walls of the churchyard. The traces of a dam built about 200 yards north of Old Shoreham Church are to be seen to-day.

But this reclaiming had been carried out without the consent of the Lady of the Manor—no less a personage than Queen Elizabeth herself, who was not the monarch to submit tamely to any such infringement of her rights of property by the people of Old Shoreham. Her receiver of rents was directed to enquire into the matter of these "concealed" lands and he reported that he "had been to the Manor of Old Shoreham" and that "Shoreham Marsh ought of right to appertain to Her Highness," that it was proved concealed and the tenants being evicted, it was worth to be "letten" at so much the acre.

The marsh affords pasture for cattle to-day, but it is now commonly known as the "saltings."

Closely associated with the history of Old Shoreham Manor was the ferry and passage over the river, the only means of crossing at this point before the timber bridge was built. It was quite distinct from the ferry at New Shoreham already mentioned.

In a survey of the time of James I. it was stated that "the Earl of Arundel, or the ferry-man, his tenant, usurps the landing of passengers upon the Prince's land at Old Shoreham and therefore it is fit he should have a rent according to the value of the moiety of the ferry, viz., £10 per annum."

Cottages, Malthouse Lane, Old Shoreham

In the Parliamentary Survey of 1651 the manor was described as "parcell of ye revenue of Charles Stuart, late Prince of Wales, as part of ye late Dutchie of Cornwall." Mention is made of the quit-rent due to the Lord of the Manor from "a certaine ffarme or messuage called 'Court Farm,'" in the parish of Old Shoreham, and also "all that fferry and passage over the river commonly known by the name of Old Shoreham fferry, which leadeth from the town of Old Shoreham toward Arundel."

At that time the Earl of Arundel claimed the profits of the ferry, "but by what right or title," said the surveyors, "ye

THE FERRY

saide Earle doe soe hold and enjoy the same we noe nott, and upon our survey we find by credible informacion that the said fferry is parcell of the Manor of Old Shoreham, neither hathe ye Earle any land lying on either side of the said river (nor neere ye same) and therefore we return the fferry to be in ye possession of the Honoble ye Trustees."

In 1652 John Urlin purchased the manor with all its rights and appurtenances, including the passage over the water, "commonly called Old Shoreham Ferry," and all rights of hunting, hawking, fowling and fishing in the manor.

Church & Bridge Old Shoreham
Arthur's Pelham

The river was sometimes fordable by horsemen but apparently this custom was attended with a certain amount of risk.

Dr. Burton, journeying to Findon in 1751, and arriving at Old Shoreham, says : " as the passage over the river did not look either convenient or free from danger, we turned to the right and traversing the country rather upward sought the security of the bridge " (at Bramber).

In 1772 Mr. John Baker, of Horsham, describes in his diary how he, with a companion, travelled from Arundel through Broadwater, Sompting, and Lancing to Shoreham ferry, and how

THE STORY OF SHOREHAM

the ferry-man rowing over, a soldier followed on horseback behind the boat. "So," says the diarist, "we rode over and landed at Old Shoreham." The two travellers put up at the "Star" at New Shoreham, "the best though poor," and were lodged two beds in one room. "Some fellows drinking under us and singing disturbed us much, and bad beds, and we forced to go through kitchen where they were, to bed."

The Act of Parliament, passed 1781, for building the timber bridge at Old Shoreham, stated that the ancient ferry was dangerous and provided £20 yearly rent of the ferry to the owner, Charles, Earl of Surrey, his heirs or assigns. The Act authorised £5,000 to be raised in shares of £100 by way of annuity, the income arising from the tolls, falling to the Duke of Norfolk on the death of the annuitants. The bridge was ten months in building and was considered at the time of its completion a marvel of engineering skill. It has a total length of 500ft. with 27 openings, the roadway is 12ft. wide with two recesses, 70ft. by 24ft., for passing vehicles. It is connected with the Lancing side of the river by a causeway built on faggots sunk into the morass, which formerly extended to the Sussex Pad. This old bridge—one of the most picturesque features of the Adur Valley—is now the property of the Railway Company, having been acquired by them at the time the line was extended to Horsham. It has recently undergone a necessary and careful restoration.

The Manor of Old Shoreham—vested in the Crown as part of the Duchy of Cornwall—was purchased by Charles, Duke of Norfolk, from George IV., when Prince of Wales.

The acceptance of the stewardship of this manor, being an office held under the Crown, formerly vacated a seat in Parliament.

Most of the thatched cottages are of considerable antiquity and give the village much of its venerable appearance. Those in Malt House Lane are especially worthy of notice. The fine old Court Cupboard shown in our picture is in a cottage in Old Shoreham Street. It was in this cottage, or the one adjoining, that a former local celebrity, blind Fanny Winton, lived for many years, bearing her affliction with cheerfulness and Christian resignation.

It may be of interest to note that the fields situated north and south of the highway running from the cross roads to Old Shoreham village are known as the Upper and Lower "Butts." It may be that the name is an echo of the fifteenth century when

OLD
COVRT
CVPBOARD

BVILT INTO
COTTAGE AT
OLD
SHOREHAM.

HEIGHT = 5 ft. 3 ins.
WIDTH = 4 ft. 11 ins.
DEPTH = 1 ft. 11½ ins.

THE STORY OF SHOREHAM

men of all towns and villages who were capable of bearing arms were required to practise shooting on every Feast day or suffer the fine of a half-penny. The cultivated lands on the Downs are known as "Laines," and other place-names not elsewhere referred to are Anchor Bottom and Crooked Moon.

Richard Budgen's Map of Sussex, dated 1724, shows two windmills on Mill Hill. One which stood there within living memory was destroyed by fire about thirty years since. From a circumstance to be noted later Mill Hill is sometimes called "Good Friday Hill."

We find a reference to three mills—a windmill and two water-mills—all situated in Old Shoreham, in a "Fine," dated St. Andrew's Day, Lewes, in the 14th year of Henry III. (1230). It sets forth that Henry de Sco Walerico on the one side, came to an arrangement with Thomas Scot and Cicely, his wife, and Agnes "de Veteri Shorham" on the other side, with reference to six acres of land in Old Shoreham. In the result, Henry granted to the first two one acre of land, "being that acre where the windmill is situated, together with the windmill itself and its appurtenances," and two acres of land "which adjoin in the field to the east of the said ville against the sewer outside on the south and one croft which adjoins the messuage of the parson of the said ville on the west . . . to be held by the said Thomas and Cicely, paying two shillings in four terms, viz. : at the Feast of St. Thomas the Apostle, 6d. ; at the Annunciation of the Blessed Virgin Mary, 6d. ; at the Nativity of St. John the Baptist, 6d., and at the Feast of St. Michael, 6d. for all service. All the remainder of the six acres of land, with *two water-mills* in the said ville and everything pertaining thereto, to remain to Henry and his heirs." He also remits to the other three persons all arrears of rent for the mills which he could have claimed up to the date of the agreement.

While making no attempt to indicate the exact position of the windmill it seems quite evident that it was near the village. Possibly the croft is identical with the small meadow which the inhabitants now refer to as "the crawt," in the immediate neighbourhood of which the windmill was probably situated.

It is quite reasonable to believe that the water-mills were situated in the hollow at Little Buckingham, where the farm buildings now stand. We will go even further and claim that the western of the two cottages was anciently one of the actual

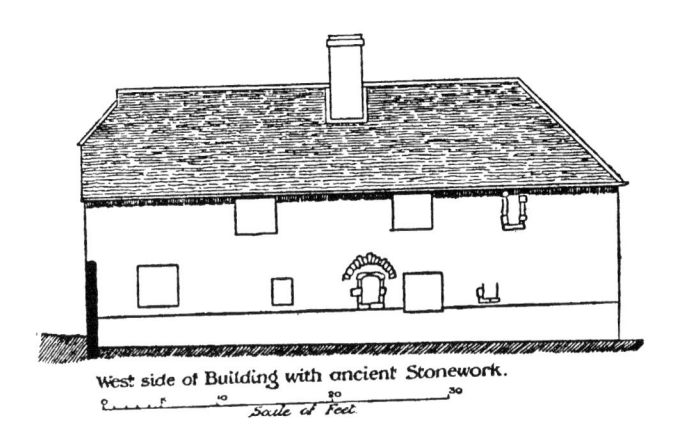

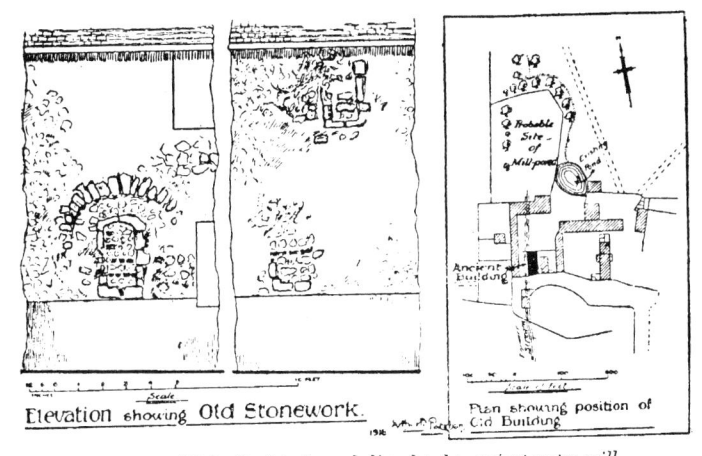

West side of Building with ancient Stonework.
Scale of Feet

Elevation showing Old Stonework.   Plan showing position of Old Building.

House at Little Buckingham, believed to be ancient water-mill.

THE STORY OF SHOREHAM

water-mills. A careful examination of the exterior of the west wall of this cottage reveals some blocked openings of 13th century date, and a blocked arch, where it is possible that the spindle of the mill-wheel came through. It is not improbable that the other mill stood a little further north, about where the barn is—and the wheel of this would have been turned by the water running over it from the pond behind, thence flowing south—or falling into another pond and turning the other wheel from *below*, which was anciently, and is, indeed, at the present day, a quite usual method of turning a mill-wheel where the exigencies of the case demand it. That it was so in this case we are led to believe from the result of calculations worked out from levels taken on the site.

Two mills are again mentioned in a "Fine," dated 52 Henry III. (1268). Though not specially defined as water-mills, it is quite reasonable to believe that they were identical with those mentioned earlier in the century.

The fine in question was an arrangement or agreement between Richard Baudefar (son of John Baudefar) and John Baudefar (the latter probably a brother or cousin of Richard) concerning 2 virgates of land, one mill, one half of a mill, and 3s. 10d. rent in Old Shoreham, and 40 shillings rent in New Shoreham, 2¼ virgates of land in Kingston and Southwick and 20 pence rent in Southwick.

At Little Buckingham.

Richard granted all the above to John for the whole life of the said John, who was to hold it of Richard and his heirs, rendering 10 shillings and ninepence at three separate dates, viz., 9d. at Easter, 5s. at the Feast of St. Peter ad Vincula, and 5s. at the Feast of St. Thomas the Apostle for all service.

After the death of John the property was to revert entirely to Richard and his heirs. If, however, Richard died before John and also left no heirs who survived John, the property in its entirety was to remain absolutely with John's heirs. There was no provision as to what was to happen if John left no heirs.

The Baudefars appear to have been noteworthy people both in

FORMER WATER-MILLS AND WIND-MILLS

Old and New Shoreham, inasmuch as we find the family continually referred to in the records at this period. It appears that some members of the family had an interest in another mill, which is, however, expressly stated to have been in New Shoreham.

A reference has already been made to Mill Lane, which is quite obviously an old road sweeping up from Shoreham to the hills, and it partly forms the parish boundary, always a sure sign of antiquity in a highway.

Dismissing from the mind the modern windmill (lately removed) which stood near Buckingham Road, we may take it that the "Mill Lane" took its name from a water-mill which was in all probability situated somewhere near the present Cemetery lodge. The lane, continued towards the hill, would have been carried on a causeway, and the water falling down from the upper mill-ponds at Little Buckingham would have been dammed back by the causeway in sufficient volume to provide a decent head of water to turn this third mill situated just within the boundary of New Shoreham.

It appears from an Assize Roll, dated 7th Edward I., that this last-named mill was owned by a certain William Baudefar and that he died, leaving a widow, Isabel, and son, John, his heir, then under age. Isabel, "who after William's death had the custody and bringing up of John and who held the mill in soccage, demised it to Master Robert de Blechington, the Vicar of Old Shoreham, for a certain term of years for 30 marks. Apparently this term had not fully expired when the Vicar was asked to relinquish his tenancy of the mill. When the case was gone into, Master Robert de Bletchington said that he claimed nothing in the said mill unless the term aforesaid, and pleaded for judgment as to whether John Baudefar was entitled to occupy the mill, before he attained his legal age. The case resulted in an agreement by which John Baudefar was to recover the mill from the Vicar, but the latter was at liberty to obtain, if he wished, a writ of agreement with Isabel, to whom the custody of the mill was to be committed until John attained his lawful age.

Isabel Baudefar had also demised ten acres of land and seven acres of meadow, with appurtenances, in Shoreham, to Master Robert de Blechington for three years and recovered possession of the same in like manner with the mill.

The widow, on behalf of her son, also made a claim respecting

THE STORY OF SHOREHAM

11 acres of land in Old and New Shoreham which were held by Robert Tregol, who said that she had demised the land to him for a term of three years " to hold according to a certain deed made between them." The Sheriff was ordered to value the 11 acres " and the chattels found in the same " and this being done, it was ordered that Robert Tregol should have the value of the crops on the land and that John should recover possession.

Yet another case records that Maud, "who was the wife of Nicholas le Taylur," held 5s. 6d. rent, with appurtenances, in Old Shoreham, and of this the Baudefars sought to recover possession. Maud, while admitting that the property in question had belonged to William, father of John Baudefar, said that he, " long before his death," demised the same to Nicholas le Taylur, her former husband, for 16 years, within which time Nicholas died and bequeathed the said term to Maud and she now claimed nothing except by reason of that term which she said was " not yet past." She also produced the deed of William Baudefar witnessing the demise to Nicholas for the term of 16 years, but her contention that the period had not expired would not hold water. " On reckoning," so runs the Assize Roll, " it is found the term is complete and past and John shall recover possession."

One more case may be mentioned in connection with the property of the Baudefar family, but in this Richard, who figures in connection with the two water-mills in Old Shoreham in 52 Henry III., again appears. Richard's father, John Baudefar, had given to Adam de Horton and his issue six acres of marsh in Old Shoreham, but with the understanding that if Adam died without issue, the same should revert to John Baudefar and his heirs, quit of the other heirs of Adam. Adam died without issue and it appears that his brother William took possession. On the case being tried the jurors said on oath that William de Horton had made a false claim and was therefore in mercy but was pardoned by the justices because of his poverty. William de Horton was described as a " chaplain " and at this time the six acres of marsh were in the tenancy of Robert de Blechington before mentioned.

This Vicar of Old Shoreham continually appears in the Assize Rolls of the period. For instance, the same " Maud who was the wife of Nicholas le Taylur " made a claim in 16 Edward I. for 2½ acres of land, with appurtenances, in Old Shoreham, in which she said the Vicar had no right or " entry " except as the tenant

ANCIENT LITIGATION

of Nicholas, her former husband. In defence, Robert de Blechington said that he purchased the land from Nicholas le Taylur, who had bought it from a certain William Forceaus, and judgment was against Maud for a false claim. Maud was certainly most unfortunate in her litigation.

At another time we find Robert de Blechington disputing with Ralph de Anyngdon (Annington) as to the possession of three acres of land in Old Shoreham, claimed by Ralph as his lay fee, against which the parson said that "a certain Florentius, his predecessor, was seised of the land as of the right of his church of Old Shoreham, but it was alienated from him."

Again, the Vicar appears as debtor to Edmund, Earl of Cornwall, who was Lord of the Manor of Old Shoreham at this time. The debt was 100s., which he agreed to pay "at Michaelmas next," and if he does not he grants that the Sheriff shall distrain his lands and goods. Moreover he found pledges—Master William de la Folde of Goringes and Simon Scherington, who acknowledge themselves the principal debtors (? to Robert de Blechington) and grant that if Robert does not pay the Earl at the time named the Sheriff may then distrain on *their* goods.

CHAPTER IV.

OLD ERRINGHAM—HELD OF KING EDWARD THE CONFESSOR—EARLY RECORDS—WILL OF JOHN COBYE—BELLINGHAM FAMILY—THE OLD MANOR HOUSE—THE CHAPEL—A RESTLESS SPIRIT—NEW ERRINGHAM HOUSE—AN OLD COACH ROAD

APPROACHED by means of an ancient track-way leading out of the old road from Shoreham over the Downs to Beeding is Old Erringham. It may also be reached from the river valley by way of the road, which takes one up through Erringham Shaw, where the trees cling to the steep sides of what we may reasonably believe to be ancient sea-cliffs of the Adur estuary. All along the eastern side of the river valley, from Old Shoreham northwards to the Shaw, the slope of the Downs is very abrupt and in some parts almost precipitous.

The Saxon Fredri held the Manor of Erringham of King Edward the Confessor and it was then assessed for five hides and worth 40 shillings. Fredri, being a free man, "could betake himself whither he pleased," such is the quaint wording of Domesday Book, and the same record also informs us that at the time of William the Conqueror's great Survey (1086) William de Braose held the manor, but it was then assessed for half a hide and its value had fallen to 20 shillings. There were two villeins and five bordars on the manor "who have nothing."

References to this place are found among the records from the 13th century onwards. In 1259 Adam Rymund was admitted to bail from the King's prison at Bramber "for the death of John, son of Celea de Erringham." In 1328, among the lands and tenements of Adam de Bavent, it was stated that "at Erringham there is a certain messuage and 64 acres of arable land, pasture for sheep and rents due at the Feast of St. Thomas the Apostle, and at the Nativity of St. John the Baptist," and the whole yearly value was said to be 104s. 1d.

By a deed, dated London, 1st July, 1344, Roger Bavent, Knt., granted to King Edward III. his manor of "Iryngham" and in 1351 it is referred to as being reserved for the uses of the King's chamber. In 1358 it was granted to Peter de Braose, and in

THE WILL OF JOHN COBYE[1]

1363 John atte Hyde of Iryngham and Isabel, his wife, gave certain property in New Shoreham to the Carmelite Friars who had settled in the town. The Hydes held Iryngham as well as certain lands and tenements in New Shoreham, of Sir John de Mowbray (of Bramber) by Knight's service and John is again mentioned as "of Iryngham" in 1372. The names of Walter Walkstede, clerk, and Richard Sonde and Pauline, his wife, appear in a document relating to Iryngham, which is dated 1411.

Old Eringham
West side
Arthur B Packham
1913

BLOCKED-UP
MEDIEVAL
WINDOW

The will of John Cobye of Iryngham, in the parish of Old Shoreham, co. Sussex, dated 6th September, 1541, and proved 20th November, 1544, is preserved at Somerset House. He bequeaths "to the mother church of Chichester 12d. and to the high altar of the church of Old Shoreham, 8d." To his wife, Isabel, £40, "and one half my household stuff if she occupy her lands herself, she to have corn enough to sow her lands, also sheep to lay her leage." Remembering the faithfulness of one of his servants he directs that his executors "shall keep old Nyman during his lifetime." After bequests to his children,

THE STORY OF SHOREHAM

Thomas Cobye, Hugh Cobye (residuary legatee and executor), Lettys Cobye and another daughter, referred to as "wife of John Harrys," the testator gives "to the reparation of the church of Oulde Schorham 6s. 8d." and "I will that an obit annually shall be kept in the church of Oulde Schorham for my soul and all Christian souls for the space and time of ten years to the annual value of twenty shillings, that is to say, ten priests, 5s. with their breakfast, the overplus in meat and drink and alms to poor people." "Maister Richard Bellingham" was one of the overseers of the will.

BELLINGHAM.
ARMS.—*Argent, three bugle horns sable, stringed gules, and garnished or. Crest—a demi-stag salient attired or, between two rose branches each bearing a rose.*

The last-named was a member of the somewhat notable family connected with Erringham for something like one hundred and sixty years, and one branch of which resided in the old Manor House for several generations.

The ancestor of this family was Sir Robert Bellingham (the name is pronounced "Bellinjum"), Baronet, of Burnishead in Westmoreland, living there in the time of Kings Henry the Fifth and Sixth. By his wife, Elizabeth, daughter of Sir Richard Tunstall, Knt., of Thurland Castle, county Lancashire, Sir Robert had issue, three sons—Sir Henry, ancestor of the Burnishead and Levens families; Richard, ancestor of the Lincolnshire family; and Thomas, who settled at Lymster, near Arundel, and became the ancestor of the Sussex families with whom we are more particularly concerned.

Thomas Bellingham, by his wife, Joan Wiltshire, was the father of three sons—Ralph of Lymster, born about 1470, Edward of Erringham, and Richard of Newtimber and Hangleton—and one daughter, Joan, who became the wife of Ralph Shirley. Thomas Bellingham died and left to his son Ralph the Manor of Yapton, near Arundel, certain property in Petworth, and a moiety of the Manor of Erringham in Old Shoreham.

Edward Bellingham, second son of Thomas, married Jane,

BELLINGHAM FAMILY

daughter of John Shelley of Michelgrove, by whom he had two sons, John and Edward.

Edward, the younger of these two sons, rose to a position of considerable distinction in the service of his country. He was brought up in the Duke of Norfolk's household and is, no doubt, identical with Edward Bellingham, described as of Erringham-Walstead, who was one of the defenders in a tilting held at Westminster in 1531. He was a soldier of distinction and served in Hungary with Sir Thomas Seymour and with the Earl of Surrey at Boulogne. He became Lieutenant of the Isle of Wight and in 1545 took the chief part in the repulse of the French attack on the Island. Edward the Sixth made him a member of his Privy Council and appointed him, 12th April, 1548, Lord Deputy of Ireland. He died in the autumn of the following year.

We find that Richard and George Shelley and Nicholas Gaynesford demised the Manor of Erringham-Walstead to John Bellingham (above-named), Joan Delve (whom he subsequently married), and others, with remainder to the heirs of Edward, father of John, then to Richard, brother of Edward, then to John of Lymster, son and heir of Ralph, brother of Richard, and then to Joan Shirley, the sister.

John Bellingham, described as of Little Horsted, died in 1541, leaving by his wife, Joan (Delve), who survived him, a son and heir not five years of age at his father's death. John's possessions included Haseholt, in Southwick, and he held the Manor of Erringham-Walstead of the Honour of Bramber. Joan Bellingham, the widow, married James Gage, son of Sir John Gage, Comptroller of the Household to Henry VIII.

John, left an infant at the death of his father in 1541, was described, at an Inquisition taken at Lewes in 1556-7 to prove his age, as "John Bellingham, gentleman, cousin and heir of Sir Edward Bellingham, Knight "(? of Newtimber), and he was then 20 years of age. He married in 1560 and by his wife, Ann, had issue—John, Thomas, Elizabeth, Ann, and Mary. He died in 1576 and was buried in Bath Abbey, November 11th of that year (see Bath Abbey registers) and his memorial, formerly in the Abbey Church, read thus :—" Here lieth the Bodie of John Bellingham, late of Earingham in the county of Sussex, Esquier." His family arms were engraved on this monument—Argent, three bugle horns sable, stringed gules and garnished or, and impaling party per bend of six, on a canton, a lion rampant

Old Erringham
(South end)

A.B.P. 1920

JOHN BELLINGHAM

(probably the latter coat depicted the arms of his wife's family). This memorial is believed to have been removed from the Abbey during the restoration of 1834. Its latest mention is found in John Britton's "History and Antiquities of Bath Abbey Church," 1825.

John Bellingham, described as of Erringham, county Sussex, esquire, by his will, dated 8th February, 1575-6, which makes no mention of a desire for interment at Bath, directs "at my funeral alms may be given to such poor as most deserve charity, nigh unto Erringham, to the amount of £6 13s. 4d., a quarter of wheat and two quarters of malt." To the reparation of Old Shoreham Church he bequeathed 10s. "At my marriage," he says, "I made to my wife, Anne, a jointure for her life of all my lands called Erringham, which descended to me from my father, and since I have purchased of Sir Thomas Shirley, of Wiston, county Sussex, knight, lands called Erringham-Bruse, being intermingled with my said lands, so now I bequeath these lands to my said wife for ten years for the bringing up of my four youngest children, and after ten years to my wife for life, with remainder to my son John in tail male, in default of such issue to my second son, Thomas, in tail male, in default to my issue, in default to the right heirs of my son John. All my stocks of corn and cattle on my lands of Erringham-Bruse to my wife. To my wife my farm, called Paythorne, which I hold of Mr. Richard Covert of Slaugham, esquier, for ten years, she at her decease to leave at Erringham a stock of 500 ewes, 20 qrs. of seed wheat, 40 qrs. of seed barley, eight drawing oxen, six kine and 20 hogs for the heir of my body." His daughter Elizabeth was to receive £300 at her marriage, his son Thomas £200 at age 21, his daughters Ann and Mary £200 each on marriage, and his son and heir, John, £100 in ten years' time. These sums were left in trust in the hands of his cousins Edward Bellingham, of Newtimber, Esquier, Richard Bellingham, his son, Edward Bellingham, of Putney, Esquier, Thomas Fenner, of Harting, and his uncle, George Goring, of Ovingdean, Esquier, who were also named as the overseers of his will, which was proved 11th May, 1577, by John Lewes, proctor to the Executrix, Ann Bellingham.

The Inquisitione Post Mortem of John Bellingham records that he "was seised of the Manor of Erringham, otherwise Erringham-Walstead, and of a capital messuage, one pigeon house, one garden, 200 acres of arable, 40 acres of meadow, 100

THE STORY OF SHOREHAM

acres of pasture, 100 acres of marsh and 100 acres of heath and brushwood, a windmill and pasture for 1,000 sheep in Old Shoreham and Beeding, and 20 acres of arable, 18 acres of pasture and 10 acres of heath and brushwood called "Walsteedes," in Old Shoreham."

He also was " seised of the Manor of Erringham-Breuses, otherwise Breuse " (Braose) and 50 acres of arable, 40 acres of pasture and 40 acres of heath and brushwood in Old and New Shoreham.

Both manors were then held of William Dix and William Cantrell, esquires, as of the Honour of Bramber by service of $\frac{1}{8}$th of a knight's fee. "Walsteedes " was held of William West, knt., Lord de la Warr by fealty and rent of 8d. in soccage, as of his Manor of Sompting-Peverell.

We may note that the Manor of Erringham-Braose was anciently part of the great possessions of William de Wiston, who had acquired it by his marriage with Agnes, daughter of William de Harcourt. William de Wiston dying in 1259, his only daughter, the wife of Adam de Bavent, became his heiress. Her granddaughter, Joan, wife of Sir Peter de Braose, left a daughter, Beatrix, from whose descendant, Thomas Shirley of Wiston, John Bellingham had purchased it in 1564.

John Bellingham's son and heir, John, also of Erringham, born in 1563, married his distant relative, Mary, daughter of Richard Bellingham of Hangleton. He died 1st December, 1613, having had issue—John, who died young, Richard and Francis, and a daughter, Mary, who married Sir Thomas Springett, of Broyle Place, Ringmer. She died in 1654. The eldest son of this marriage, Herbert Springett, created a baronet in 1660, was M.P. for the Borough of New Shoreham in 1661 and died in 1662.

Richard Bellingham, of Erringham, who succeeded his father at the age of 24, married Jane, daughter of Thomas Bowyer (sister of Sir Thomas Bowyer) and died 20th August, 1625.

His eldest son and heir, Thomas Bellingham, of Erringham, born about 1612, who married (1633) Margaret, daughter of Henry Shelley of Patcham, Esq., sold Erringham in 1650 to John Juxon, of Albourne.

The subsequent descent of the united manors of Erringham-Walstead and Erringham-Braose may be given in a few words. Sir William, son of John Juxon, sold in 1664 to the Hon. Cecil Tufton, with whose descendants the Erringhams remained until

THE MANOR HOUSE AND CHAPEL

1765, when 5/6ths were conveyed to Colville Bridger, Esq., and the remaining 1/6th to him in 1774.

Among the Burrell MSS. in the British Museum is a water-colour drawing of Old Erringham House as it appeared when visited by Sir William Burrell in 1782. That gentleman, in his notes on Old Shoreham, says :—" at Erringham in this parish a branch of the family of Bellingham formerly resided. It was a building of considerable extent, now occupied by a farmer, and the chapel on the north-west angle is converted into a stable."

REMAINS OF MEDIÆVAL BVILDING AT OLD ERRINGHAM.
From a drawing by Gremm (about 1787) in the British Museum.

The water-colour, which is of the east front of the house, shows that a wing running out at right angles from the main building was then ruinous and this has since entirely disappeared, and also a double-storied porch, which formed the principal entrance, since removed.

On the west side this old manor house seems to have been but very little altered for some centuries. It retains several features which indicate that parts of the building date back to the Middle Ages. Not the least interesting are some blocked

Remains of a Mediaeval Building at Old Erringham.

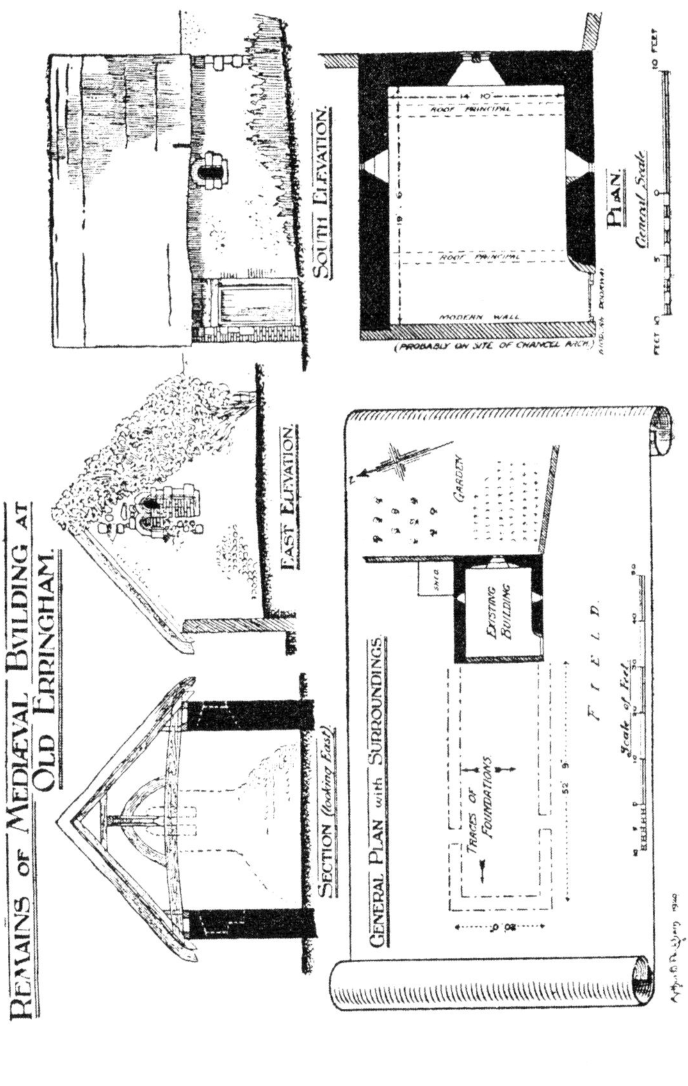
REMAINS OF MEDIÆVAL BUILDING AT OLD ERRINGHAM.
SECTION (looking East).
EAST ELEVATION.
SOUTH ELEVATION.
PLAN.
General Scale
14' 10"
ROOF PRINCIPAL
19' 6"
ROOF PRINCIPAL
MODERN WALL
(PROBABLY ON SITE OF CHANCEL ARCH.)
GENERAL PLAN with SURROUNDINGS.
GARDEN
SHED
EXISTING BUILDING
TRACES OF FOUNDATIONS
52' 9"
20' 0"
FIELD.
Scale of Feet

THE STORY OF SHOREHAM

openings with stonework still *in situ*, one of which is shown in the inset of our drawing on page 51.

Some restoration seems to have taken place early in the 18th century, as the date " 1710 " may be seen on a stone built into the projecting chimney at the south end.

The chapel referred to by Sir William Burrell (of which there is also a water-colour in the British Museum) is, without doubt, a relic of the Middle Ages. It is part only—the chancel—of a larger building, and in dry weather the lines of the nave foundations are quite easy to trace. The east window of two lights, partly blocked, belongs to the Transitional period and two small Norman openings yet remain in the north and south walls, the original stonework, still in good preservation.

Mr. A. Stanley Cooke, in " Off the Beaten Track in Sussex," recording his visit some years ago to the chapel at Erringham, mentions that he noticed "the remains of a holy-water stoup and piscina" (no trace of either of these features can now be found), and that the building was then known to the farm-hands as the synagogue !

It is, perhaps, quite natural that such a spot as Old Erringham should enshrine the legend of a ghost—a headless lady, who was wont to wander about in the evening twilight "wringing her hands," presumably in search of, but unable to find, the lost head. This apparition—real or imagined—said to haunt the Shaw and its neighbourhood, must have served as a valuable ally of the old-time smugglers, who were wont to conceal their contraband merchandise at Erringham and such like out-of-the-way places.

The restless spirit of the headless lady, was probably the means of preventing the intrusion of the too-curious into the abode of a more tangible and fiery spirit, brought from overseas, in handy and convenient tubs. In these days, or nights, we are told, she seldom appears. Possibly with the decline of smuggling, she retired from the ghostly business, or her nightly search may at last have been rewarded by the discovery of the missing head, and her wandering spirit found "a well-earned rest."

The usual wild and incoherent stories of underground passages are told at Erringham. One is supposed to connect the house with the chapel, and another, described to the writer as " a submarine passage," to lead direct from the cellars to the sea, a distance of two miles !

NEW ERRINGHAM

New Erringham House stands in the valley north-east of Old Erringham. It was at one time a Coaching Inn on the road from Brighton to Horsham and London, which crossed the Downs

New Erringham 1917
Arthur O Peckham

hard by. This Brighton-London road was one of the most frequented in old coaching days and is marked on Richard Budgen's Map, 1724. It left Brighton by way of the Old Shoreham Road, which it followed for some distance, diverting

THE STORY OF SHOREHAM

from it westward of Southwick, passing Holmbush and running through Mossy Bottom (the "Happy Valley" of Shoreham Camp). Thence it crossed the Downs by New Erringham to Beeding Bostal or Bramber Gorge, as it was then more generally called, and passed through Beeding, over Bramber Bridge, through Steyning, Horsham, Dorking, and Epsom to London, the whole distance being 56 miles.

During the palmy days of the Southdown Foxhounds one of the most popular meets of that popular pack was at New Erringham, at that time the residence of Mr. Thomas Pearson, who then farmed the land. As many as from four to five hundred equestrians of both sexes would frequently assemble on these occasions.

Many years ago small race meetings were sometimes held on the adjacent Downs. Much of the action of George Moore's racing novel, "Esther Waters," takes place in the immediate neighbourhood. Many of the scenes are laid in the town of Shoreham, and Buckingham House is easily recognised under the thin disguise of "Woodville."

The training of racehorses was much in evidence at New Erringham just before the outbreak of the war, the farm having been let for that purpose.

CHAPTER V.

OLD SHOREHAM *alias* "RUSPAR"—BUCKINGHAM FAMILY IN EARLY DEEDS—BLAKER, MONK, and BRIDGER FAMILIES—BUCKINGHAM HOUSE.

There is another manor, known as "Old Shoreham *alias* Ruspar," but its early history is somewhat obscured by the mists of antiquity. It became separated from the chief manor before the middle of the 14th century and as been held successively by the families of Fitzalan, Cobham, Bowyer, Boorde, Gage, Blaker, Monk, Elliston, Elliott, and Bridger, following much the same line of descent as the Manor of Buckingham, with which it has apparently been closely associated from early times. Its limits extend beyond the boundaries of the parish, and it is a curious fact that the General Post Office in Ship Street, Brighton, is actually in the manor of Old Shoreham-Ruspar.

It seems to have derived its *alias* from the Priory of Ruspar near Horsham. In 1326 Isabel, Prioress of "Roughsparre," and William Bernard and William de la Stocke of Old Shoreham, were the defendants against William de Borughersh and Isabel, his wife, who had made a false claim to 2½ acres (doubtless part of the manor lands) in Old Shoreham.

Thomas de Bokyngham died in 1395, an outlaw, and his lands and tenements, "by reason of his outlawry taken into the hands of the king," included a messuage in New Shoreham which he held of Lord de Poynings, two shops in the same town held of the Prior of Sele, and eight acres in Old Shoreham "held of the Prioress of Ruspar."

The family above mentioned derived their name from the Manor of Buckingham, and we find frequent reference to them in early deeds relating to Shoreham and the neighbourhood. John de Buckyngham, seneschal to John, Lord de Braose, was one of the witnesses in 1220 to a deed relating to Sele Priory; Richard de Buckyngham is mentioned in an Assize Roll of 1271; a Richard de Bockyngham was M.P. for New Shoreham in 1300-1; and a Thomas de Bokyngham represented the town in 1357-8 and 1362. In 1397 Robert de Bokyngham is mentioned as son and next heir of Thomas, who had been outlawed. A Thomas Bokyngham held the estate in 1403.

THE STORY OF SHOREHAM

In the reign of Edward VI. (*i.e.*, 1550-1) the Manor of Buckingham was quit-claimed to Thomas West, Lord La Warr and others against Richard Lewknor, * gent. Edward Lewknor, when admitted to the Inner Temple in 1603, was described as "of Buckingham," and in 1606 the widow of one of the Lewknors held the mansion of Sir John Gage.

Edward Blaker, who was living in 1645 and died October, 1653, is described in the memorial to his widow, Susannah, in Old Shoreham Church, as of Buckingham.

He was succeeded by his son Edward, who possessed the manor and estate and was Sheriff of Sussex in 1657 and M.P. for New Shoreham from 1658 to 1678.

By a deed, dated 11th July, 1657, Edward Blaker, therein described as of Old Shoreham, gent, in consideration of the love which he bore to Dorothy, his wife, and for further jointure in case she should outlive him, granted to her "the manor house called Buckingham House," which he had newly erected, with the dovehouses, barns, stables, gaterooms, courts and appurtenances and the closes called Northfield, Newfield, Eastfield, Tenne Acres and Southfield, all which were parcel of the farm called Buckingham Farm, and all other lands in Old Shoreham in his tenure. Edward Blaker, of course, rebuilt on the site of an older house which went by the name of Buckingham.

BLAKER.
ARMS.— *Argent, a chevron ermine, between three blackamoors' heads in profile couped proper.*
CREST. — *A horse's head sable, bridled and maned or.*

The memorial to this gentleman in Old Shoreham Church informs us that "his piety, loyalty, charity, humility and sweetness of disposition engaged the love and admiration of all that knew him in his life and noe less their lamentation at his death," and that "he exchanged this life for a better, 13th September, 1678, in ye 49 year of his age, whose sorrowful relict, Dorothy, ye daughter of Henry Goreing of Heydown in this

* Old Shoreham Registers record the burial of Richard Lewknor, August 28th, 1570.

county of Sussex, Esq., as a testimony of her never dyeing affection, hath paid her last tribute in this monument."

Dorothy Blaker's "never dyeing affection" for her first husband did not prevent her from entering a second time into the bonds of matrimony. She remarried, 9th April, 1681, at Kingston-Bowsey, Robert Hall, of Old Shoreham, son of Robert Hall of Rye, and found a last resting-place February 4th, 1683-4, in the north cloister of Westminster Abbey. Her second husband was also buried there 8th November, 1690.

After Edward Blaker's decease, the property devolved (subject to his widow's interests) on his brother William Blaker, who was Sheriff of Sussex in 1684 and died 6th October, 1703. He was buried at Old Shoreham. By his first wife, Ann, he had an only daughter, Susannah, the wife of John Monk, of Kingston-Bowsey (Member for New Shoreham in the Parliament summoned to meet at Westminster, 22nd January, 1688-9, and dissolved 6th February following). He died in 1701 and his wife in 1690 and both were buried at Kingston.

Their son, William Monk, married Hannah, one of the daughters of Stephen Stringer, of Goudhurst, in Kent. The mother of this lady was an Austen, and it may be noted in passing that Jane Austen, the gifted novelist, was a descendant of the same family. By his will, William Blaker devised his property to his grandson, William Monk.

MONK.

ARMS—*Gules, a chevron azure, between three lion's heads erased argent, langued.*

CREST.— *A dragon volant.*

The memorials to William and Hannah Monk, in Old Shoreham Church are interesting. He died May 2nd, 1714, at the early age of 29, and his epitaph records his "principles of honour and justice, laid concealed by reason of his early fate, tho' long since implanted and which shone out so gloriously in one of his illustrious family," that he was "generally beloved and esteemed while he lived and lamented by all at his death, but especially by his loving consort Hannah . . . by whom he left issue, Jane, Barbara and John, which last died in the 3rd year of his age and lies in the same vault with his father."

THE STORY OF SHOREHAM

His widow, " whose most tender and affectionate care inducing her to a personal attendance in London on the education of the two heiresses of this most antient family, dyed there of the small pox, January, 1722, aged 39."

The co-heiresses, Jane (who married Thomas Brodnax, who by Acts of Parliament took the name of May in 1726 and Knight in 1738) and Barbara Monk, sold Buckingham in 1734 to Edward Elliston, of South Weald, in Essex, whose only daughter and

Buckingham Park in 1782. After Grimm

heiress, Catherine, married in 1756 Edward, 1st Lord Elliott, who, in 1766, sold Buckingham to Colville Bridger, Esq.

The family of Bridger resided at Buckingham House for some generations and to them a long series of monumental inscriptions will be found in Old Shoreham Church and Churchyard.

The illustration of the east front of Buckingham House (from the original water-colour in the British Museum) shows it as it appeared in the year 1782. It would seem to be of somewhat later date than that referred to in Edward Blaker's deed of 1657 as then " newly erected," but possibly it had been added to.

BUCKINGHAM HOUSE

There was another rebuilding, or very considerable alteration, after 1782, as the " ruin " of the late Buckingham House bears witness, although there are evidences that portions of the more ancient house were incorporated in it.

It will be noted that the road from Brighton to Shoreham formerly ran quite close to Buckingham House, as shown in the picture. Its course may still be traced in front of Little Buckingham out to " Cockeroost."

Some years ago, the family of Bridger retired to Adur Lodge, where they still reside, the present head of the family being Lieut.-Col. Bridger, Deputy Lord Lieutenant of the County of Sussex.

BRIDGER.

ARMS. — *Argent, a chevron engrailed sable, between three sea crabs gules.*
CREST. — *A crab as in the arms.*

Buckingham then became the residence of Henry Head, Esq., whose connection with the town of Shoreham will long be remembered. This gentleman interested himself in every good work for the welfare of the inhabitants and was beloved and esteemed by all. He died at Buckingham House on July 1st, 1905, at the age of 70, and memorials to his memory, to his widow and four of his sons will be found in the chancel at Old Shoreham. One son was a victim of the ill-fated "Titanic" and one was killed in action in Gallipoli in 1915.

After Mr. Head's decease Buckingham was without a tenant for several years, but ultimately it passed by purchase into the possession of W. G. Little, Esq., the present owner, who built a new mansion in the park somewhat to the north of the old.

The former house was the scene of a tragedy during the 'fifties. A series of robberies occurred in the neighbourhood and culminated in one at Buckingham. The robber, attempting to escape by a window, was shot by one of the men-servants, wounded, and afterwards found dead in the park. The body, in a coffin with a glass lid exposing the face to view for purpose of identification, was placed in an out-house at the Red Lion Inn. Strange as it

THE STORY OF SHOREHAM

may appear, some hundreds of people from the surrounding district visited this gruesome exhibition. A dog, recognising in the exposed face that of his master, would not leave the coffin. So the man was identified as one, John O'Hara, and was buried in the Churchyard.

CHAPTER VI.

NEW SHOREHAM—THE MANOR AND THE TOWN—DE BRAOSE AND DE MOWBRAY FAMILIES—FORMER AND PRESENT GOVERNMENT OF THE TOWN—FAIRS AND MARKETS—MARKET HOUSES—SUSPENSION BRIDGE —INNS—OLD HOUSES—PLACE-NAMES—BUNGALOW TOWN.

THE Manor of New Shoreham belonged to the Lords of Bramber and so followed the same line of descent as that Barony, being held successively by nine of the de Braose family.

In 1316 William de Braose (the last of that name), holding his manors of the King in chief as of his crown by knight's service, granted the manors of Knappe, Shoreham, Horsham, Beaubusson, and Bramber, and 3,000 acres of wood in Bramber, to Richard Haclut and William Moigne, with remainder to John de Mowbray and Alina his wife, daughter and heiress of William de Braose, and their issue. De Braose retained a life-interest.

John de Mowbray above mentioned was the founder of the Carmelite Priory at Shoreham. During the reign of Edward II. he joined with other nobles against the Despensers. The plot to overthrow these notorious favourites of the King failed. Sir John was beheaded at York (1322) and his wife and son imprisoned in the Tower. "Alina, late wife of Sir John de Mowbray," was compelled by order of the King to grant the estates to Hugh Despenser the younger, Earl of Winchester.

In 1324 there was a grant for life to William de Braose of £70 yearly by the hands of the Sheriffs of London "out of the farm of the city in return for the castle and manor of Bramber and the town of Shoreham, which he has granted to the King for that term."

After the death of William de Braose an Inquisition was taken at Steyning (1326), and it was found that he "late held the castle and manor of Brembre, with the town of Shoreham, for life, as part of the Barony of Brembre as of the heritage of Hugh le Despenser, Earl of Winchester, as appeared by a fine levied between Alina, who was the wife of John de Mowbray and Hugh, Earl of Winchester. And the castle and manor of Brembre he (William) demised to the King for the term of the life of the said

William." The next heirs of William de Braose were stated to be Alina de Mowbray and John de Bohun, son and heir of Joan, who was the wife of James de Bohun.

After the death of Edward II. and the execution of the Despensers, King Edward III., in the first year of his reign, sensible of the services rendered to the Crown by the Mowbray family, restored them to favour.

John de Mowbray, son of the Sir John who had been executed in the previous reign, held the Castle and Manor of Bramber and the town of Shoreham of the King in chief by Barony. He attended the King in two expeditions to France and when the French threatened to invade the coast of Sussex he was directed to remain in his Castle at Bramber, which was to serve as a stronghold from whence he and his men at arms might sally forth and annoy the enemy. He espoused a daughter of Henry, Earl of Lancaster, and died of pestilence at York, 1362.

The Mowbray family continued to hold the Castle and Barony of Bramber for several generations, passing from the above-named John to his son John, who was slain at Constantinople in 1369, then to the latter's son, John de Mowbray, Earl of Nottingham (died 1383, aged 19), to his brother, Thomas Mowbray, who was created Duke of Norfolk and died at Venice, 1399, to his son, Thomas Mowbray, Earl Marshal and of Nottingham (beheaded at York) and to his brother John, who was 14 years of age at the time of his succession and to whom the Dukedom was restored.

After the death of Thomas, Duke of Norfolk (1399), his widow married Sir Robert Gonshill, and at the death of the latter (1403) it was stated that " he held the Borough of Shoreham." His widow, Elizabeth, died July, 1425, and it was then stated that she " held in dower the day she died the manors of Fyndon, Knappe, Grenestede and the Borough of Shorham, which, after her death, reverted to John, Duke of Norfolk, son and heir of the late Duke and Elizabeth." In the Borough of New Shoreham certain rents of assize are mentioned and a sea-port held of the King in chief by Knight's service.

Sir John Arundel, who died in 1422, held the Manor of Shoreham with appurtenances of the Earl Marshal, and when Thomas, Earl of Arundel, died in 1427, he held the Manor of Shoreham " of John, Duke of Norfolk, his nephew, by what service is unknown."

John de Mowbray, Duke of Norfolk, died in 1432 and the

LOCAL GOVERNMENT

Barony of Bramber descended to his son, John, Duke of Norfolk, who, dying (1461) left a son, John, created Earl of Warenne and Surrey in his father's lifetime. He died (1476) without issue surviving and the Honour of Bramber devolved on the Howards, Dukes of Norfolk, with whom Bramber descended as Arundel, the present Duke of Norfolk being Lord of the Manor of New Shoreham.

In the first year of Henry VII. the Manor of Shoreham was granted to Thomas West, Lord de la Warr and the borough and town of Shoreham granted in fee farm to Sir Thomas Seymour in 1st Edward VI.

The Manor is co-extensive with the parish but extends seaward from the Harbour Mouth to Old Shoreham Bridge, being bounded on the south and west by the river bank. It formerly comprised the rights of fishery, anchorage, boomage (a tax on every ship, possibly at so much per mast), and meterage (the right to license meters and taking a fee for the licence) for which officers were appointed, but in 1760, when the Board of Harbour Commissioners was appointed and authorised to levy tolls, the rights of anchorage and boomage ceased.

There prevails in this Manor the custom of "borough English," by which land held by copyhold descends to the youngest son, daughter, or collateral heir, as the case may be. A peculiar rule of descent, the real origin of which is lost. The copyholds are somewhat numerous and are held at small fines certain and there are also some freeholds held of the Manor by quit-rents and heriots.

The local government was formerly in the hands of two High Constables (an office dating from the reign of Edward I.), who, together with a headboro', two ale-conners, two leather-searchers and sealers, coal-meters and a pound-keeper and town-crier, were annually appointed at the Court Leet. More recently the only officials appointed were one High Constable and the Town-crier. Major T. B. Gates was the last High Constable of New Shoreham. James Chapman was the last Crier officially appointed. But an unofficial crier and his bell still lingers and his "take notice" is heard from time to time as he makes known to the public any forthcoming event of local interest.

The "Local Government Act, 1858," was adopted by the town 6th December, 1865, when a Local Government Board was formed, but under the Act of 1894 the town is now governed by an Urban

THE STORY OF SHOREHAM

District Council of 15 members. By a Local Government Board order which came into operation October 1st, 1910, New Shoreham extended her boundaries and was re-named Shoreham-by-Sea. The Urban District comprises the town of New Shoreham, Old Shoreham, Kingston-by-Sea, and the greater part of Bungalow Town, and has been divided into North, South, Marine, and Kingston-by-Sea Wards.

The following gentlemen have held the office of Chairman of the Urban District Council :—W. H. Harker, 1894-1901 ; C. Howard, 1901-2 ; H. Reeks, 1902-3 and 1905-6 ; T. B. Gates, 1903-5 ; E. R. Harmsworth, 1906-7 ; A. Chubb, 1907-8 ; S. Gregory-Taylor, 1908-9 ; Ellman Brown, 1909-11 ; H. G. Evershed, 1911-13 ; A. Eade, 1913-15 ; M. L. Cook, 1915-17 ; A. Chapman, 1917-18 ; W. P. Glazebrook, 1918-21 ; S. Gregory Taylor, 1921.

The Custom House, being no longer required for that purpose, was leased to the Local Government Board for a Town Hall, and was opened on Lady Day, 1890, by Sir Henry Fletcher, Member for the Parliamentary Division of Lewes. It has recently been purchased by the town from the Hooper family. The building which formerly served as a Town Hall, in East Street, is now part of St. Mary's Hall.

The important part which fairs played in the life of a town during the Middle Ages and later is well known. In the reign of King John (1202) a fair lasting eight days was established at Shoreham. In 1220 a fourth part of the fairs held in the town was granted by John de Braose to Sele Priory. At the beginning of Edward the First's reign we learn that William de Braose possessed the town and port of Shoreham, with toll and other lawful customs thereto belonging. At that time there was a free market on Wednesdays and Saturdays and a fair of two days at the Feast of the Exaltation of the Holy Cross (September 14th) " at which he takes his accustomed tolls and assize of bread and ale." The Lord of Bramber also possessed the rights over the seacoast and fishery by his mariners of Shoreham, " from Beauchef (Beachey Head) as far as the Isle of Wight and to the middle of the sea."

It is probable that these early markets and fairs fell into abeyance with the decay of the town during the 15th century, but as it began again to be a little more prosperous about the beginning of the 17th century the need of a market again became apparent.

At Shoreham. 1906.
Arthur B. Packham.

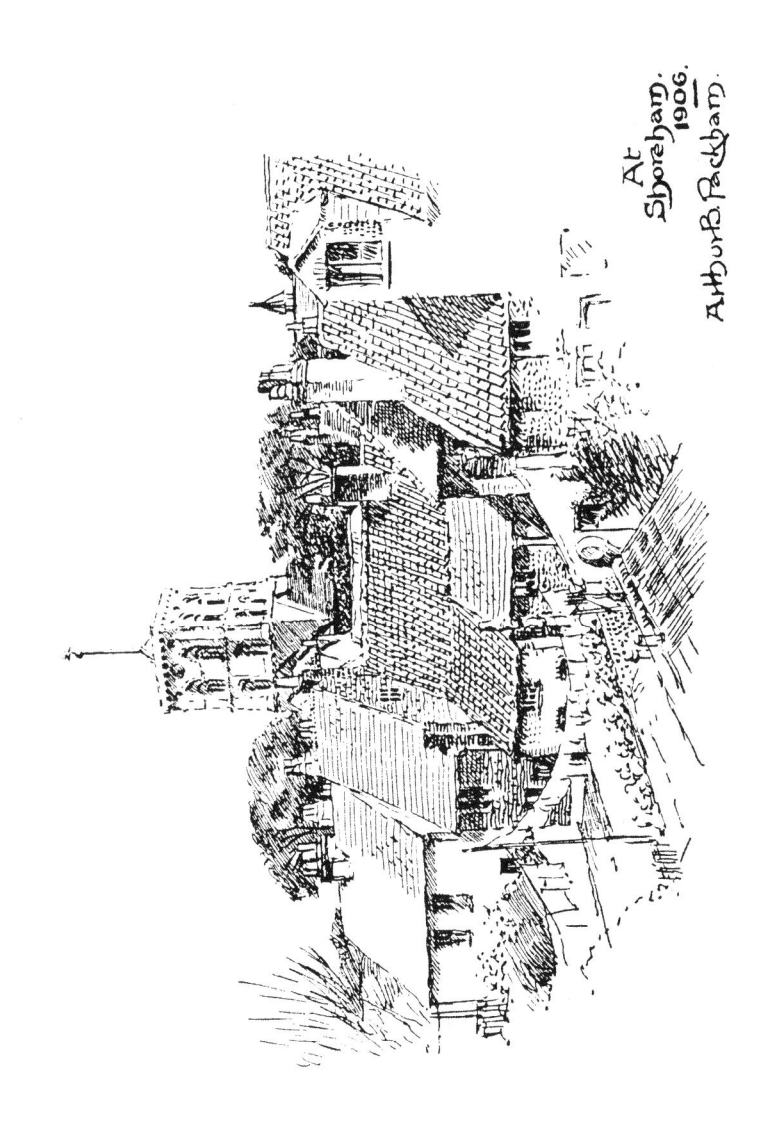

THE STORY OF SHOREHAM

The original Charter, granted by James I., to hold a weekly market on Tuesdays, is preserved at the Town Hall. It is inscribed on a sheet of vellum, ornamented with a portrait of King James and some floral work and has the Great Seal of England attached. This Charter was granted at the suit of Thomas, Earl of Arundel, to his uncles, Thomas, Earl of Suffolk, and Lord William Howard, conceding them full licence to hold a market in the town of New Shoreham every Tuesday and to take all tolls arising therefrom. It is dated June 9th, 1608. The Earl of Arundel, at whose suit the Charter was granted, being at the time a minor, probably accounts for the grant itself being conveyed to his uncles. The document provides also for a Court of Piepowder to be held on market-days. This name is a corruption of the court of *piedpoudre (curia pedis pulverizati)* said to be so called from the dusty feet of most of the suitors who frequented the court, although, perhaps, a more satisfactory derivation is *pied puldreaux* or the court of the pedlars. It was a court wherein the steward of the owner of the market or fair was judge, with power to administer justice for all commercial injuries or disputes, transacted at the gathering of trades, and on all commercial complaints its authority was absolute. An offender might be taken, a jury of similar trades empanelled on the spot, evidence heard at once, and the offender commence his punishment all within an hour.

In later years Saturday became the market-day and is so noted in a Gazetteer of 1770 and in Bailey's British Directory of 1784. There was also a corn market every alternate Monday.

According to De Foe, the original Market House, "an antient and very strong building, was blown flat to the ground " in the great storm of 27th November, 1703, and at the same time, he tells us, " all the town shattered."

Some years later a new Market House was erected at the expense of Sir Nathaniel Gould, Member for the Borough. This building is described as having consisted of " an oblong canopy of freestone, embellished with gothic ornaments, supported by ten columns " and is said to have been a fine piece of architecture. It stood almost in the centre of the town, immediately in front of the present Crown and Anchor. Two of its columns yet remain in use as lamp-posts, one at each extremity of the ancient Market-place. It is almost needless to state that neither are *in situ*, although not far removed from their original position

TRADE TOKENS

Why this building was removed in the year 1823, to make room for its successor, which is described as having been "a mean building of brick," we are not able to say.

The annual fair held at Shoreham is within the memory of the present generation. It took place on the 25th July (St. James' Day) and the stalls were arranged in the Market-place—on the Custom-house Stones and the south side of the High Street. It was discontinued about 30 years ago, having then dwindled to a mere collection of toys and pedlary—a ghost of its former self.

The tradesman's half-penny token issued in the 17th century has on the obverse " Richard Glyd of New " and a griffin in the field. The reverse has "Shoram in Sussex " and the letters G./R.A. in the field.

The Shoreham Shilling.

The very beautiful shilling token issued by Clayton and Hyde in 1811 shows a view of the church. In June, 1920, two of these "Shoreham shillings" were sold by auction in London for £3 10s. The firm named carried on business in the premises at the south-west corner of John Street, afterwards Tillstone's, and more recently Ayling's.

An important event in the history of the town was the building of the Suspension Bridge to carry the main coast road over the Adur. It was designed by W. Tierney Clarke, the architect of Hammersmith and Marlow Bridges, and the masonry work performed by W. Ranger of Brighton. It was opened May 1st, 1833, with an appropriate ceremony. Old Shoreham Bridge having been locked up by the High Constable of Shoreham, the keys were delivered to the Duke of Norfolk. His Grace was accompanied by the Earl and Countess of Surrey, the Duke and Duchess of St. Albans, Sir C. F. Goring and Sir James Lloyd,

THE STORY OF SHOREHAM

Baronets, and these notables headed a procession to the new bridge, where the Duke performed the opening ceremony. A luncheon followed. The Lion and Horse surmounting the arches carrying the chains upon which the bridge is suspended represent the crests of the noble Duke whose name it bears. In the words of the Press at the date of opening—"an elegant structure, reflecting much credit both on the architect and builder."

Of Inns, the most famous in former times was the Star. It was an old coaching house and the premises extended from the corner of Church Street (Star Lane) to, and including, the site now occupied by Eade's Stores. Its sign formerly was suspended over the High Street by means of two uprights and a cross-beam, from which it hung high above the traffic which passed under it. In more recent years the premises have served as an ordinary public-house, and as such are now closed. The Dolphin Chambers was formerly an Inn, but the successor of a still older Dolphin. Part only of the ancient Fountain Inn, adjoining the Old Ship-yard, remains. Until superseded by the modern Bridge Inn this house of entertainment had been known to travellers for generations. The "Old George Inn" stood practically on the site of the Primitive Methodist Church. A King's Arms, possibly the present day King's Head, and a Ship are both mentioned in the 10th year of George I. The White Lion (the arms borne by the de Mowbray family, anciently Lords of Shoreham) gave name to White Lion Street, now West Street.

An examination of the interior of many of the houses in New Shoreham reveals an antiquity not always apparent from a glance at the outside. Many have been refronted and in some cases "post and panel" work has been plastered over. Low entrances and ground-floors much below the level of the street, stout oak beams and chimney-corners—the latter adapted to modern requirements—bespeak the antiquity of the homes of many of the townspeople.

A very ancient tenement, in which the business of harness making and saddlery is carried on still remains in East Street. It shows unmistakable signs of extreme old age. An examination of the interior will lead to the assumption that it has been standing not less than four hundred years and it is not at all unlikely that, in the distant past, it was a farmstead.

OLD HOUSES

The property adjoining to the north is "Lladloes" and is so named in the title deeds, but the origin of such name is lost.

"Bank House," on the opposite side of the street, though altered and adapted to the requirements of modern business premises, retains some features of interest. Several of the rooms, originally forming one very spacious apartment, are

The Saddler's Shop, East St., Shoreham.

panelled from floor to ceiling. These panels were formerly decorated with paintings, now unfortunately obliterated by one uniform colour. In the deed of conveyance the premises are described as "formerly in the several tenures of James Mitchell, William Stevens, Hugh Roberts, Sir Ralph Moore, Widow Muggridge, Charles Annington" and others.

It may be of interest to note that the present vicarage house was formerly known as "Cupola House," so called from the

THE STORY OF SHOREHAM

cupola with lantern which then surmounted it. It is said to have served the purpose of signalling to smugglers to warn them of danger or to assure them of safety when a cargo was waiting to be "run."

There are two or three old houses of interest remaining in the High Street and of these may be mentioned "Stone House," "Ye Olde Red House," and some cottages at the corner of West Street. Others showing signs of antiquity are to be found in West Street, John Street, Ship Street, and Church Street. The "Three Houses" at the north end of Southdown Road (formerly New Barns Lane) have been robbed of their old-time quaintness by recent restoration.

Most of the "field" names are marked on the map. The "Longcroft" is mentioned in a will, 16th December, 1618. Some land described as "part of Clubb's Hall" (east side of Brunswick Road) was sold early in the last century for building and so was the "Seven Acres" on which stand the houses in Queen's Place and Western Road and over part of which runs the line to Worthing. Other fields, some of them also built on, are Ravenscroft, Baron's Croft, Stonegate Field, and Bayfield. Gordon and Rosslyn Roads are built on part of the Ham Field (Old Shoreham).

Few of the elm trees, for which the town was once so famous, now remain. They grew on either side of some of the principal streets and the churchyard was surrounded by them. It is said that many were cut down to supply the wood for gunstocks for the Army during the French Wars. A venerable specimen is still standing on the north side of the churchyard, two very fine trees at the north end of Ravens Road and one or two in Mill Lane and elsewhere, while at Old Shoreham they are more plentiful, though many have been laid low by the storms of recent years.

The Shoreham Grammar School is one of the chief educational establishments of the district. It was founded in 1842 by the late Mr. W. H. Harper. It has for many years been carried on with conspicuous success by the present Head Master and proprietor, S. Gregory Taylor, Esq., M.A.

An excellent boarding and day-school is conducted by ladies at Longcroft and there are several good preparatory schools, both in the town and on the beach. The Council Schools are in Ham Road. They were the former Board School buildings, the

A NEW TOWN

foundation stone of which was laid in 1874 by Mrs. Clara Gates, wife of Mr. Thomas Gates, Chairman of the Local Government Board. The new Council Schools are in Victoria Road, on the site of the Swiss Gardens. The Roman Catholic School stands on the site of the old cottages shown in the accompanying picture.

The former lonely and desolate beach is now almost covered with bungalows, which have been erected in an endless variety

Old Cottages formerly on site of Catholic School
Arthur B Packham
(from photo) 1918.

of styles. Some are fantastic, some grotesque, many are beautiful, and some are—not. To a certain extent the place has still something of the appearance of a town in the making, and although its condition is not quite that of "Eden" in Dickens' "Martin Chuzzlewhit," it certainly " aint all built yet."

But some day it will be a large town and meanwhile bungalows rapidly increase in number. Many have had their origin in disused railway carriages. It is remarkable to note the very

THE STORY OF SHOREHAM

roomy bungalows which have been formed by placing two carriages in parallel position a few feet apart, building a saloon in the space between them and a verandah at either end. But they are not all so composed and a more picturesque and permanent type is now in fashion.

The Ferry Shoreham

The names which have been given to these bungalows are as varied and as fanciful as the styles of building. Some, very appropriately, have reference to the marine surroundings, others bear the names of flowers, some of Sussex hills and villages or of places far distant. A few suggest the repose of a seaside resort as yet not quite spoilt by the noise and bustle of the modern

THE BEACH

sea-coast town. Some bear the titles of well-known nursery stories, pantomime and light opera.

It is curious to note that visitors to Bungalow Town often refer to Shoreham itself as "the village." "I am going over to the village," you will sometimes hear them say. Others, who seem to have a somewhat hazy notion of the geography of the district, will refer to Bungalow Town as "the island."

Although included in the Shoreham area for purposes of civil government, Bungalow Town is wholly in the parish of Lancing, and a chapel-of-ease erected some years ago is dedicated to "the Good Shepherd."

In spite of the fact that a large and populous town is quickly covering the beach many beautiful wild flowers still flourish in abundance, one of the gayest being the yellow-headed poppy.

At high tide, in genial weather, the passage across the river to and from Bungalow Town by ferry-boat is a pleasant experience. At low tide it is otherwise. You may then almost, —but not quite—walk over and there is a ford for horses and carts. At high tide the Adur presents the appearance of a fine lake. At low tide she trickles through a waste of mud.

The foot-bridge, opened with appropriate ceremony February 3rd, 1921, by Earl Winterton, Member for the Horsham and Worthing Parliamentary Division, is a great convenience to Shoreham and Bungalow Town. It brings up the number of bridges now crossing the Adur at Shoreham to four and is already justifying its existence. Our aged townsman, Mr. Thomas Stow, present at the opening of this latest bridge, saw the Norfolk Bridge opened in the year 1833.

CHAPTER VII

GRANTS TO ANCIENT RELIGIOUS HOUSES—KNIGHTS HOSPITALLERS AND TEMPLARS—CARMELITE PRIORY—ITS GRADUAL RUIN BY THE SEA —HOSPITALS OF ST. CATHERINE, ST. SAVIOUR, AND ST. JAMES.

MENTION has been made of the founding of the Priory of Sele by William de Braose and of the property with which he endowed it. The same baron also made considerable grants to the great Abbey of Battle which William the Conqueror had founded on the site of his triumphant victory over the last of the Saxon kings.

De Braose granted to the Abbey " 8 messuages in the Borough of Bramber in the Rape of the same name in Sussex, and three others in Sorham, and one hide of land in Sorham to be held for ever without molestation." He also gave the Abbot and monks, annually, 400 bushels of salt and 10 bushels of wine, which the Abbot of Fécamp paid him yearly for a certain land of his which he held called "Wurmincgeherste" (Warminghurst, near Steyning), near Lenglentune. In like manner he freely gave for one of his knights, named Haseline, another hide of land called "Herincgeham" (Erringham). At the same time another of his knights, named Ralph, the son of Theodore, with his consent and confirmation, gave another 400 bushels of salt to the Abbey. Tetbert, one of the tenants of William de Braose, "influenced by the example of such benevolence and piety, earnestly desired to become a monk and devoutely dedicated himself to the Abbey." With the assent and confirmation of his Lord, he gave with himself the lands which he possessed, viz., 1 hide at Lenglentune in Heregrave, called "Wulfran's hide" in "free and eternal possession."

All these gifts Philip de Braose, son of William, confirmed in his father's presence. The latter, in accordance with the liberties and royal dignities of Battle Abbey, granted that the burgesses whom he had given with their houses "should have full possession to buy and sell within their houses without molestation and without toll, except on market-days when wares were publicly exposed."

GIFTS TO RELIGIOUS HOUSES

Among other gifts to Religious Houses may be noted that of Matilda, the wife of John de Beauchamp. Early in the reign of Henry III. she " gave and confirmed to the Prior and Canons of Calceto (near Arundel) all the rents which they had received from Bernard de Hagia, her husband's father." In addition "the plain with a messuage thereupon of which he became possessed in the town of Shoreham, by marriage with her mother, Matilda." These gifts were made for the express purpose of providing a lamp to burn constantly before the altar of St. Mary, in the Church of Calceto, as a perpetual alms. The remains of this Priory of Calceto stand on the left-hand side of the road leading from Worthing to Arundel in a small enclosure at the foot of "Causeway Hill," the descent which leads down to the lowlands of the river Arun.

About the middle of the thirteenth century William of Arundel, son of Edward King, " for the salvation of the souls of his father and mother and all his ancestors," gave three shops in the town of Shoreham to St. Mary's Hospital at Chichester. They were described as " adjoining the house of Robert the Minter on the south side and extending to the corner."

Some reference has already been made to the former existence of Religious Houses in Shoreham. The Knights Hospitallers and Knights Templars had a contemporary existence in the town. There is ample proof that the establishments of both these Orders were situated on land south of the present High Street, but long since swallowed up by the sea, before the shingle-bank was formed and the river forced to take its present eastward course. The Adur, therefore, runs over the site of the conventual buildings and the shingle-bank covers up much of the land with which both Hospitallers and Templars were endowed.

The Knights Hospitallers were founded in the year 1113, but the exact date when they acquired land at Shoreham cannot be ascertained. The first reference to their existence in the town is found in the Cottonian MS. (Nero E VI.) in the British Museum. It tells us that " William de Braose (probably the grandson of the first William) confirmed to the Hospital of St. John of Jerusalem in frank almoigne all the land which William Trenchenote held at Shoreham and the tolls and pontage and all customs and exactions which should come to the said William or his heirs from his goods and chattels at Shoreham for the good of the souls of the said William, his father and mother."

THE STORY OF SHOREHAM

We also find that Alan Trenchemere made a grant to the same religious body of " a selion of land "—a long narrow strip of indeterminate area—in front of his house at Shoreham, " extending from the door of that house to the sea, to hold the same in frank almoigne." This grant was witnessed by Philip and Ralph de Hastings, Roger de Wyka, Berenger de Apineto, Viel, son of Berenger, Siward de Bolonia, William Trenchemere, James the Clerk, Master Richard de Hastings, and Jordan, his esquire.

These grants, as the term " frank almoigne " implies, rendered the grantees for ever free from every kind of earthly service to the grantors in respect of them so long as the lands remained in their hands, being perpetual tenure by free gift of charity.

The Knights Templars, a military Religious Order, having its origin in the Crusades and known as the Brothers of the Temple of Solomon, was founded in the year 1118, but, it is believed, had no possessions in England until about the year 1134. In the county of Sussex they had a Preceptory at Shipley, near West Grinstead, and another at Saddlescombe, near Poynings. How they came to acquire their land at Shoreham is not quite clear, but during the Pontificate of Alexander III., who reigned from 1159 to 1181, they were already established in the town. The setting up of this military-monkery had become a thorn in the flesh of the Abbot of St. Florent, who, as patron of the parish church, regarded the Templars with jealous eye and no little disfavour.

The Abbot complained that the Knights Templars " had built an oratory within the parish of his Church at Shoreham, infringing thereby on the rights of a monk of St. Florent, who held the same by the authority of the Roman Pontificate." A covenant was therefore entered into between the Abbot and the Templars. In this document it was stated that " the Templars having received full papal licence to build and maintain a church and chantry on their own lands, it is agreed that the chapel shall be upheld where it is on condition that the Templars collect no tithes and do not admit the parishioners to daily service or to burial, but that after hearing mass in their own parish church on solemn days and Sundays they may resort for devotion to the chapel, while passengers and strangers only are allowed to make voluntary oblations there."

By the middle of the thirteenth century the Templars had

TEMPLARS AND HOSPITALLERS

apparently ceased to exercise their religious functions at Shoreham although still owning the property. In 1253 Brother Rocelin de Fos, Master of the Templars in England, entered into a covenant with William Bisshop of Staninges (Steyning) and Dionisia, his wife, granting to them a messuage in Shoreham which Maud de Temple held of the Templars. They were to hold it for life at a yearly rental of 20s. and were to maintain the houses and chapel in that messuage. On William's death a third part of his goods was to go to the Templars as an obit and on the death of the longer liver the property was to revert to the Templars. This covenant was signed at London during Eastertide, 1253, and was witnessed by Hugh Waldefare, Philip de Hollburn, John de Beauchamp, William le Mercer, Finian de Shoreham, John Swele, and Peter de Bosco.

In 1292 Guido de Foresta, the Grand Master of the Templars, granted to John and Matilda Lote the lease of the tenement and chapel in New Shoreham called "La Temple" so long as they should pay to the Templars at Saddlescombe the sum of 20s. per annum and should keep the house and chapel in repair.

In the year 1308 Edward II. seized every Knight Templar in the realm and committed them all to prison on charges of practising profane rites. By the application of cruel tortures confessions were wrung from many of them. Some were burnt at Smithfield and the order was totally abolished. In the valuation of their property in Sussex mention is made of their house and chapel at New Shoreham. This, and all other Templar possessions, was granted to the Knights Hospitallers of St. John of Jerusalem, which order, as we have before noted, had long been their near neighbours at Shoreham.

Disputes between the Knights of St. John and the Abbot of St. Florent quickly followed. At length the former were forbidden to appoint one of their own order to officiate as a priest in the chapel. Finally it was agreed that they were to be permitted to nominate a secular clerk to minister there but he was to hold his appointment as from the Bishop of Chichester, to whom he was to pay the same canonical obedience as was due from the incumbent of the parish church.

You will find in the street nomenclature of the town, John Street; formerly it was St. John Street—probably a faint echo of those far-off days when the Knights Hospitallers of St. John of Jerusalem flourished in the town. The street in question,

THE STORY OF SHOREHAM

crossing and continuing south of the High Street, possibly was the highway to their property.

Another Religious House was founded at Shoreham in 1316 by Sir John de Mowbray on land apparently quite near to the "Temple" and certainly south of the High Street. This was the Carmelite Priory of the Blessed Virgin Mary. A year or two later the visitor and chapter of the Hospital of St. John of Jerusalem in England was requested to grant to the order of St. Mary of Mount Carmel "the chapel and plot of land that the Templars formerly had in Shoreham." The Carmelites required the property so that they might "construct a house and oratory for them to dwell in there" and agreed to render the brethren of the Hospital as much yearly as was rendered therefore to the Templars.

The result of this request was a grant by Thomas Larchier, Prior of the Hospital of St. John of Jerusalem, to the Prior and Carmelites of New Shoreham of "a messuage called the Temple with a chapel therein, to him and his Priory for ever." The grant was dated "in the celebration of the Chapter of St John of Clerkenwell, by London, 4th Ides of February, 1325."

About the same time the Carmelites acquired from William de Braose, father-in-law of the founder, land adjoining their house, formerly built upon but then vacant. De Braose held this land of the King in chief as a burgage of the town. It was later the subject of an Inquisition held at Shoreham by the King's Escheator for Sussex. Certain men of the town said on oath that it would be to the prejudice of the King to allow the Carmelites to retain the property in question. It had been acquired after the publication of the Statute in Mortmain and without first obtaining permission of the King. However, in spite of this, we find that the Carmelites were pardoned for acquiring in mortmain this property and entering therein without licence. Moreover they received licence to retain the same.

Although Thomas Larchier and the brothers of St. John had granted to the Carmelites the Templar property and renounced all claim to it in their favour, the lease of the "house and chapel" called the Temple seems to have been held by the Lotes until 1336. In that year, on the death of her husband, Matilda Lote, described in the deed of gift, as "of the Temple," gave the house and chapel to God and the Blessed Mary and the Carmelite Friars of Shoreham. Two of the witnesses to this deed were Thomas

THE CARMELITE PRIORY

Mouraunt and Richard Serle, whose names are to be found as those of men who represented Shoreham in Parliament in 1326 and 1360.

Meanwhile, in 1330, John Kingswoode of Findon gave the Friars a tenement in the town of New Shoreham, which he held under the Temple. This tenement was described as having the house of Simon Crabwych on the south side of it and that of Robert Herryngs, together with other houses the property of John le Blaker, John de la Knauc, John le Ferur and Simon Trenchmere on the west, and the marsh of the Templars, called " le Templestead," to the north and east. Among the witnesses to this deed was a John de Bokyngham. Kingswoode also gave them at Christmas in the same year, by the hands of their Prior, Nicholas de Bedinges, six marks sterling of good and lawful money, in addition to twelve marks due to him on the purchase of the house alluded to.

In 1336 Margaret Covert, of Sullington, willed to the Friars 1 qr. of wheat, 2 qrs. of barley and 15s. for six trentals for the souls of her late husband, Sir John Covert, herself and others.

In 1348 the Prior and Brothers of the Order of the Virgin of Mount Carmel of Shoreham petitioned King Edward III. to allow Sir John de Mowbray, son of the founder, to assign to them a vacant piece of land containing one acre and a half which Sir John held of the King in chief as of his Barony of Bramber. The piece in question adjoined the dwelling-house of the Carmelites and *extended to the High Street on the north.* It was required for the purpose of enlarging the said dwelling-house "which," said the petitioners, " *is on the coast of the sea-port, at the extreme end of the town of Shoreham, and is subject to devastation and destruction towards the east by the ebb and flow of the tides, and the same is likely to become a ruin unless a remedy is very quickly applied.*"

An Inquisition into this matter was taken before the King's Escheator at Shoreham on Saturday, after the Feast of St. Gregory the Pope, in the presence of William atte Helde, bailiff of the town, and twelve of the inhabitants, who stated on oath " that it is not to the damage or prejudice of the King or others if the King grants the petition of the Prior and monks."

Thus it is apparent that the encroaching sea was already considerably damaging the property of the Carmelites and causing them no little anxiety as to its preservation.

Again, in 1363, the King was petitioned to allow John atte

THE STORY OF SHOREHAM

Hyde of "Iryngham," and Isabel, his wife, to grant a messuage with appurtenances adjoining the dwelling-house of the Prior and Friars in New Shoreham to enlarge their dwelling-house.

A few years later the Carmelites appear to have enlarged their church, as in 1368 Sir Michael de Poynings left them £20 for that purpose. Small bequests were also made to them by John Borle in 1373 and William Laxman in 1374.

Ralph Double, citizen and fishmonger of London, whose will was proved 29th March, 1392, in addition to other bequests, left to " the Prior and Convent of Friars of New Shoreham " 6s. 8d. to celebrate for his soul and for the souls of his parents and brothers and others. This testator also left £15 for a chaplain to celebrate for his soul in New Shoreham Church, 6s. 8d. to the Vicar for the same purpose and 6s. 8d. to the church fabric. One of the witnesses to this will was Thomas Brydham, "Vicar of New Schorham." Robert Rede, Bishop of Chichester, left the Carmelites a small bequest in 1414.

In addition to the property already mentioned the Carmelites owned three roods of land " in the meadow of Burstall," given them by Richard Stapleton. Early deeds relating to this describe its situation as " near the land of Amicia de Wayte," and as running from that belonging to the Templars to the water's edge. Robert de Lindon gave them a meadow adjoining this land.

This southern part of the town was too unprotected from the encroachments of the sea to suffer any other fate than complete ruin. By the year 1493 the sea had made such overwhelming inroads that it threatened to sweep away the little that remained of the Carmelite Priory and eventually it disappeared beneath the waves. The waters of the Adur now flow over the site of the church and conventual buildings. The shingle-bank, heaped up after the sea had overwhelmed much of the town and destroyed several streets, covers up part of the Priory lands.

Driven out from their home the Friars were obliged to seek another asylum. They migrated to the Priory of Sele. As it had belonged to the Abbey of St. Florent it had reverted to the Crown at the suppression of Alien Priories in 1450, and nine years later was annexed to Magdalen College, Oxford, by Bishop Waynfleet. In 1493 it was tenantless and here the Carmelites from Shoreham, whose house " was not only falling into decay but in danger of being entirely washed away by the sea," found

RELIGIOUS HOSPITALS

a refuge, the college leasing to them the house, chapel, and four acres of land. They appear to have been, at the Dissolution of the Monasteries, the poorest of all the Sussex Friars, against none of whom, we are told, could charges of luxury be levelled. When the Bishop of Dover came, in July 1538, to the White Friars of Sele he "found neither Friar nor secular, but the doors open ; there was none to serve God and had not been for some time."

The only recorded names of the Priors of Shoreham are :— Nicholas de Bedynge, in 1329 ; Nicholas, in 1342 (possibly the same individual) ; John Bromlee, before 1383, and John Crawle, in 1414. It is recorded that in 1438 Brother John Bolney was ordained a Deacon of the Convent of Shoreham, in Boxgrove Church.

The Hospital of St. Katherine of Shoreham is known from its occurrence in the Subsidy Roll of 1327 and in several mediaeval wills. Margaret Covert, in 1366, John Borle, rector of West Tarring, in 1373, and Andrew Peverell, in 1375, left small bequests to it, and the will of Richard Jay, of Crawley, 1466, mentions "the almspeople of the hospital of St. Kateryn." It probably survived the religious changes of the Reformation by abandoning its patroness and becoming "the Hospital of Our Saviour, Jesus Christ," from the fact that much prominence is given to St. Katherine's emblem on the sixteenth century seal, by which alone the existence of a Hospital of St. Saviour at Shoreham is known. If this conjecture is correct the reconstituted Hospital was no doubt "the spytyll" at Shoreham to which Henry Marshall, Vicar of Wilmington, left 20 pence in 1550.

The seal just referred to is a pointed oval. Our Lord on the Cross on a mount between two trees of peculiar form, in base, a Catherine wheel. Legend :—"The sele of O' Saviour Jesus Christ of the 'ospital of Shoram in Sussex."

Very little is known of the Hospital of St. James. It was in existence in 1249, when, at an Assize held at Lewes, "Letitia, who was the wife of Ralph Beaufz," brought an action against

THE STORY OF SHOREHAM

the master of St. James of Shoreham, Ralph, son of Agnes, and Robert Deth, to recover two acres of land "in Suwyk" (Southwick) which she claimed in dower against them. The defendants did not appear at Lewes and judgment was given that the property should be taken into the King's hands, but they were summoned to appear on St. Hilary's day, three weeks later, at Winchester.

The Brothers of the Hospital of the Blessed James, in the Borough of New Shoreham, contributed to the subsidy levied in 1296, and again in 1327, and John Borle and Richard Jay, mentioned above, left small bequests to it. Nothing further is known of this Religious House until 1574, when its site and buildings were granted to John and William Mersh, of London. Whether this is the Hospital mentioned in the Valor Ecclesiasticus of 1535, or whether the reference is to that of St. Katherine is not clear. A faint echo of its former existence in the town is to be found in the will of Walter Farley of New Shoreham, mariner, dated 30th June, 1628. "Being sick in body, I make my will and desire to be buried in the church of New Shoreham. I bequeath to my wife all my household stuff and a tenement of cellars called *Hie Cakge*, and a croft called *St. James*, containing 3 roods of land, for her life, and after her death to my brother, John Farley and his heirs for ever ; if he die without heirs then the same to the heirs of my cousin, John Farley, of Benham Bridge (?Bineham Bridge) and Thomas Farley of the same."

CHAPTER VIII.

THE ANCIENT FERRY—THE "MARLIPINS"—FORGOTTEN STREET NAMES—OLD-TIME TRADERS—CUSTODY OF THE "COCKET"—WOOL TRADE—"OWLERS.'

The ancient ferry at Shoreham, approached from the west end of the High Street, crossed the river to the Lancing side. It was entirely distinct from the ferry at Old Shoreham mentioned in previous pages, nor must it be confused with the modern ferry to the beach, which had no existence in the Middle Ages.

It is mentioned in a Charter which King John granted to the burgesses of Shoreham in the year 1209, when they paid the King 30 marks " to have their town at farm for £70 " and also " to have their *ferry* during the King's pleasure, so that no horse above the value of three marks, nor any dog, nor any unknown messenger, burgess or merchant, shall have passage without the King's writ and unless they swear that they are carrying no message except it be to the honour of the King."

Somewhat later William Bernehus, of Cokeham, gave to the monks of Lewes Priory " the right of paying nothing at the passage of Shoreham beyond the harbour, provided the person really belongs to the Priory." For this concession he was promised a perpetual anniversary to his honour.

It is evident that the right of these monks to a free passage across the river to the Lancing side was sometimes disputed. This is disclosed in a case tried at Lewes " in the morrow of All Souls, 33 Henry III." (1249), when Roger de Hyda was summoned to answer the Prior of Lewes in a plea " that he permit him—the Prior and his men—to have free passage over the water of Shoreham in the boat of the said Roger free of freightage as he has always been wont to have." This privilege had been granted, so the Prior maintained, and as noted above, by William de Bernehus, father of Agnes (the former wife of Roger de Hyda), whose heir she was, and he produced the deed under which de Bernehus had made the grant to his Priory. " Nevertheless," said the Prior, " Roger demanded freightage for the ferry," whereby he had suffered damage to the value of 40s.

THE STORY OF SHOREHAM

Roger de Hyda, in defence, said that "he cannot answer thereto because he does not hold the ferry-boat or ferry, nor has any claim thereto." He said that John de Gatesden held the ferry, and the Prior, "who could not contradict this," was "in mercy."

Some years after this (1263) Thomas de Brom granted the ferry to Walter de la Hyde and Joan, his wife, on the basis of their paying him one pair of white gauntlets, or alternatively one penny each Easter and rendering the customary service of the town to the over-lord. They gave Thomas 40 marks (about £500 of our money), which must have constituted what would

"Roger demanded freightage for the ferry."

be a practical buying up of the entire rights, subject only to the small "peppercorn" rental of one penny at Easter, or the pair of white gauntlets.

At the same time Andrew de Lichepole "laid on " or, as we should say, " put in " his claim, probably for the services referred to as those due to the over-lord, which position he doubtless occupied in the manor of Lancing, to which the ferry was attached. A farm in the neighbourhood is still known as Lichpool or Leechpool.

In 1302 there was an enquiry as to whether "John de Gatesden, father of Margaret, the wife of William Paynell," was in possession of "a ferry across the water of Hulkesmouth, with appurtenances in New Shoreham," which Henry de Guldeford,

High St Shoreham

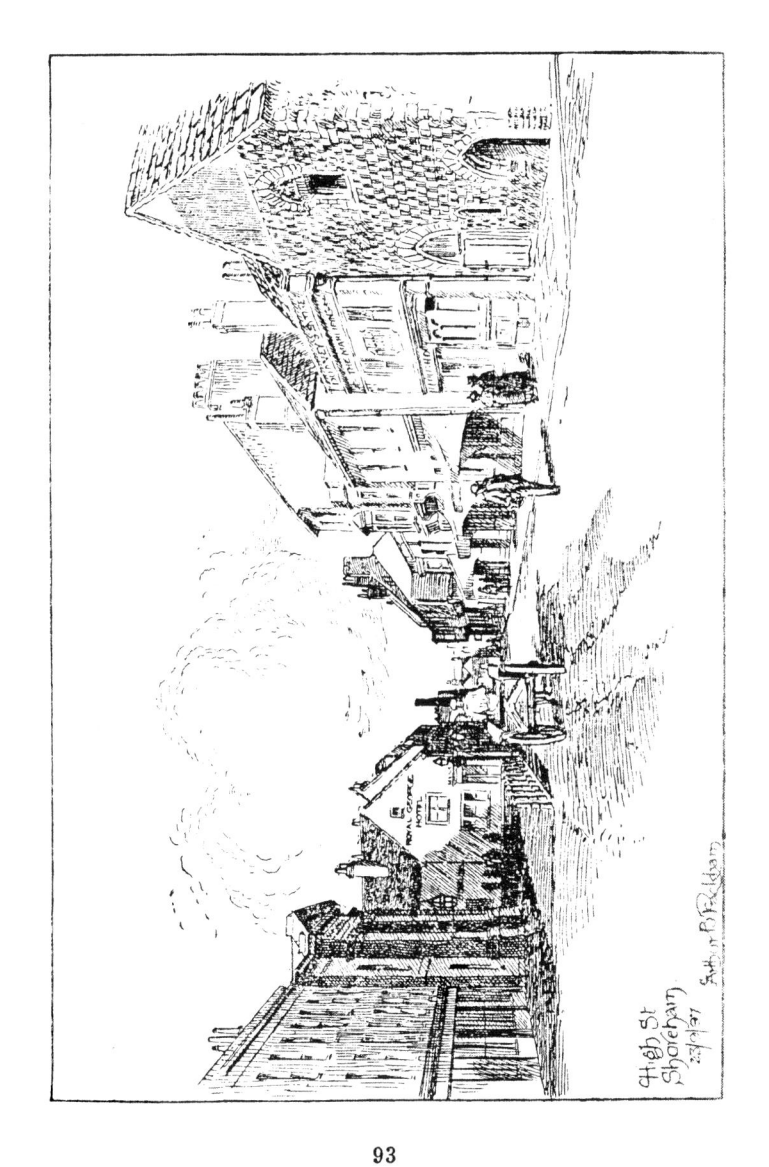

THE STORY OF SHOREHAM

Hawise, late the wife of Roger de Veel, Richard Serle and Maud, his wife, Walter Burgess and Isabel, his wife, held at that date.

Fourteen years later William Paynell granted to the Prior and canons of Herryngham (Hardham near Pulborough) on account of their poverty, " his manor of Cokeham and 32 acres of land in Lancing, together with a ferry (passagium) over the water of New Shoreham." It was stated that the ferry was then held of William de Braose by service of 4s. yearly, " de Braose holds of the King, and the said manor lands and ferry are worth £18 a year." In 1327 the profits were stated to be worth £20 per year.

In return for the endowments made them by William Paynell the monks of Hardham were to find four secular chaplains to celebrate divine service daily in their church for the souls of the King, Edward II., and his progenitors, and for the souls of William Paynell and his ancestors " for ever."

But the appointment of these secular chaplains led to unseemly daily strife in the Priory of Herryngham. In 1332 Matilda, daughter of John Paynell and heiress of William Paynell, while confirming the grant " of the passage over the river at New Shoreham " and the other endowments, seems to have deemed it a wise policy to allow the monks, for the future, to appoint four of their own order to celebrate the services. The unseemly quarrels which continually arose " on account of the difference of the rule of seculars and regulars " were thus to be avoided.

The remarkable building, known as the " Marlipins," which stands in the High Street (the ancient highway to the ferry) has survived the changes of at least six hundred years. A venerable relic of the Middle Ages, it may claim to be one of the very few buildings remaining in this country or elsewhere in Europe, erected during the late 13th or early 14th century for, and devoted to, entirely secular purposes.

Its time-worn appearance never fails to arrest the attention of the most casual observer, and many conjectures as to its origin and former uses have from time to time been put forward. Some have supposed that it was part of one of the Religious establishments previously dealt with, while others have vaguely referred to it as " a chantry."

It is built of Caen stone and knapped flints in chequered squares. On the south side, fronting to the High Street, pointed door-openings give access to the cellar, which is, however, very little below the level of the street, and to the stairs leading

THE MARLIPINS

to the loft above. Both cellar and loft have pointed windows. The window and door openings have no mouldings, only a plain chamfer to arch and jambs. On the Middle Street side the building shows evidence of somewhat rough repairing.

The original purpose for which the Marlipins was built is a matter of much uncertainty. It may have been erected to serve as a store for wool and hides, or for wines. There is no evidence to show that it was part of a Religious House and it certainly has nothing in common with a chantry.

Some years ago the writer, in searching the Calendars of Ancient Documents preserved in the Public Record Office, discovered that among them are several deeds relating to the Marlipins, which throw some light on its history.

The earliest is a grant by John le Pottere, of New Shoreham, to Juliana, late the wife of Reginald le Cartere, of the same, of a stone-built corner tenement called "Malduppinne," in the market place called "Otmarcat" (Oat Market) in New Shoreham, to hold for life, with remainder to Richard, her son. John Hemeri, bailiff of the town, was one of the witnesses to the grant, which is dated 1st August, in the 20th year of the reign of Edward III. (1347).

One hundred and thirty-two years later, that is to say, on the 31st August in the 18th year of Edward the Fourth's reign (1479), John Stempe, John Martyn and John Sharpe granted to Thomas atte Vanne, "of Suthampton," a stone-built corner tenement called "Malduppynne," in the market-place called "Cornmarket" of New Shoreham, late of Robert Coleman, deceased, adjoining the garden called "Prede," John Cookson, bailiff, being one of the witnesses.

On the 8th September in the 4th year of the reign of Henry VII. (1489) John Sharpe the elder, of New Shoreham, husbandman, granted the building to Thomas Dymocke, of Suthampton, merchant. It was then described as "a cellar with a chamber or loft above it," called "Malappynnys" in New Shoreham between the street called "Moderlove Strete" and a garden of the Lord of the said town, and another street called "Procession Strete."

Three years later, Thomas Dymocke, of Suthampton, merchant, granted the building to Richard Benjamin of Lewes. In this Deed it is described as "a cellar with a chamber or loft (camera sive lofta) over it," in New Shoreham, called "Malappynnys,"

THE STORY OF SHOREHAM

adjoining a street called "Moderlove Strete" and "Procession Strete." A letter of attorney authorises John Hunt to deliver seisin (possession) of the premises, 14th March, 11th Henry VII. (1496).

Four years after this there was a grant by Thomas Adam, clerk, and Thomas Thaccher, gentleman, to Henry Coby, Richard Rolle, Thomas Filde, Thomas Trower, John Cheverell, and John Delve the younger, of "a cellar with a chamber or loft above it," called "Malappynnys," in New Shoram, "bequeathed to the grantors by Richard Bengemyn, deceased," with letter of attorney authorising Thomas Garston to deliver seisin of the premises 1st October, 15th Henry VII. (1500).

The words "Malduppinne" and "Malappynnys" present a problem which is not easy of solution. It is possible that the terminations "ppinne" and "ppynnys" (pin and pins) suggest a connection with "pin," which is a barrel of brandy or wine containing ten gallons. In such a connection the word would possibly mean "place (or house) of the pins" (*i.e.*, of wine or brandy).

Standing in the Market Place for something like six hundred years, this old building must have witnessed many changing scenes as the centuries passed and many quaint ceremonies and customs long since forgotten.

Ceremonies, both religious and secular, doubtless gave to the High Street its ancient alternative name of "Procession Strete." Whether this street-name was common in other towns during the Middle Ages we do not know. So far the writer has met with no other reference to such a name in England, but—this only in passing—thousands of years ago ancient Babylon had a "Procession Street."

During the Middle Ages processions played a very important part in the observance of high days and holidays and all towns of any importance had trade gilds. It is clear that such existed in our town during the fourteenth century because the general writ issued for a return respecting gilds, 1st November, 1388, was proclaimed in the Borough of New Shoreham 15th December following.

There was a strong religious element in the organization of trade gilds at this period, and the custom of all the fraternities going in procession to the church of their town on certain feast days, carrying their banners and symbols, gradually developed during the 15th century until it became a sort of pageantry.

FORGOTTEN STREET NAMES

These pageants represented scenes from the Bible. They were really a series of tableaux and would appear to modern ideas somewhat profane. Each scene was enacted by a separate group of mechanics and tradesmen, who dressed in costumes suitable to the parts they were to play, and each tableau was usually " set " on a trolley or cart, which took its appointed place in the procession. The favourite subjects for such displays were the Creation of the World, Paradise, "Helle," Cain and Abel, Noah's Ark, Abraham and Isaac, Moses and Aaron with the Children of Israel, and Pharaoh and "his knights," David and Goliath, the Birth of Christ, the Baptism of Christ, and others. You will doubtless conclude that " Procession Strete " was so named from having been the scene of some such religious drama as the above.

Probably here, too, as elsewhere there was the religious ceremonial observance of Rogationtide, when it was customary for the priests and people to perambulate the streets and boundaries of the parish and ask the blessing of God upon the fruit of the field.

"Moderlove Strete" was the present Middle Street, and its ancient name presumably had some connection with the cult of the Virgin Mary. Possibly in those far-off days the rents of the property in this street were devoted to the upkeep of " the chantry at the altar of the Blessed Mary " in New Shoreham Church and for the maintenance of the chantry priest. The "garden called Prede" may have some reference to Predial tithes (tithes of that which grows from the ground only). The site of this garden appears to have been between the Marlipins and St. John Street.

The building has long served the purpose of a builder's store and carpenter's shop. For a short time after the outbreak of the war, the cellar was adapted to the practice of rifle firing, but has now resumed its former peaceful uses. It is to be regretted that such an interesting relic of the past has never been acquired for the housing of the antiquities of the neighbourhood. For such a purpose it would be well suited and would thus be saved from the destruction which, we fear, will one day overtake it.

In addition to the documents named above there is also in the Record Office a grant by John atte Corner to Roger atte Corner, his brother, of his corner tenement in New Shoreham, in a street called "Sowterystrete." It is witnessed by Reginald

THE STORY OF SHOREHAM

Goldismark, bailiff, and others, and is dated Monday after the Annunciation in the 10th year of the reign of Henry VI. (1432).

It would appear that the "corner tenement" mentioned in this grant does not refer to the Marlipins. "Sowterystrete" was probably situated in another part of the town—it may have been south of the High Street—and it is possible that the origin of this street-name may be found in the once common expression for a shoemaker—"souter." It is of frequent occurrence in old writings and a Simon le Souter is mentioned in one of the Assize Rolls relating to Shoreham. It was a common practice in ancient times for each trade to congregate together in its own street or locality, and so we find a "Mercery Lane" and a "Butcher's Row" in old cities such as Canterbury; and London abounds with similar examples. At Shoreham anyone requiring the services of a worker in leather would have sought such an individual in the particular street where he and his fellows carried on their special trade, which was in "Sowterystrete."

It seems that the term "souter" is even yet not quite obsolete. A shoemaker in one of the Sussex towns so described himself when claiming exemption before a Military Tribunal during the war.

Trade-names abound in the early Assize Rolls and we find at Shoreham mention of such individuals as Reginald the Smith, William le Goldsmith, Robert le Baker, John le Sopere, Nicholas le Taylor, and Richard le Barbour. John le Botiler was, no doubt, a maker of leather bottles, and John le Pottere probably fashioned most of his vessels from pewter and not clay. Ernald le Isemonger must have dealt in hardware, for the name is an old form of writing ironmonger, while the names of German le Brazour and Gervase le Brasur sufficiently indicate that they were workers in brass. John le Peleter probably got his living by preparing the furry skins of wild animals, and his name was derived from the "pell" or "pelt" applied to any undressed skin, doubtless brought into Shoreham in large numbers by ship from distant lands. Godfrey le Pilcher was a maker of "pilches" (the large outer tippets made of fur), Richard le Percur was a maker of leathern purses to suspend from the girdle, William le Ferur was probably a farrier, and German le Brewer a maker of strong liquor. Robert and Thomas le Tabler, both of whom are met with at Shoreham in the reign of Henry III., were makers of writing tablets at a time when paper was far too expensive to be

THE COCKET

merely scribbled upon, and tablets supplied its place. They were formed with a framework, sometimes of ivory, sometimes of cypress wood, overlaid with smeared wax, on which the characters were impressed with a sharp instrument known as a "pointel."

Among names which have no reference to trade we have found that of "Hamo Sourale," probably one whose somewhat crabbed and peevish nature earned him this very unenviable sobriquet.

A reference to the office of Controller of Customs is found during the reign of Edward I. in connection with the export traffic of wool to Flanders. Prior to that period several instances are mentioned of the infliction of fines on those who shipped it from the port without licence.

"During the discord," so runs the Assize Roll, referring to the war between Henry III. and his barons, William de Braose sent certain sacks of wool over sea and sold them to Flemings against the prohibition of the King. Also that Nicholas Dytton, his bailiff, "struck a bargain" with William de Chamond of Shoreham to send wool over the sea and to pay de Braose, his lord, a custom. De Chamond, failing to keep his part of the agreement, "inasmuch as he made no custom with de Braose for wool sent away," the baron put him into prison and kept him there until he paid him a fine of 10 marks. William de Braose was himself afterwards fined 20 marks for his share in this matter.

The Cocket.

In 1282 "Peter Jordan, of Lucca, and two others, men of Shoreham," were appointed to collect the new customs. The office included the custody of a "cocket," with which the merchandise was sealed before it left the port. The matrix giving the obverse of this seal is now in the British Museum and was found with a lot of oddments in the Pyx Chamber, Westminster Abbey, on the 21st June, 1842. The legend running round the "cocket" informs us that it is the seal of

THE STORY OF SHOREHAM

Edward I., King of England, and the words "de Sorham" at once identify it with our town. On a shield are the three lions of England, passant guardant. The reverse of the matrix is lost.

This "cocket," which was used at Shoreham for the collection of the tax on wool and hides, should not be confounded with the Borough Seal. It is recorded in 1304 that Arnald de Ryver, a merchant of Bayonne, forged an imitation of the "cocket."

It is apparent that this instrument was not always kept at Shoreham. After the execution of Sir John de Mowbray and the grant of his estates to Hugh le Despenser the younger, that baron, as lord of the town, influenced the King to transfer the "cocket" from Chichester, where it had been kept for some time, to Shoreham. Doubtless this was with an eye to the profits which the town and he himself would enjoy thereby, as the wool might be shipped only from the port where the "cocket" was kept. Thus in 1325, when Nicholas Tunstall was granted the office of Controller of Customs, it was directed that he was to receive in wages "as much as other controllers have had." At the same time William Vyvian and Germanus Hobelit were required to deliver to him the custody of "one part of the seal called 'cocket' and other things pertaining to the office," which were in their custody.

After the death of Edward II. and the execution of the Despensers the citizens of Chichester petitioned Edward III. to restore the "cocket" to their city. Vyvian and Hobelit were thereupon ordered to carry it back and exercise there "what pertains to the collection of the customs until otherwise ordered."

In 1341 Edward III. laid a wool tax on England, for the purpose of his French wars, and during the latter part of his reign there are further references to a "cocket" at Shoreham. Payment of customs was at times evaded by the wool merchants. In 1363 a ship freighted with over 100 sarplars of wool (a sarplar contained 40 tods) sailed from Shoreham to Calais. The sum of £400 realised by the sale of this merchandise was arrested by the searcher of the King's forfeiture because it was discovered that William Chaunterell, the master of the ship, had smuggled over from Shoreham and sold some wools "not cocketted." The King, "although he might for such deception proceed to

WOOL SMUGGLING

forfeiture of all the wools, and the body and goods of William Chaunterell, nevertheless has pardoned him in consideration of his confession."

Those who engaged in the export smuggling of wool became known as "owlers," because, like one who goes abroad o' nights, they usually carried prohibited goods to the seaside and shipped them off under cover of darkness. This traffic, which was extensively carried on for many centuries along the Sussex coast, came to an end during our last war with France.

CHAPTER IX.

SCENES IN THE MARKET PLACE—ASSAULT AND ROBBERY—MURDER—THE CHURCH AS A CITY OF REFUGE—REVENGE FOR PIRACY.

DURING the period from 1275 to 1289 many complaints were made against William de Braose (mentioned in the previous chapter) as to the manner in which he exercised his feudal powers in Shoreham, often "in contempt of our lord the King."

At one Assize Court William de Gyselham, who sued for the King, complained against the baron that he took in his town of Shoreham of each ship calling there with wines, "one cask from before the mast and one cask from behind the mast," and made a prise of wax and other merchandise against the will of the merchants and without warrant.

De Braose attended to answer these charges and denied them, saying that he did not claim any prise of merchandise in the town, but that of ancient custom he took toll of merchandise coming to the town, that is, for each cask of wine, 1d., for each last of hides, 10d. "and other small tolls" as his ancestors were wont to make, but that he took no prisage.

There were other charges against the baron, to wit, he had forbidden the traders of the town to sell victuals or other necessaries to Robert Aquilon, his heirs or others on his behalf, or to allow them lodging in Shoreham, or even to admit them into its precincts. Robert Aquilon went with his grievance to the King and an order was made that he should be permitted to trade with the men of the town. In spite of this de Braose still forbade them to have any dealings with him.

Nicholas Dytton also took of wine and other goods "partly paid and partly unpaid" and retained them against the will of the owners and amerced them many times against the statute, and "because he was bailiff of William de Braose," his master was directed to bring him before the Assize for judgment.

Nor was this all. By his bailiffs, we are told, de Braose took at his pleasure, corn, meat, and fish from the poor, to their great damage and against the King's statutes. On one occasion

THE STORY OF SHOREHAM

it would appear that the castle fires were burning low and the wood-stack in the court-yard diminishing. " Certain poor men taking 30 cart-loads of wood to the market at Shoreham " were waylaid by Nicholas Dytton, constable of Bramber Castle, and other servants of William de Braose, who wounded the men, seized the carts and their contents, and took them to the castle.

Further, William de Braose, Nicholas Dytton, William Frewyn, and William Tester came to the house of a certain Richard de Tutting in Shoreham town, and there wounded Nicholas Brench, and against the King's peace " took and spoiled him of one tabard worth 5s., a sword worth 3s., a cap worth 4d., a tripod worth 2s. and a burse containing 5s. 8d." De Braose also took the owner captive and carried him off to Bramber Castle, where he was imprisoned until ordered to be liberated by the King. It appears, however, that the property of his somewhile captive, was still detained by de Braose ; and, indeed, a very suitable motto for that baron might have been found in the words " What I take, I hold fast."

With such an example before the men of Shoreham it is small wonder that they, too, were charged with offences against the laws of the Realm. So we find it recorded that Arnold the Draper and Richard de Mansiot sold cloth against the assize ; that John le Franckelin, John de Bedinges, and Gregory Caldwell unjustly took money in tolls. In the seventh year of Edward the First's reign, eleven of the inhabitants sold 260 tuns of wine, " since the last itinerary, against the assize." Nine years later eighteen of the townsmen sold 220 tuns ; and Arnald le Isemonger, William and Robert Chamond sold bread against the assize.

We must now go back some years and relate an incident which occurred in the market-place of New Shoreham on Saturday in Easter week, in the forty-second year of the reign of Henry III.

The townsmen and others from a distance, engaged in their various callings, were ready to supply the wants of all comers.

Among those gathered there " in full market " was Edmund de Adberton (Edburton) " selling his wares." William Baudefar, member of a well-known family in Shoreham at that time, came into the market. He made his way to Edmund's stall, and— they were somewhat quarrelsome folk, those old-time traders— angry words were soon bandied about from one to the other. During the dispute, Edmund carelessly fingered a hatchet lying

"Beat and knocked him to the ground."

ASSAULT AND ROBBERY

on his stall. William, probably seeing what was coming and determined to "get his blow in first," the record tells us, "beat and knocked him to the ground and pressed his throat so that the blood flowed out of his nostrils." Moreover he "took away a silver buckle to the value of 2s." and did other damage against Edmund, which the latter assessed at 20 marks.

When the case was tried at Lewes "William Baudefar comes and defends the injury and says that he wishes to know the truth." He stated that Edmund insulted him on the said day at Shoreham market and "tried to strike him with a hatchet." He repulsed him but did not strike him nor take his buckle nor do him any harm, but only defended himself. Both men "put themselves on the country" and the jurors said that "William insulted Edmund and hit him with his fist but did not take the buckle nor pressed his throat." Therefore William was to satisfy Edmund his damage by the blow, which they put at half a mark, and was to remain in custody for transgression, while Edmund was "in mercy" for a false claim as to the buckle.

The records of these cases of assault—sometimes accompanied by robbery—are numerous. One or two others which occurred during the Edwardian period may be mentioned.

William le Irish or le Erisshe—the name is written both ways in the Rolls—had put up a paling to protect his ground from trespassers. His neighbour, Henry le Bourne, promptly "pulled it up and threw it on the ground and wounded and ill-treated" the owner who subsequently at the assize complained that he had damage to the value of £10. "And Henry came," says the Assize Roll, "and defended himself, and as to the assault, says he is not guilty. As to pulling up the paling, he says he has a certain way to his grange in the town of Shoreham and William put the paling there to block up that way and that therefore he pulled it up and threw it down, without thereby doing any trespass." And William says "he put up the paling on his own ground, the whole way," and reiterates that Henry acted against the peace. The case was adjourned and meanwhile the two men seem to have settled their quarrel amicably as we learn further, that "afterwards the said William le Irish does not prosecute Henry le Bourne."

The same Assize Roll records how John de Goringe "beat and wounded" John Wodemer, in the town of Shoreham, "at a county court held there" He went also to a certain house in the town and beat William Goldsmith, the owner, "so sorely" that for fear of him the latter fled the town.

Questioned as to how he will acquit himself of the said trespass, John de Goringe says "he is in no way guilty," and on this puts himself on the country. The jurors say on oath that "the day the county court was held, John de Goringe beat John Wodemer and wounded him in the middle of his arm with a knife, and injured William Goldsmith so that he fled the town; and that the said John is a common brawler." John was committed to gaol but afterwards paid a fine for these transgressions, while certain of his fellow-townsmen became pledges for his future good behaviour.

In 1327 "certain persons broke open the chests and coffers of William Vyvian at Shoreham, and finding therein £600, carried it away." Now this sum was probably money which had been collected as dues on merchandise brought into the port; William Vyvian having been appointed in 1324 and again in 1325 and 1327 deputy for the King's chief butler "in the port of the town of Shoreham."

Another case, which assumed somewhat serious proportions, occurred in 1330. Thomas de Weston was concerned with many others of the townsmen in an assault on Richard de Peshale, knt. He came to the house of the latter "with force and arms" and not only wounded and ill-treated the knight himself, but "took and carried away his goods and chattels to the value of £500, assaulted his men and servants and maltreated them so that for long he was without their services."

The names of some of the "malefactors and breakers of the King's peace," concerned in this robbery and riot, occur with frequency in the records of the time. In several instances they are those of men who represented the town in Parliament !

A commission of Oyer and Terminur,* in this matter, was issued to Richard de Wylughby, Philip de Ifeld, and William de Northou; and those summoned to appear at Chichester in Pentecost week, 4 Edward III., on the plea of Richard de Peshale, were Thomas de Weston, John de Pevense and John, his son, German Hoblyt, Reginald le Cartere, Robert le Puffer, William and John Bernard, Guy de Ely, John Ivory, Ralph Stacy, John de Beauchamp, Nicholas le Taverner and Elias le Taverner, Master John le Bulter,

---

* A commission granted by the Crown to "hear and determine" cases of treason, felony, and trespass.

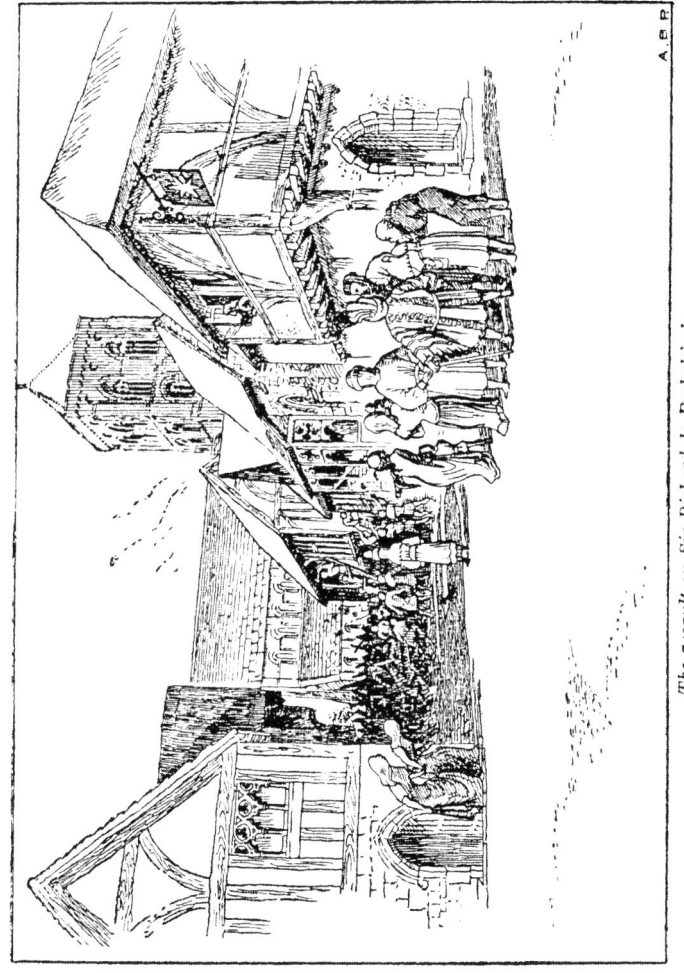

The assault on Sir Richard de Peshale's house.

THE STORY OF SHOREHAM

Mathew le King, Thomas Coxtyll, John Judde, Thomas Wedende, James le Best, David Fynian and Thomas his brother, Richard, Stephen, and John Must, Roger Germayn, Richard and John Vigerous, Ralph le Groonde, John de Perchyng, John le Spicer, John le Crouchepreste, John Swele, Ralph le Baker, Reginald de Washington, Henry de Blechyngton, and Henry Alleyn.

The jurors found that "Thomas de Weston and all the others, except Henry Alleyn, Ralph le Baker, Reginald le Cartere, Reginald de Washington, and Henry de Blechyngton "were guilty of the trespass and that they were to pay Richard de Peshale damages to the tune of £500.

The following year we learn that German Hobelit, probably the same individual whose name is recorded in the above list, " put himself against Thomas Comyn " in a plea that he " with force and arms " took and carried away his goods and chattels to the value of £30 and did " other grave damage, to the hurt of the said German and against the peace." This case was adjourned several times and its conclusion is not found in the Rolls.

" On Saturday next after the Feast of St. Matthew the Apostle," in the sixth year of Edward III., William, Hugh, and John Panethorne, brothers, " with other malefactors " broke into the house of John le Younge at Shoreham, and carried away his goods. These included a silver coffer " full of florins," gold buckles and precious stones, eight cups of mazer, belts of gold and of silk, silver spoons, gold rings, seals and silver chains tied together, cloths of linen and wool, which the owner valued at £300. They also " hurt and wounded " Agnes, wife of John le Younge, and, carrying her off, kept her imprisoned at Shoreham for 15 days " and badly treated her, against the peace." John Panethorne seems to have been the ring-leader in this affair. After the case had been adjourned several times he was found guilty, both as to the robbery and the assault, and was fined £50 for the former and £10 for the latter ; " and John is taken," says the record. The process against his brothers was continued and many adjournments followed, without, as regards their case, any decision being recorded.

It is yet early morning and the mists have scarcely lifted from the Downs above Shoreham. A woman hurries down from the hill-side and along the road into the town ; her hair is unkempt, her skirt be-draggled, she wears a " hunted " look. With fearful glance, again and again she half-turns her head, as one in fear of pursuit. "Isabel, who was the wife of John le Chapelier of Beeding," has committed a crime. The hue and cry has been raised and she knows well enough that pursuit follows hard upon her heels.

The parish priest of Shoreham, concluding his early ministration at the altar, is disturbed by a slight commotion at the far end of the church. As he turns thitherward, a panting, hunted creature runs toward him and falls exhausted at his feet. Isabel has sought refuge in the Church of Shoreham, or in other words claims the privilege of sanctuary, and thence none dare drag her forth to answer for her crime.

The priest is familiar with such cases. It is not his duty to question this poor wretch as to the reason why she has sought this city of refuge. Possibly it is robbery, it may be murder—anything short of sacrilege. In due time the Coroner will pay his visit and then all will be enquired into. But for the present the woman is safe and safe for forty days. The priest commends her to the care of some women-folk standing there and passes out to his vicarage.

Isabel claims the privilege of Sanctuary.

But news of the crime has already reached Shoreham. Isabel's two children have been found, murdered. The mother has fled and is suspected of having killed them. Some of the men of Beeding, knowing full well that the crime will be put upon their village unless they can take the woman, have hunted for her all night long and are even now in the town, whither they have traced the fugitive. They are too late to take her, for none dare violate the privilege of sanctuary.

In due time comes the Coroner and Isabel confesses her crime—the homicide of her two children. She was destitute, it seems, for the record tells us "she had no goods." So is the story of this tragedy handed down to us—the murder of two helpless infants. Yet may it not be possible to read between the lines ? "She had no goods " is a statement which seems to give a clue to the mother's unnatural crime. Without money to buy bread or other sustenance for her children, in the madness of her own hunger she killed them. Such crimes have been known even in our own day.

However, as this may be, in accordance with the law of those times, Isabel had to take an oath to depart from the Realm within a given time and never to return "without special grace of our lord the King." And so we see her no more.

More heartless, it would seem, was the crime of "a certain strange woman" who killed her male child and threw him down a well in the town of Shoreham and at once fled—"no one knew whither." In this case, as the murderess could not be traced, the verdict was "murder upon the town of Shoreham "—a quite usual method of fastening the crime on the community and making them responsible when they failed to produce the criminal, or, in some cases, when there was no property to confiscate, as in the following cases.

John de Edulnebregg, a stranger to the town, was taken for burgling the house of Henry Hobeday, and imprisoned, but escaped from custody. Judgment of escape was made against the town while the criminal, "who had no goods in the tithing because a stranger," remaining a fugitive, was outlawed.

"Simon de Ponte of Beddinge " having been murdered in Shoreham, " the first finder and four neighbours come and are not suspected " (*i.e.*, of the crime). Afterwards it was discovered that John Baudefar and others who fled out of the town had committed the crime. Later these men returned "and because the inhabitants did not take them" judgment was pronounced against them.

The Baudefars seem to have been a very lawless family. John, son of John Baudefar, and Adam le Mounier, having killed Godfrey le Beicher, Adam fled, but John sought sanctuary in the church, whither Joan, his wife, followed him and "stayed with

A LAWLESS FAMILY

him for three days," but whether she was a party to her husband's crime does not appear. John confessed to the Coroner the crime of murder and robbery, abjured the Realm and his goods were forfeited. Joan had no desire to share her husband's banishment. She seems to have left him to his fate. When the three days were up " she came out of the church " only to be taken by Robert de Haleghton, the constable of Bramber Castle, who promptly clapped her into prison and "kept her there for fifteen days." This was a high-handed action for which he was subsequently rapped over the knuckles by the Sheriff. The latter informed him that "no one taken anywhere in the county, except in the Castle of Pevensey, ought to remain more than three nights (in custody) before being put in the King's prison."

Nicholas de Barlynglyde and Roger le Fishere, having waylaid John Mahun outside Shoreham town and " beat and wounded him so that he died the next day, fled, and put themselves in the church," and took the usual oath to depart from the Realm. They were strangers to the town and because " they had no goods in the tithing " the murder was put on the Borough of Shoreham.

But the case did not end with this decision. We learn that Isabel, the widow of John Mahun of Shoreham " called in the county court " Nicholas and Roger for the death of her husband, but did not appear when the case was to be heard. Later, she withdrew her charges against Roger who, it appears, had already fled overseas. The case was finally wound up at an Assize held at Chichester " on the morrow of Ascension Day, 16 Edward I," when Nicholas appeared to answer the charge against him, and the jurors and witnesses from the neighbourhood of Shoreham said " he is not guilty, therefore he is quit."

In the same year (1288) another sanctuary case is recorded. It was the sequel to a murder and robbery at Findon, in which the dramatis personae were a man, a woman, and a priest.

Agnes, the wife of Robert Cole, who seems to have been as faithless as she was doubtless fair, had fallen in love with a priest —Richard le Chanceleur. She admitted him to her dwelling, and the intercourse of the guilty pair eventually led to the murder of the goodman of the house. While the woman found a city of refuge in her own parish church the priest fled for sanctuary to the Church of Shoreham. Richard, the priest, confessed to the Coroner that he had killed Robert Cole, and also William de Wynton. It is possible that the latter had made an attempt to

THE STORY OF SHOREHAM

hinder his flight to sanctuary. The woman also confessed her share in the crime at Findon and both abjured the Realm.

Probably this guilty pair embarked at Shoreham, and there being no record to the contrary, it may be assumed that they crossed to the land of their exile in safety, but, apparently, pardoned criminals were not always so fortunate in "going over" as you will presently see.

In the year 1355, two pirates, John Colet and Stephen Sherman, "plundered the king's men with their ships and goods on the sea." They were captured by some men of Shoreham and placed for safe keeping in the dungeons of Bramber Castle. It is evident that the treatment they received at the hands of their warders left something to be desired—possibly they were tortured in order to wring confession from them. At all events we learn that " they escaped and fled to the church (of Bramber) for sanctuary " and afterwards received pardon on promising to abjure the Realm.

"*They were thrown out of the boat.*"

As usual in such cases, the nearest port was assigned these men. In going towards it each would be required to carry a cross in his hand, to keep to the King's high-way, turning neither to the right nor to the left "until he be gone out of the land." The two pirates took passage at Shoreham. but while crossing to Normandy "*they were thrown out of the boat.*"

Some half-dozen men, Laurence Absolon, Richard atte Hurn, William le Blake, Philip atte Hale, John Judde, and Harry Gower,

REVENGE

doubtless those who had suffered loss at the hands of the two pirates, seem to have embarked on the same ship and were concerned in the business of casting them overboard. They were subsequently charged with the murder of the two men, but on the supplication of Richard, Earl of Arundel, they received pardon.

CHAPTER X.

A GATE-WAY TO THE SEA—KING JOHN'S VISITS TO THE TOWN—MARITIME TRAFFIC—THIRTEENTH CENTURY "SHIP-CARPENTERS"—PIRACY—SHIPS FOR THE WARS OF EDWARD III.—A "PILGRIM" SHIP—AN ACTION FOUGHT OFF SHOREHAM—RECOMMENDATIONS FOR "DEFENCE"—THE ROYAL FUGITIVE—THE KING AND THE QUAKER.

As a well-frequented highway to and from the Continent for at least three centuries after the Norman Conquest, Shoreham held no secondary place among the ports of Sussex. The extent of its maritime traffic may be gathered from an examination of the Rolls preserved in the Public Record Office. In these are found frequent references to the arrival or departure of notable personages, the demands of the King for ships to serve in war-time, exports and imports, and to frequent cases of piracy.

Shoreham, indeed, has played no small part in the making of English History, and you may find if you follow our story to the end, that a few side-lights are thrown upon the larger page, perhaps to illumine it with a new interest.

It is a far cry from Shoreham to Lincoln, and the two places, it would seem, have little in common, yet, curiously enough, during the twelfth century, the old Cathedral City of the Fenlands and the Sussex seaport were linked together in a somewhat interesting and dramatic way.

At Lincoln lived "Aaron, the Jew." He was the chief financier of his day, and his house, still remaining, is one of two in that ancient city built in Norman times. These are believed to be the earliest private houses of stone still extant in England. Both are still inhabited.

Aaron's speciality in money-lending seems to have been that of making large advances to monasteries. It was his proud boast that, but for him, even the great Abbey of St. Albans—one of the most important in England—would be a ruin and "St. Alban have no roof to his head."

Few, indeed, were the great ones of that day—cleric or layman—whose names were not to be found on Aaron's books. Many

The King's retinue accomplished the long journey from Lincoln to Shoreham in safety.

THE STORY OF SHOREHAM

a mitred Abbot and Prior in financial straits was fain to take the road to Lincoln, and toil up the Steep Hill for a business interview with the Jew at his house just below the Cathedral. Having pledged for so many marks this, that, or the other property belonging to his monastery, Abbot or Prior wended his way home again with the coin jingling in his money bags, yet withal an uncomfortable feeling that the Jew would require the heavy usury, which he had demanded in return for the loan, to be paid punctually.

Aaron's terms were indeed high—sometimes he charged a penny per pound per week, sometimes twopence, or in other words from above 20 per cent. to 40 per cent. per annum. At such a rate of interest he speedily became "Aaron the Rich" and continued to heap up treasure for many a long year.

But, in 1186, another and less welcome visitor knocked at Aaron's door and the old money-lender died. His chests and coffers were then full to over-flowing, while the debts owing to his estate were enormous—nine monasteries in Yorkshire alone were indebted to him for the large sum of 6,400 marks.

King Henry II., viewing this vast accumulation of wealth and securities with greedy eyes, seized both treasure and debts. Although Aaron left several sons they were allowed to inherit only a very small portion of his riches.

Henry Plantagenet intended to send the treasure to Normandy, and doubtless it was with the idea of making the sea voyage as short as possible, and so reducing the risk of piracy, that Shoreham was chosen as the port from whence it was to be shipped.

The King's retinue accomplished the long over-land journey from Lincoln to Shoreham in safety and this seems to argue the existence of good roads at that period. In February, 1187, the treasure was put on board ship for Dieppe. It never reached the Continent. A violent storm arose, the angry sea swallowed up the wealth which the greedy King had stolen from the Jew's sons, and the greater part of the royal retinue went down with it to a watery grave.

That impetuous and fiery monarch, Richard I., having asserted that the King of France had "connived at the invasion of Toulouse" and thereby given great offence, sent Archbishop Baldwin to the French court to "pacify Philip," January 16th, 1188. Prince John followed the Archbishop, embarking at Shoreham for Dieppe, apparently on the same mission.

KING JOHN LANDS

After his crusade and subsequent captivity in Germany, Richard I. returned to England in his favourite galley, "Trench-le-Mer" or "Cleave-the-Sea." She was commanded by Alan Trenchmere, one of a notable family which flourished at Shoreham in the twelfth century.

On the death of the last-named monarch, King John, setting aside the claims of his nephew, Prince Arthur (the son of an older brother) seized the crown. In the then reigning lord of Bramber, William de Braose, he had a very powerful adherent, who was one of the foremost in urging that John should be crowned King of England.

Possibly this fact decided the King to make Shoreham his landing-place when he came to assert his claim, six weeks after Richard's death. When he landed with his army on the 25th May, 1199, he came to a town whose people were friendly disposed toward him and were to remain so during the greater part of his restless and unsatisfactory reign. The first part of his progress to Westminster was through friendly territory—the Rape of Bramber—which owned his powerful friend as lord.

Shortly after his Coronation, King John commenced that restless journeying from town to town and to and from the Continent, for which his reign seems so remarkable. In less than a month after his arrival he was again at Shoreham (16th June, 1199) accompanied by his friend de Braose, busy assembling the fleet and embarking an army for the invasion of France, the King of that country having declared war against him and favouring the cause of the young Prince Arthur. On this occasion, King John sojourned in the town four days, and in all probability he was lodged at the house of the Templars. Before his departure for Normandy he dated from Shoreham a Charter, which conferred certain privileges on the City of London.

The commercial activity of the town and port greatly increased during the reign of this King. The fair of eight days established in 1202 was an important event. The bailiffs were continually receiving letters and mandates to provide ships for the King's use or for the use of his servants in their voyages to and from Normandy. At one time they are required to provide a ship "to convey the Master of Knights Templars, and Walter de Wells, our clerk, whom we are sending as mesengers to Normandy." On another occasion they are commanded "to give conveyance and safe conduct to Petrus de Leonibus, our clerk, who is bringing

THE STORY OF SHOREHAM

to London from Caen, the rolls and charters which belong to us."

On the 18th June, 1205, King John sent greetings to the bailiffs of Shoreham, having charge of the fifteenths, and informed them that certain Gascoyne merchants had brought to the Council a fifteenth of £300 and 50s. Anjou money. They were, therefore, to be permitted to remain fifteen days from St. John the Baptist's Day (June 24th) when they were to be conceded "a safe return to their own parts."

In the same year they were required to provide a ship for William de Aune " our knight and twenty bowmen to carry them over in our service." The following year " Alan, the younger " was commanded by the King to impress all the ships that should be found at sea, as a fleet was again being assembled for the invasion of Normandy, the King of France having assumed supremacy of the Dukedom

At this time the King had fifty-one royal galleys, five of which were, from 1205 to 1208, stationed here (no port, inclusive of London, had more than five). In the latter year we find " Alan, the younger " appointed to the command of the royal galleys then stationed at Shoreham. Authorities on Naval matters tell us that this Alan was the son of Richard Coeur de Lion's captain. It may be noted that John was the first of our sovereigns to retain seamen with permanent pay, and, under his rule, the English Navy considerably improved. This reign is notable as the first instance of our country claiming to be the " Sovereign of the Seas."

On January 4th, 1214, King John, then at the Tower of London, ordered Reginald of Cornhill to pay William de Beauchamp and Humbald Luffard, merchants of Shoreham, for " ten casks of wine taken to our use in London." After his capture of the Castle of Rochester, John dated from thence, November 25th, 1215, a letter to the constable of Bramber Castle concerning means for conveying " our messenger, Robert le Mutenir " from Shoreham to Winchelsea. On December 5th of the same year the bailiffs of Shoreham are commanded to deliver a ship to " Alexander de Fortune " and to allow him to depart without hindrance. The constable of Bramber by letter dated April 3rd, 1216, from Windsor, is required to provide horses and men without delay for " our faithful and beloved Walter de Lacy who is detained at Sorham." Letters of conduct to Sorham are

KING JOHN AT BRAMBER

also required for Richard de Coggeshall, monk, and Master Stephen de Sparham, "whom our lord the King is sending as messenger."

John was at Bramber 25th May, 1216, probably his last visit to the neighbourhood. It was in that year that he addressed a mandate to Shoreham and the other ports of Sussex, promising them additional privileges in order to secure their loyalty, and requiring them "to return to the allegiance and service due to him notwithstanding the oath they had taken by constraint and by reason of his irresistible power to Lewis, the son of the French King."

Shortly after this the greater part of the King's army, while crossing the Wash, was overwhelmed by the incoming tide. John narrowly escaped with his own life and lost the greater part of his treasure and baggage. This disaster hastened his gloomy end which came only a few days later.

During the reign of Henry III. numerous briefs and orders were addressed to the town. Most of these relate to the maritime traffic of the port. In 1223 the bailiffs of Shoreham were commanded to suffer to depart without hindrance the two ships which Hugo Baldefare arrested and brought to Shoreham; Hugo is to take charge of them.

In 1227 the Sheriff of Sussex is instructed to proceed personally to Shoreham, and, with the assistance of good and lawful men of the vicinity, to enquire into what has happened with respect to a ship belonging to Peter Androeni and his fellows, merchants of the Territory of the Count of Toulouse. The ship lately came into the port of Shoreham damaged by tempest of the sea and her cargo of goods and merchandise had been carried off. The Sheriff is to enquire diligently as to the culprits and arrest them. "He has our command to make restitution to Peter Androeni and his fellows and full power to act in the matter."

The shipbuilding industry seems to have been firmly established at Shoreham at this time, and the townspeople were probably expert at their trade by the beginning of the thirteenth century. In 1231 "ship carpenters" were ordered to go from Shoreham to Portsmouth on the King's service, and, in 1235, Hugo Baldefare and Robert Niger were appointed to take charge of the work (probably building) to two galleys of the King, at Shoreham.

In 1238, mandate was sent to the bailiffs of the town that from the ship lately put in at Shoreham they cause to be seized,

THE STORY OF SHOREHAM

for the use of the King, "baskets of figs to the weight of 300 lbs., 50 baskets of dried grapes and 4,000 (? lbs.) Dates, and 1,000 (? lbs) of wax." This is interesting as showing the sort of merchandise which came into the port in those days.

It was about the middle of the thirteenth century that a somewhat curious case of " invasion " occurred at Shoreham and is worth noting. It arose from the following circumstances.

In the year 1251 a band of shepherds and peasants led by a Hungarian, who styled himself "Master of Hungary," rose in revolt in France. They were known as the "Pastoureaux," and their avowed objects were the reform of the abuses in the Church and the release of the Holy Land from Moslem rule. The outbreak, directed in the first place against priests and scholars, was accompanied by wild excesses but was soon suppressed, the master being killed in an attack on the town of Bourges. One of the leaders, however, landed in England at Shoreham but was "cut to pieces." It would appear from this evidence that the town was not always a desirable place to "land at." We are not surprised to learn that this heresy, which is said to have been the greatest menace to the Church since the time of Mahomet, was so quickly suppressed when its followers met with such a warm reception as that given them by the inhabitants of Shoreham.

An order, dated 30th January, 1254, required the town to provide ships to convey Henry the III.'s Queen (Eleanor of Provence) and her suite to France. Four years later, Simon de Montfort, Earl of Leicester, brother-in-law to Henry III., sailed from Shoreham for France. This was before the outbreak of open hostilities between the King and his barons. Henry was then on a visit to the French Court, and the Queen of France, hoping to bring about a reconciliation between the King of England and his powerful noble, arranged a meeting to take place between them. Before Earl Simon's arrival at the French Court, King Henry was "seized with a fever," possibly caused by the prospect of meeting his powerful relative. At all events, he was not able to be "at home " to the Earl and so the meeting never took place. Shortly after this came the "appeal to the sword." In the conflict known as the "Barons' War " we note that Shoreham remained loyal to the King while the Cinque Ports ranged their forces on the side of the barons.

In November, 1257, there was an enquiry touching a ship of

EDWARD THE FIRST AT SHOREHAM

Segwin and Ellis Barbe, two brothers, citizens of Bordeaux. Their vessel, laden with 116 tuns of wine, had suffered shipwreck near Shoreham. The wine was seized as wreck of the sea, "which ought not to be, because the captain, mariners and others in the ship came safely to land." The Sheriff of Sussex was directed to find into whose hands the wine had come and to make restitution to the owners. The law in such cases directed that, should anyone escape from a wreck alive, the ship should not be treated as lost and her cargo should not have ceased to belong to her owner.

In 1289, the "St. Mary," a Bayonne ship laden with cloth, metal, and other goods, ran aground off Shoreham. Her crew, reaching land, made an agreement with the townsmen for 123 marks, but it seems that they were not content with the receipt of this sum. They were later accused of stealing much of the cargo.

A writ addressed to Shoreham in 1291, ordered the inhabitants to observe a truce with France. In March, 1301, and again in the following year, the town was ordered to join with other ports in providing ships for the King's use.

In 1304, the "St. Mary" of Shoreham was engaged in a case of piracy on the high seas. Her master, Robert Alisaundre, in company with other pirate-ships from Yarmouth, Bristol, and the Isle of Wight, boarded a Seville ship while on her voyage from that city to England. They plundered her of her cargo—doubtless a very valuable one, consisting of silks, fruit, oil, and wine : exports for which the city of Seville has been famous for many centuries—and even carried off her cordage and anchors, conveying the spoil to their various ports.

Edward I. and his Queen visited Shoreham June 21st, 1305, during a progress from Chichester to Canterbury. A payment of 20s. was made to Thomas de Weston for supplying grass for the use of the Queen's horses while in the town. Possibly this was not the only visit which Edward I. had paid the town, for he had certainly been in the neighbourhood on former occasions. He was at Bramber in 1285, 1297, and 1299, and at Beeding in 1302.

In 1308, when Edward II. was making a levy of ships for the Scotch War the men of Shoreham were ordered "to prepare immediately a ship of that port with all armaments and appurtenances, and to choose and arm forty-two of the strongest and most able-bodied men of the port, of whom one shall be master

THE STORY OF SHOREHAM

and another constable of the ship." She was to be ready by the Feast of St. Peter ad Vincula and to set out then at the latest, in the King's service and at his charges, to Scotland, to be at Skyburnease (Shoeburyness) on the morrow of the Feast of the Assumption of St. Mary. The letter in which these commands to the men of Shoreham are set forth continues : " The King proposes to set out shortly for Scotland to repress the rebellion of Robert le Brus and his accomplices, and needs a great fleet. He has caused 20 marks to be delivered to his clerk, the bearer hereof, for the wages of the men from the day when they leave the port (Shoreham) until they arrive at the port of Skyburnease, and will cause them to be satisfied for their wages while in his service." The town was again asked to provide another ship in 1310 and two more in 1311, " at the King's charges."

When William Vyvian and Bertrand Champeneys, in 1312, made a voyage in their ship " la Margarete," of Shoreham, to Berenger, near St. Matthew, and landed there " to attend to their affairs," they were assaulted by William le Gras, the steward of Arthur, Duke of Brittany, " and other malefactors." The Shoreham merchants and crew of the ship were taken prisoners, and meanwhile, their captors broke open the vessel's chests and coffers and stole goods and money to the value of £20. The steward kept the merchants and mariners in prison, until they had paid a fine of £50 and even then " refused to restore them their ships and goods." Edward II., requesting the Duke to make restitution and amends for all that these men had suffered, " so that they should not come to him with renewed complaints," makes use of the covert threat " lest it should behove him to provide them with another remedy."

Between the merchants and mariners of France and England, piracy seems to have been very much a matter of " tit for tat." The men of Brittany concerned in the above case were not much worse than the men and masters of some twenty-five ships concerned in an attack on the " St. Marie " of Winchelsea, in 1317. This vessel laden at Rochelle by certain merchants of that city with 93 tuns of wine valued at 930 marks was intended for Calais. Contrary winds probably drove her far out of her course. We learn that as she was coasting along the shores of England she was attacked near the port of Shoreham by the fleet of pirate ships. The pirates " drove the merchants' men out of her, took the ship and the wines and disposed of them at their pleasure."

SHIPS FOR THE WARS

In the year 1314, the town was ordered to send another ship to take part in the War with Scotland, and it is probable that the latter vessel was the "Alysetta," of Shoreham, whose master, John Drake, after Carrickfergus was taken, was paid the sum of £7 2s. 6d. for the wages of one constable and thirty-four men. The "Sainte Marie," of Shoreham, was employed in the transport of corn for the use of the royal army in Scotland.

To anticipate a few years. It may be mentioned that, in 1327, we have the record of a considerable number of horse-shoes and nails exported from Shoreham to Newcastle for the use of the army. At that period the iron-working industry was in full swing in the forests of Sussex, and the following amounts were paid to the Sheriff : £4 3s. 4d. for 1,000 horse-shoes ; 3s. for the carriage of same from Roughey, near Horsham (where they were made), to Shoreham ; 4s. 8d. for the purchase of 14 barrels to put these horse-shoes, 3,000 others, and 80,000 nails in ; 4d. for wooden hoops for the barrels ; 2d. for iron nails to strengthen the bottoms of the barrels ; 7d. for the wages of a workman, cleaning and hooping the barrels ; 14d. for the porterage of them to the ship ; 100 shillings for the freight from Shoreham to Newcastle-on-Tyne ; and 10 shillings for the wages of a clerk to take care of them on board ship.

In 1324, William Vyvian, probably the same individual who held the office of deputy for the King's chief butler in the port of Shoreham, was required to select mariners in Shoreham, Brighton, Hove, Aldrington, Rottingdean, East Kingston, West Kingston, and Worthing for the equipment of Shoreham ships—probably two—which had been ordered to be at Plymouth by the Feast of Holy Trinity. In 1326, two ships of Shoreham were at Portsmouth on the King's service and their crews were "to have aid of their expenses" from those who remained at home. This was a levy upon the inhabitants to provide 6d. a day for each master and 3d. a day for each mariner ; in favour of Robert Loudeneys, master of the ship called "La Messager" and 22 mariners ; and Ralph Graunger, master of the ship called "La Jonette" and 24 mariners.

In 1328, all masters and owners of ships of 40 tons and upwards were required to bring them back to port and arm them, as a great many ships were assembled on the coast of Normandy "to aggrieve and rob merchants."

War with Scotland again broke out in 1332, and the continual

THE STORY OF SHOREHAM

demands of the King for ships caused much injury to trade and led to great discontent in all the coast towns of Sussex. It was therefore deemed advisable to summon masters of vessels to the Council at Westminster to enquire into the state of Navigation. To the first meeting of this kind, delegates were sent from all the principal ports of Sussex and subsequent councils were held in 1341, 1342, 1344, and 1347, and probably were found successful in persuading ship-owners to supply their ships for the wars.

Shoreham ships played a considerable part in the wars of Edward III. against the French. In one fleet which sailed from England in 1342, numbering 347 vessels, 56 were supplied by the Sussex ports and of that number Shoreham contributed 21. Another fleet sailed the same year and in this were two ships belonging to our port, the masters and mariners of which, as well as many others, deserted at Brest, and returned home "leaving the King and his army in very great peril." The Shoreham ships were "la Laurence" and "la Nicholas" and their masters, Simon Bak and Thomas Robyn, with their crews, were arrested on their return to Shoreham and committed to prison.

In 1346, in which year the inhabitants were ordered to make war on the French "by sea and land," King Edward collected a large armament for the Campaign of Crecy and the Siege of Calais. The Sussex ports furnished 60 ships and 1,257 men, and of this number Shoreham provided 26 ships and 329 men. This was a larger number of ships than supplied by London, Dover, Bristol, or Southampton, and can only lead to the conclusion that, at this period, the town was in a flourishing condition, had a considerable population, and the port was a leading one.

But King Edward's military achievements, brilliant as they were, against a gallant foe who seemed to have little power to resist the transport of his armies, resulted in a number of local invasions along the coast, which, for many years during the latter part of his reign, was continually harassed by the French. Possibly Shoreham suffered in this way more than once. Certain it is that the French visited the immediate neighbourhood and left traces of their invasion, for, in 1359, a commission was instituted to repair some sea-walls at Pende—described as situated "between Bramber, Shoreham and Lancing"—which had been damaged, not only by the inundation of the sea but also by the ravages of the French and Spànish.

PIRACY

Phillip Bagge and William Snellyng, of Shoreham, were appointed by the King to levy in their town and port a subsidy of 6d. in the pound on all merchandise imported or exported, from December, 1360, to the Michaelmas following. This was "for the expenses of mariners, armed men, and archers of a ship of war going to sea to safeguard the merchandise of his subjects and friends." Phillip Bagge failed to render an account for the time when he was receiver and was outlawed, but after surrendering to the Fleet Prison, was pardoned.

As an illustration of some of the exports from Shoreham at this period we find reference to wheat and beans sent to Ireland in 1364 "for the sustenance of the King's lieges there." In the following year sixty gammons of bacon, eighteen dozen of cheese, and twenty quarters of wheat were shipped to be taken to the Abbey of Fécamp for the use of the Abbot and monks.

The port was again ordered to supply ships for the King's Navy in 1366. In 1368 "the keepers of the passage in the port of London" were directed to allow William Brykles, a merchant of that city, to put on board a small ship "certain victuals and armour for the furnishing of a ship new made at Shoreham, called La George, of London," and to take them with "other things useful for her gear" to Shoreham "and not elsewhere."

Throughout the reign of Edward III., we find numerous references to piracy, and ships were continually plundered of their cargoes by the mariners of the port. During the time of truce between France and England (at the beginning of the reign) a merchant of Amiens came with his "woad" and other goods to the value of £28 to Shoreham to trade there. Thomas Mourant, bailiff of the town, seized the goods but was ordered by the King to restore them to the merchant. In July, 1352, John de Ellerton, King's serjeant-at-arms, was required to make inquisition "on the oaths of good men of Shoreham, touching two ships of Spain which were taken by men of the port and brought in, contrary to truce between the King (of England) and men of Spain." In the following year a Flanders ship, laden with goods for England, to wit, 5 bales almonds, 48 dozen cordwaine worth 500 florins and other merchandise "to no small value," was taken by pirates who plundered her of her cargo, which they took into Shoreham and detained there. Measures were ordered to be taken for the restitution of the property to the rightful owners.

THE STORY OF SHOREHAM

A somewhat curious case occurred in July, 1354, when the goods of Thomas Paterlyng and other merchants of London were plundered at sea by the French. Shortly after this the goods of Ralph de Sancta Fide, of " Depe," Normandy, were taken at sea by mariners of England, brought into Shoreham and there arrested by the bailiffs of the town. An agreement was then made by which Ralph promised " as far as he may " to cause the merchandise of Thomas Paterlyng and his fellows, " which can be found in the ships of those that took them," to be brought safely to England. In the meantime, two-thirds of the French goods brought into Shoreham were to be delivered to Ralph. The third part was to remain in the keeping of John Bernard, burgess of Shoreham, Ralph's host, until the Frenchman had fulfilled his part of the contract, and, moreover, his two sons were to be delivered to Thomas Paterlyng as hostages.

In March, 1359, a ship of St. Malowe, in Brittany, " which is of the King's enmity," laden with wines and " other wares and things" and lately driven into the port of Shoreham by a storm at sea, was ordered to be arrested and delivered to the bailiff and "two or three of the good men of the town to be kept for the King's use."

Very frequent are the references to " goods and merchandise by certain pirates plundered at sea, and put ashore at the town of Shoreham," but it is impossible to notice them all. During the year 1371, several vessels, some of them English, were relieved of their cargoes in this manner. It is interesting to note the goods with which they were laden.

One cargo consisted of 35 bales woad, 6 bales " alum," 4 cases (casi) " sope," 3 tons flax and 14 reams paper—valued at £140. Another vessel carried 31 dozen fells of foynes (the hides of that animal), 5 mantles of fitchews (fur of the polecat), one timber and a half, 8 fells of greywork, 7 dozen fells of roes, $13\frac{1}{2}$ lbs. green thread—of the value of £22 10s. Another ship was laden with 334 pieces of kerchief of " Wermoise," every piece containing 4 plights, 4 pieces of "camaca bleue"(a fine fabric, probably of silk), containing 34 ells, and 500 ells of " canavace "—valued at £100.

Another vessel was laden with 3 cloths of "motele," divers pieces of "roys " of Deest, 12 dozen " sadelskirtes," 6 dozen " redlash," 1 fardel of linen cloth, 3 rydels, and a great number of nails, " bokeles " of iron, and hides " silvered by the saddler's craft " in divers bags—to the value of £40 3s. 4d.

MURDER AND PIRACY

Sometimes the crime of murder was added to that of piracy. This was the case in August, 1371, when there was an enquiry, "touching the evil-doers who boarded a ship of Durdraght, whereof Yonge Bond was master, laden with goods and wares on the coast near Shoreham." After killing the master, mariners, merchants, other men and some women who were in the ship, they took the goods and wares "to no small value," put them in a barge, sank the ship and brought the barge and goods into Shoreham.

In 1380, William Lenchlade, citizen and mercer of London, was granted protection for two years in respect of his ship "la Margarete," of Shoreham, and for its mariners and goods.

A levy of 3d. was made on every noble's worth of fish landed at Shoreham, Pende, and other ports, to be expended on their defence, when an invasion by the French was considered imminent in 1385.

In 1399 the agent of the Abbot of Fécamp was building a vessel at Pende. It was seized while yet unfinished because he had taken the timber for her construction from the wood at Warminghurst without first obtaining the King's licence.

We find very little record of maritime activity at this period. Signs of the exhaustion and depression following after the French wars of Edward III. are apparent. A small vessel, known as a balinger, was ordered in June, 1400, "to be ready by the following April."

In July, 1406, the "Barthelemewe," a balinger, of Shoreham, was concerned in the capture and spoliation of a ship of Prussia, called "Crystofre of Gypswold," and Alexander Pynson, John Gate, and John Bradbrege, all of Shoreham, and probably the owners of the vessel, were ordered to pay £10. In October of the same year, John Gascoigne, of Foweye, and John Mayhewe, of Dartmouth, masters of two balingers, and many other persons "arrayed in warlike manner" attacked and captured a Portuguese ship carrying a cargo worth 500 marks. They brought her into Shoreham, imprisoned her captain and crew eleven days, and sold the ship and cargo to John Scullie, John atte Gate, Alexander Pynson, and Symon Manyngfield, men of the town, who were ordered to be arrested and taken before the King's Council.

A ship sailed in 1420 from Pende-juxta-Shoreham to Rouen, carrying provisions (probably wheat), together with many others employed in the same service. This was at the time

THE STORY OF SHOREHAM

when large supplies were being sent over from England for the use of the garrisons after the recovery of Normandy by Henry V. We may note that, so far, the above is the latest reference to the village of Pende which has yet come to light. Its exact locality, though somewhat conjectural, was somewhere at the mouth of the river. Gradually overwhelmed by the sea, before the middle of the fifteenth century it was totally washed away.

The Duke of Bourbon, one of the French nobles captured by Henry V. at the battle of Agincourt, and who had since been a prisoner in England, sailed from Shoreham to Dieppe in 1421. He was in the custody of Robert Poynings, who, for this service, was to receive 4s. a day for himself, 12d. a day each for 19 men-at-arms, and 6d. a day each for 40 archers. He was ordered to take as many ships as should be necessary to conduct the nobleman and this retinue to France, Shoreham being required to supply the transports.

In the following year licence was granted to Thomas Attehalle to convey pilgrims in his ship the "Trinity," of Shoreham, to perform their devotions at the shrine of St. James Compostella, at Santiago, Spain. This was a profitable traffic during the fifteenth century, for the shrine was one of the most frequented in Europe. In the same year James Thomas, of Shoreham, was granted a licence to export grain, and William Curteis and Thomas Hoore were ordered to proceed to Brittany for the release of John Purfote, a prisoner.

In July, 1468, there was a commission to Richard West de la Warr, knight, and others, to enquire into the complaint of John Robbyn, of Abvilde, "subject of the King's brother, Charles, Duke of Burgundy." Robbyn had laden 250 quarters of wheat in a ship of Cornelius Johnson, of Vangoose, in Seeland, at Abvilde, to take to England or Flanders, but one "John Waynflete, with others of his retinue, in two balingers of England, came upon the ship thus laden, captured it and took it to Shoreham, contrary to the form of truce between the King and the Duke." De la Warr was to cause restitution to be made and to arrest and imprison the offenders.

These acts of piracy were continued during the 16th century. A general letter from the Privy Council at Westminster, dated 1st December, 1545, addressed to "all justices, maiores, sherieves," orders the arrest of the "bodies, shippes and goods of John Burgess and John Gravesend, of Shoreham," who were

D'ANNEBAULT ATTACKS

required to answer the charge of having plundered the ship of Diego de Astodyllos, and they were to be "deteigned in saulf custodie" until they should put in sufficient sureties, with bonds, to appear before the Council.

In 1550, the merchants owning "a Britton vessel" which "gave travers" at Shoreham, complained, through the French Ambassador, to the Lords of the Council, asking for the restitution of the goods and "takling" which had been taken from the vessel to be restored to them, and again Lord de la Warr was directed to see that this was done, or otherwise, "if any refuse the delivery thereof upon due proffe to committe them to prison till they conforme themselves to the delivery of the same."

When Gilbert Horsley, a pirate, seized two hoyes, laden with coals, belonging to Nicholas Arundel and John Russell, and brought them into Shoreham, they were claimed by the officers of the Earl of Surrey. The claim was disputed by a Commission appointed by the court of the Admiralty, which court decided that the Earl's claim to the hoyes "had no ground or collor in law and justice" and his officers, Cantrell and Dix, were required to deliver the two hoyes to Russell and Arundel and "thereof not to faile, as they will answer to the contrary at their perilles."

There is a tradition that Shoreham suffered from the attack of the French during the fifteenth and sixteenth centuries, and that, in one of their descents, they burnt part of the town. Aldrington, Hove, and Brighton also had a share of these unwelcome visits. In the summer of 1545 D'Annebault, the French Admiral, made a desultory attack on Seaford. A landing was effected and the place pillaged and set on fire. The hardy Sussex Volunteers, roused by the smoke of the burning town, armed themselves and came down upon the French in swarms, destroyed their boats, and only a mere fraction of the invaders recovered the Fleet.

Meanwhile the English Fleet, commanded by John Lisle, Henry the Eighth's Lord High Admiral, was greatly handicapped by weather conditions. August brought with it light easterly winds and calms and it became sultry beyond the ordinary heat of an English summer. The beer supplied to the fleet turned acid, fresh meat would not keep for two days, and the English Admiral was obliged to hang along the shore, where boats passing to and fro continually could furnish a succession of supplies. After a fortnight of ineffectual cruising, the two fleets, on the

THE STORY OF SHOREHAM

morning of the 15th, were in sight of each other off Shoreham. The light air which was stirring came in from the sea. The French were outside and stretched for five miles along the offing. Having the advantage of the wind they could force an engagement if they pleased, and Lisle hourly expected that they would bear down upon him. Indeed, the French galleys came out, but the English were better provided. They had several large galliasses and "shallops with oars." One of the former, commanded by Admiral Tyrrell, of four hundred and fifty tons, was as swift as those of the enemy and more heavily armed. An indecisive battle lasted until the evening, when the French retreated behind their large ships and by that time the whole line had drifted down within a league of the English. Admiral Lisle cast anchor to show that he was ready for them if they cared to approach nearer. As darkness fell the enemy appeared to be imitating this example and a general action was confidently looked for in a few hours. A breeze, however, sprang up at midnight. As day broke, the space which they had occupied was vacant and the last vessel of the Fleet of D'Annebault was hull down on the horizon in full sail for France. (Froude's Henry VIII.)

The proper defence of this country has been, and is, an ever present and important question. Not less so was it to our ancestors in the reign of Elizabeth, when an invasion by Spain was considered imminent.

A survey of the coast of Sussex, taken in 1587 by the deputy-lieutenants of the county, makes certain recommendations for its defence, but the batteries would now be of little use against an enemy and give but small sense of security.

Dealing with our own immediate neighbourhood the survey stated that " between Lancing beacons and Shoreham is a marsh and therefore needith but a small trench, flancked at the sayd beacons for small shotte." There were "two beacons on Cissbury Hill for signalling to Chanctonbury." Between Shoreham and Brighton there was " good landing, for defence of which two demiculverins and two sacres should be kept in some good house to be ready at sudden and in sundrie places to be entrenched aptly for small shotte."

The Civil War does not seem to have affected Shoreham very closely, but during the period 1624-31 there are references to the billeting of soldiers in Steyning, Tarring, Shoreham and the

SHORTAGE OF CORN

neighbourhood. The mayor and jurats of Rye were ordered to dispatch six of the biggest and most serviceable pieces of ordnance in that town to Shoreham, and Captain Temple " took order to hasten the work at Bramber and Shoreham by the Pioneers and Captain Fuller to man them when completed."

Captain Temple was probably the same individual whom Chillingworth mentions in these terms :—" I visited a brave soldier of my acquaintance, Captain James Temple, who did that day defend the fort of Bramber against a bold daring enemy to the wonder of all the country, and I did not wonder at it, for he is a man that hath his head full of stratagems, his heart full of piety and valour and his hand as full of success as it is of dexterity."

The town contributed to the unpopular tax known as " Shipmoney," in 1635 and 1636.

In February, 1637-8, the people of Shoreham and the neighbourhood were suffering hardship caused by a shortage of corn. They complained that " one sack in two market-days at Steyning was all the proportion sent thither, nor would the farmers sell any to the poor." This shortage seems to have been due to the fact that William Avis and one Lawrence, both of Shoreham, had engrossed great quantities of corn for the use of the King's Navy, " it was said," and by the order of John Crane, chief clerk of His Majesty's kitchen, had sent away one ship-load which was entered in the custom's book in the name of Mr. Alcock for London. On the return of the ship to Shoreham she brought a certificate from Southampton, in which port " it was said the corn had been sold for the private benefit of Alcock, Avis and Lawrence, and in no way expended for the King's service." This charge was denied by Crane, who stated that, although Alcock's name was used in the business, " it was only as his (Crane's) deputy for victualling the Navy." Other corn stored at Shoreham was waiting to be shipped in a bark already hired, but Sir John Leedes, of Wappingthorne, would not allow it to be sent away " until he had examined the business," stating that the outcry of the poor was so great that not only did they threaten to break open the places where it was stored, but " Avis went in fear of his life by the inhabitants of Shoreham."

We need give only a passing reference to the escape of Charles the Second from Shoreham Haven on October 15th, 1651. Here he terminated his six weeks of wandering after his defeat at

THE STORY OF SHOREHAM

Worcester on September 3rd. His exciting adventures have often been recorded as well in the pages of romance as in those of sober history. We may mention the fact that, about twenty-five years ago, Henry Hamilton and Augustus Harris produced

King Charles's Cottage
SOUTHWICK
A.B.P. 1921.

at Drury Lane Theatre "The Royal Oak, a historical and romantic drama of 1651." This play, as its title implies, was founded on the adventures of the King after his defeat at Worcester, and the scenes in Act IV. were laid at (1) the George Inn, Brighthelmstone, and (2) the Beach, Shoreham.

THE ROYAL FUGITIVE

With two faithful friends to bear him company the King had ridden through Sussex by way of the Downs. He crossed the Adur at Bramber, where he narrowly escaped recognition by a troop of Roundhead soldiers. He again ascended the Downs by way of Beeding Borstal, his intention being to make for Brighton, where he was to remain until Captain Tattersall's brig, which had been engaged to take him to the Continent, should be ready to sail.

There is a tradition that the King tarried for awhile in a cottage on the west side of the Green at Southwick, while the final arrangements were being made, and thence went on to Brighton. A former tenant of "King Charles' Cottage" once informed the writer that there is, or was, a secret place where the King is said to have been concealed during his visit. Other accounts state that the King rode direct to Brighton, and, at any rate, he spent some hours at the George Inn, in Middle Street of that town, where he partook of supper, and was recognised by the landlord, who was a loyalist.

To quote from the King's own account of the conclusion of his six weeks of wandering. He tells us that :—

"About 4 o'clock in the morning, myself and the company before named (those who were aiding his escape and had been present with him at supper) went towards Shoreham, taking the master of the ship with us on horseback behind one of our company, and came to the vessel's side. It being low tide I and my Lord Wilmot got up with a ladder into her and went and lay down in the little cabin till the tide came to fetch us off. But I was no sooner got into the ship and laid down upon the bed but the master (Tattersall) came in to me, fell down upon his knees and kist my hands, telling me that he knew me very well and would venture life and all that he had in the world to set me down safe in France. So about 7 o'clock in the morning, it being high tide, we went out of the port."

Charles had assumed the role of a bankrupt merchant, flying from the bailiffs, but, with the events which had so recently transpired fresh in the minds of the crew, it is small wonder that some of them seem to have made a very shrewd guess as to the identity of the "merchant." Moreover, the brig had been chartered for Poole and not for France, whither she was now sailing so merrily. The King is said to have made himself remarkably agreeable with the crew. One of the latter was observed standing to the windward of the King, with whom he was chatting, so that Charles had the full benefit of the smoke from the pipe which the mariner was smoking. On being reproved by one of his mates for this familiarity, the man is said to have replied "a cat may look at a king, surelie."

Charles received important aid from the mate of the brig, Richard Carver, who was a quaker. He, too, recognised the King, but assured him that his life was quite safe in his hands. When they arrived, about 10 o'clock the next morning, off Fécamp,

' *Fell down upon his knees and kist my hands.*"

he rowed him ashore and in shoal water carried him on his shoulders to the land.

It had been a favourable voyage, but "they had noe sooner landed but the wind turned and a violent storm did arise in so much that the boatman was forced to cut his cable and lost his anchor." The brig then made for Poole, no one discovering that she had been out of her course.

Some eighteen years later King Charles and Richard Carver again met, but then under very different circumstances. The

THE KING AND THE QUAKER

King had again "returned to his own." Richard Carver, who had been in the West Indies, came back to find a great number of his friends the quakers in prison. Some of the leading members of the Society of Friends entreated his sympathy, and, with him, obtained access to the King. Charles at once recognised him and enquired why he had not been to claim his reward before. He replied that he had been rewarded with the satisfaction of having saved His Majesty's life, "and now, Sir," said he, "I ask nothing for myself, but for my poor friends, that you should set them at liberty as I did you." The King offered to release any six, and we may imagine the sailor's blunt reply. "What ! Six poor quakers for a King's ransom !"

The King is said to have been so pleased as to invite Carver to come again and ultimately ordered the release of the prisoners, but this would seem not to have been the case during Carver's lifetime, if we may judge from the evidence of a request which his widow, Mary Carver, afterwards made to the King. In this document, which is preserved in the Record Office, Mary Carver reminds the King that her husband "carried over His Majesty in his great distress from near Shoreham into France at the risk of his life, when, by discovering him, he could have gained £1,000, and has desired no favour in return but the liberation of some of his friends, the quakers, which was not granted him."

Possibly after this the quakers were liberated, and it is to be hoped that the King also "remembered the widow's poor estate."

The name of Carver has been known at Shoreham for generations, and although Captain Tattersall's mate was a quaker, it is more than probable that his baptism as an infant is recorded in the New Shoreham Registers thus :—"Richard Carver, son of Derick Carver, bapt. 1 Jan., 1609."

It is also recorded in some early Quaker Registers, relating to the meetings of quakers at Steyning, that "Joan Apps, of New Shoreham, widow, who died in 1696, "was of ye stock of ye Carvers, yt suffer matredum in Queen Mary's days."

Joan Apps' house had been a place of meeting in 1676 and probably she was a near relation of the Richard Carver beforenamed—possibly his granddaughter—while the "matredum" mentioned refers to the burning of her ancestor, Derick Carver, in the High Street, Lewes, in 1557, during the Marian persecution.

CHAPTER XI.

PRIVATEERING—PRIZE SHIPS—LOYAL PRIVATEERS—SMUGGLING—CUSTOM HOUSES.

THE licensed form of Piracy, known as Privateering, was very general during the wars of the seventeenth century, and there are records of the owners and captains of Shoreham ships obtaining from the Government of the day, letters of marque or commissions "to set forth to take pirates" and plunder the ships of the enemy.

Several such licences were granted from 1625 to 1627 to Capt. Richard Gyffard for the "Peter," and in 1628 to Capt. William Freeland for the "St. Peter," from 1627 to 1629 to Capt. William Scras, Tuppyn Scras and others for the "Dolphin," and in 1628 and 1629 to Tuppyn Scras for the "Fortune," and to Leonard Cross for a vessel of the same name in 1632.

Frequent letters passed between Capt. Gyffard and Edward Nicholas (Secretary to the Admiralty) as to the adventures of the "Peter."

Apparently the vessel was a prize ship, as she is referred to as the "Peter of Dunkirk" in a deed of covenant, by which she was conveyed to Capt. Gyffard by order of the Duke of Buckingham. She was then (October, 1625) in Portsmouth Harbour and it was agreed "for the setting forth of the ship on a voyage, with commission of reprisal," that Edward Nicholas should receive for the Duke's use (over and above the usual tenths) a third part of all goods that should be taken, one third to go to Capt. Gyffard for victualling the ship and the remaining third to the captain and crew, "according to the custom of commissions of this nature."

In the following February, Thomas Paynter took workmen from Shoreham to Portsmouth to receive the ship and prepare her for sea. Later she was brought to Shoreham and a warrant issued to the officers of the port to permit Capt. Gyffard to put eight pieces ordnance aboard his ship, the "Peter," her captain being Henry Parrant.

Apparently the vessel met with some success, for, in June,

PRIVATEERING

1626, the goods in the "Peter of Dunkirk" were valued at £60 5s. 6d. A few days later in the month Capt. Gyffard, sending his servant to Nicholas for a commission for the "Peter," says "the ship will be ready before Midsummer," and he hopes she will bring them "some spending money," but in July he informed Nicholas that "the shipwrights have found that all the floor-timbers of the Peter are rotten."

Captain Gyffard, in the spring of 1627, was confined to his house at West Blatchington through illness, and in a letter to Nicholas he laments that he cannot follow the Duke of Buckingham in his expedition for the relief of Rochelle, which was then fitting out at Stokes Bay, and in which were two Shoreham ships.

In July of the same year a Dutch ship was brought into Shoreham, and the captain, informing Nicholas of the fact, refers to his continued ill-health and states that their ship "went to sea on the 5th with instructions to go into the bay towards Nantes;" he hopes that she will yet do something that will return Edward Nicholas his money, and adds that he "would rather lose all his own than Nicholas should lose a penny."

The hope that the ship might do more "business" seems to have been realised later in the year, when a bark of St. Malo or Grenville, the "Sea Horse," was driven to the mouth of the harbour and brought in by the captain's men. She was laden with linen, cloth, wines, and other commodities, and Gyffard claimed her as a prize, begging for a warrant "whereby there may be judgment given and every man have his due." He stated that the proceeds "will be about £500, of which the savers claim half."

In November, 1629, Sir Henry Mervyn, Admiral of the Narrow Seas, from his ship the "Lion," then in the Downs, reported that he had "stayed the Peter." She was laden with barley, and her master, Richard Graseden, "had no papers and gave contradictory accounts of himself." Sir Henry prayed for immediate instructions, as the corn "began to heat." These were given and the vessel was ordered to London, from which port, ten days later, he informed the Admiralty that "the master of the bark has brought certain papers from Shoreham" which he (Sir Henry) encloses, and he thinks they are not counterfeit, "whatever was the cause of the master's double tales."

In March, 1628, Captain William Scras, in his ship the

THE STORY OF SHOREHAM

"Dolphin," captured seven Dutch ships. The following April he took a French bark, the "Peter," of Conquet, laden with sugar, and in July, the "Rose," of Conquet. On a later occasion the "Dolphin" gave chase to a Dutch man-of-war, which had captured a Swansea bark and was making off with her prize. Captain Scras engaged the Dutchman and succeeded in re-taking the bark, but retained her as his prize, taking from her, according to the owner, the sum of £600. The "Dolphin," sailing into Cowes Harbour with her prize, was seized by the Vice-Admiral of the Isle of Wight. Scras was taken into custody and his ship condemned to be sold, but some months after this the captain petitioned the Lords of the Admiralty for the release of his ship and for his own discharge out of custody. He "apologised" for the resistance which had been offered by his servants to the arrest of the ship, and was eventually allowed to buy back the "Dolphin" for £230 and again obtained a letter of marque in respect of her. The owner of the Swansea bark, although petitioning the Admiralty more than once, does not appear to have obtained redress.

Edward Alford, of Offington, writing to Nicholas on July 10th, 1628, reports on prize matters at Shoreham, and states that *"the fish prize lies at waste in Shoreham Haven and savoureth,"* and that his man will deliver the account of the Dunkirk ship, "St. Michael," the cargo of which vessel sold for £226 4s. 3d. Sixteen days later Nicholas was asked to give definite instructions concerning "selling the fish in the prize at Shoreham," which matter must, indeed, by that time have required urgent attention. It had been "lying at waste" for over a fortnight, and if it already "savoured" on the 10th, its condition on the 26th could only have been such as to fill the town with an odour not only fish-like but "ancient."

But although Shoreham captains were often successful in capturing prize ships, it is apparent that their vessels were as liable to be taken. During the period we have been considering there were continual petitions to the Lord-Lieutenant of the County that the coast might be well guarded, as "by the ravages of the Dunkirkers, they dare not put to sea to follow their fishing or vent their commodities, but are daily chased and taken, and they pray for two small ships for securing that coast."

In August, 1628, three ships took a bark of Shoreham Haven, and the country people, coming down to rescue her, were driven away by ordnance till they fetched a "piece from Brighthelmstone." Afterwards the enemy cast anchor before Shoreham all night. During the same year frequent requests were made for ships to convoy Shoreham barks laden with timber for Portsmouth, Plymouth, and Woolwich, "the French men-of-war being very busy on the coast." Some fighting occasionally took place, and the burial of "a man slain by the enemy off Shoram" is recorded in the Registers of St. Clement's Church, Hastings, on August 24th, 1628. In 1629, barks laden with quantities of Chichester and Shoreham wheat "look for a convoy, otherwise their captains will not put to sea, for the enemy lies well upon the coast so that none go out but are taken."

"The Narrows swarm with Privateers to the westward." Such was the complaint in 1672. "They daily do much damage, but four or five of His Majesty's small frigates would prevent the daily loss and do much service to the King and country." When a ship was chased ashore by a Dutch caper of eight guns, her crew "cut a great hole in her side, purposely to sink her, but the privateers, following her so close, got her off and carried her away."

"*The fish prize lies at waste and savoureth.*"

Christopher Coles, timber merchant to the Navy Commissioners, had three vessels lying at Shoreham in March, 1673. They were laden with timber for Sheerness and he asked for a convoy for them.

The "St. John," of Dieppe, bound for St. Malo in December, 1673, was chased by two Dutch privateers. She ran into harbour at Shoreham, only, it would seem, to escape from one enemy to

"*They often drink their Majesties' health.*"

LOYAL PRIVATEERS

fall into the hands of another. Richard Forty, doubtless the officer of customs, went on board, and, with others, seized the cargo for the King of England's use "and his own," setting the broad arrow on some of the merchandise. This action resulted in an enquiry, held at the "Lyon," Steyning, but it transpired that, although the officer had detained the goods "till last night," he had then delivered them to Mr. Michael St. Avory, and they were then shipped on board.

When a privateer was being fitted out at Shoreham in February, 1689-90, the Government of the day displayed some uneasiness as to the intentions of those who were interested in the venture.

Edward Lawrence, the Collector of Customs at Shoreham, received instructions to enquire into the matter. From his letter to John Sansom, Secretary to the Commissioners of the Customs, which is preserved in the Public Record Office, we learn that in obedience to commands he had "been diligent in getting the best account" that he could, "both of the shipp and men." "Here are now," he says, "in ye towne and on board, about eighty men, of which between twenty and thirty call themselves seamen, and others have been, some troopers, some tradesmen, and some formerly privateers in ye West Indies, as they themselves say." The ship was then in great forwardness, her captain, John Wood, being expected hourly, and it was said that they intended to sail in eight or ten days. Edward Lawrence assures "their honours" that, having been often in the company of these men, he "cannot perceive they are any way disaffected to the Government, as I humbly assured your Honours ye 11th February last, but contrarily they often drink their Majesties' health, and seemingly with great respect."

Whether the doubts of the Government were dispelled by the assurance that the privateers "often drank their Majesties' health," we cannot say. William and Mary had not long been seated on the throne, and it is just possible that there was a lurking suspicion in high places that the privateers had on hand some secret business in the interest of the exiled James the Second, whose adherents, we are reminded, were much given to the practice of drinking the health of "the King over the water."

The wars with France, in the time of William III. and Queen Anne, revived and greatly increased the custom of import smuggling, for which the export system, already well organized, gave every facility.

For this traffic no district could be better suited than the low-lying coast between Shoreham and Lancing. In the days when the river ran quite close to the Sussex Pad (destroyed by fire some years ago and since rebuilt) that house was a favourite resort of those engaged in smuggling. Its lonely position was of no small account in "running" a cargo with the secrecy necessary to such a business. Its capacious cellars and hiding-

Ye Olde "Sussex Pad" Inn Lancing

places formed convenient receptacles for the contraband goods until they could be conveyed into the interior of the county by way of Shoreham Gap.

There are one or two references to the appointment of riding officers at Shoreham, a preventive system which was in existence prior to the establishment of the coast-guards, but very few captures are recorded as taking place in the immediate neighbourhood.

Some French and English sailors were taken near Shoreham in May, 1703. In the following May, 29 packets of lustring (a glossy silk) and 15 bales of raw silk were seized and delivered into the Custom House by Mr. Wade (probably the Customs Officer). Notice of the smugglers' arrival had been given by Charles Goring, esquire, who, on account of this information, claimed a share in the value of the goods, but apparently without success. In July, 1735, the preventive officers had a short encounter with smugglers at Kingston and seized the brandy which the latter had landed and carried it to the Custom House, but the smugglers escaped.

Nearly every class participated in this contraband traffic and made "a very good thing" out of it. The parson, preaching on Sunday to the squire, the farmer, tradespeople, and fisherfolk, on "the sinfulness of sin," was, like as not, as deeply interested as his flock in the business of smuggling carried on o'dark nights.

In his "Tour through Britain," Defoe noted that the Shoreham, Brighton, and Rye boats went in numbers to the Yarmouth Fishery, but in 1785, such was no longer the case. A writer of that date tells us that the Sussex boats had given up going to the fishery, and that the owners were "supposed to have taken to smuggling," a trade which doubtless paid them much better.

In June, 1790, the "Nimble" cutter seized off Shoreham 105 casks of contraband spirits. In August, 1791, two luggers, waiting a favourable opportunity to land their cargoes, were seized by H.M.S. Pomona and sent into Shoreham.

The vessels employed in this traffic carried about sixty tons, and their cargoes were tea, silk, spirits, and tobacco, loaded by merchants in France. On the arrival of these vessels the cargo was rowed ashore in small boats and delivered into the charge of forty or fifty armed men, previously warned of the impending arrival, and who were lying in wait at some convenient spot. The goods were quickly loaded on horses and into carts and carried away to a hiding-place. More than once has a "little lost Down Church," nestling in its quiet coombe, served as a temporary warehouse for smuggled merchandise. An empty mansion—especially one having the reputation of being "haunted"—found great favour with these gentlemen. In such places the goods were stored until an opportunity for their final disposal could be found. The horses of the squires, parsons, and farmers were often employed in the transit of the goods, while their servants assisted in the bestowal. A favourite method of concealing kegs of spirits, was to rope them together and sink them in the river or brooks, until an opportunity occurred for their removal.

In the early years of the nineteenth century the Revenue Cutter "Hound," Captain John Butler, was stationed at Shoreham. Captain Butler was sometimes allowed to disguise his vessel by having a trawl-net hanging over the side and took a number of smuggling craft. Smugglers were the "Hound's" principal prey, but she took several small enemy privateers during the French war. On one occasion a Frenchman having taken an English vessel, Captain Butler turned the tables by opening fire upon the French ship and capturing her. Captain John Butler's cocked hat, sword, and pistols are still preserved by his descendants at Shoreham.*

Adventurous and daring as the old-time smugglers undoubtedly were, it may safely be said that for " coolness " and audacity the events now to be noted would be hard to beat.

About the middle of August, 1855, a celebrated wild beast show visited the town and took up its position near the Custom House (the present Town Hall). Even in these days such an exhibition proves no small attraction, and sixty or more years ago they were less common. Among those to whom the Science of Zoology proved an attraction were the officers and men of the coast-guards and customs. Possibly this is not a matter of surprise ; complimentary tickets of admission had been distributed with liberal hand, and to a man they all went to the show.

Never had there been such a splendid opportunity for "running a cargo." It was too good to be lost. The local smugglers had laid their plans with consummate skill and acted accordingly. Moored to the Custom House Quay was a vessel laden with about eighty or ninety tons of stone. She had entered the harbour earlier in the day. To the curious, her captain vouchsafed the information that he was ordered to lay there until a purchaser could be found for her cargo.

She looked an innocent craft as she lay there. Who would have dreamed that the fragrant weed was so cunningly concealed beneath her stony load ? Yet there it was, bale upon bale, and, so to speak, right under the noses of the Customs officials ; but these worthy men, almost within a stone's throw of the smuggler,

---

* Some very fine ship models, built by one of this family—Robert Butler —are in the possession of Capt. Purse, of Shoreham.

AN OLD CUSTOM HOUSE

were so fascinated with performing lions, tigers, and elephants, that they detected nothing amiss.

As the gloom of evening crept over the river many bales of tobacco were quietly put over the side of the vessel into a barge, which, with the flood-tide, went merrily off up the river as far as Beeding chalk-pits. Four vans, drawn by stout horses, were there waiting, and into these the bales were quickly loaded and they departed. Subsequently one van was traced as far as Horsham and another found to have passed through Hurst and Cuckfield, but there the trail ended. Of the other vans no clues were discovered and nothing more has been heard of any of them

from that day to this. A man concerned in "running" the cargo, who had been left behind, drunk, boasted to an inn-keeper that fourteen tons was about the quantity of tobacco which had been "run" with so much success.

The vessel which had brought the stone—and tobacco—to Shoreham, left the harbour early next morning, and before the events of the previous night began to leak out, the captain stating that he had found a customer for the stone at Brighton.

For "supposed negligence" in this affair, nearly all the officials at Shoreham coast-guard station were "replaced."

Our picture of a former Custom House at Shoreham is from a drawing in the British Museum. It was situated in Church Street, just south of the Manor House, and the building

145

L

THE STORY OF SHOREHAM

depicted was doubtless the residence of the Comptroller of Customs. This house and the adjacent offices and warehouses occupied the site of the modern cottages which are " set back " on the west side of Church Street, and beneath one of which there is still existing a large tunnel-like vault built entirely of chalk blocks. It probably dates from the late seventeenth or early eighteenth century and was used for bonding purposes.

In former times much of Church Street seems to have been given up to the convenience of those who engaged in the same profession as " the late Mr. Bardell." The Star Picture Theatre stands on the site of former Custom House buildings. In 1812, George Browne, then of Rotherhithe, but formerly of New Shoreham, shipbuilder, sold to the trustees under the will of Selina, Countess of Huntingdon, " all that piece or parcel of land, scite or ground on which two several buildings were lately standing, one of which was lately used as a Custom House and the other as a Warehouse to the same, situate, lying and being in New Shoreham and lately under the care of the Collector and Comptroller of Customs there." This property was further described as " part of certain hereditaments late John Roberts, who by last will and testament devised to his son, John Oldham Roberts, and before that, part of the estate of William Foster of New Shoreham, gent." On this site the Chapel of the Countess of Huntingdon's Connexion was erected.

The Custom House buildings and warehouses in Church Street were superseded by one designed in pseudo-classic style by Sidney Smirke, and erected in 1830 on the south side of the High Street, having spacious vaults beneath and adjacent wharfage to the river-side. It served its purpose up till the end of 1886, when the business formerly transacted in it was transferred to a new Custom House at Kingston-by-Sea.

Mr. J. B. Norton, Collector of Customs here, was, in 1795, murdered and robbed between Southwick and Shoreham by a drummer and private of the Westminster Militia, which regiment was encamped in the neighbourhood.

CHAPTER XII.

SHIPS OF SHOREHAM—REVIVAL OF INDUSTRY IN ELIZABETH'S REIGN—SHIPS FOR EAST INDIA COMPANY—A RELIC OF THE SHIPWRIGHT'S ART—A SEVENTEENTH CENTURY BUILDER AND HIS SHIPS—MEN·OF·WAR—LATER BUILDERS—THE LAST OF HER KIND—CONCRETE SHIPS AND "MYSTERY" TOWERS—THE HARBOUR IN MODERN TIMES—OYSTER INDUSTRY—STEAM PACKETS—WAR'S EFFECT ON HARBOUR TRADE.

THE reader will have gathered that much of the town's ancient prosperity was due to shipbuilding, which flourished for many generations, and that during the latter part of the fifteenth century there came a time of serious depression due to the encroachments of the sea and the raids of the French. To these causes the industry owed its decline.

In the reign of Elizabeth there are, however, signs of its revival. To encourage the building of merchant ships, suitable for use in time of war, the Queen had settled a grant of 5s. a ton on all vessels of 100 tons and upwards. In 1571 Thomas Fenner was paid this bounty for the "Bark Fenner" of 150 tons, and in 1576 the owner of the "Margaret Speedwell" also obtained it. Both these vessels were built at Shoreham.

Thomas Fenner of Shoreham was summoned to appear before the Lords of Her Majesty's Council on 2nd January, 1579. It appears that there was a little matter of "trading with the enemy," which their lordships wished to hear satisfactorily explained. When Thomas Fenner appeared before them he was charged with "the sending over of cast-iron ordnance out of this Realme into Spain," and doubtless the "Bark Fenner" was used for this purpose. He confessed his fault and was committed to the Fleet Prison on 28th January, but was released on 7th February following. On 10th November, 1584, he was returned to Parliament for New Shoreham.

Ships were being built for the East India Company in 1614-15. In the latter year Richard Furbisher was appointed as overseer for the building of one of these vessels at a salary of 14s. per week!

An interesting relic of this period remains in the carved oak chimney-piece (before referred to), removed from what was

THE STORY OF SHOREHAM

formerly part of the Fountain Inn, adjoining the Old Shipyard, and recently restored and placed in the Town Hall.

The centre panel of this interesting relic has, with very slight difference, a well executed representation of the Arms of the Shipwrights' Company of London, granted in the year 1605, viz. :—On a shield the hulk of a vessel, above which a cross, a lion on the latter. Crest—On a helmet, a Noah's Ark with dove with wings expanded.

The dove does not appear in the Shoreham carving, and the motto of the Company, "Within the ark safe for ever," is likewise absent. The left-hand panel shows a ship afloat; the right-hand panel gives a view of the Parish Church.

OLD CHIMNEY-PIECE,
SHOREHAM.

Robert Tranckmore, who may have been a descendant of the Trenchmeres who figured in the history of the town during the twelfth century, was the noted shipbuilder at this time. Possibly he was a member of the Shipwrights' Company, and it may have been for him that the chimney-piece was carved. We learn from the Minutes of the East India Company that they agreed with him, in July, 1619, to build a ship at Shoreham.

It was the usual custom at this period for a vessel, on her completion, to be furnished with as many pieces of ordnance as her owner deemed necessary for her defence, and for this purpose, warrants, known as Trinity House Certificates, were issued. They are known to have been granted in respect of the following ships, built by Tranckmore at Shoreham. Five of them were of 300

TRANCKMORE'S SHIPS

tons—a fair size for those days—four of 200, and one each of 180, 150, and 140 tons. The dates given are those of the certificates.

27th September, 1625, the "Thomas Bonaventure"; 4th January, 1626, the "Garland," of London; 28th October, 1627, a ship on the stocks unfinished; 15th July, 1629, the "Mary and John," of London; 14th October, 1629, a ship unnamed; 25th November, 1629, the "Content," of London; 5th June, 1630, the "Charles," of London; 27th July, 1631, the "Joan Bonaventure"; 5th May, 1632, the "Confident"; 6th July, 1633, the "Joseph," of London; 28th September, 1633, the "Thomas and John," of London, which vessel was "furnished with 18 pieces of cast-iron ordnance, from the usual market in Smithfield"; 7th May, 1636, the "Blessing," of Dover; 25th June, 1636, the "Ann and Sarah."

In February, 1628, Robert Tranckmore obtained the contract to build one of ten pinnaces for the Government. These were small craft of about 185 tons and were provided with sweeps as well as sails. They were three-masted and square-rigged, carrying ten guns on two decks and were built after the model of a ship called the "Lion," and so were named "Lion's Whelps," being numbered from one to ten. Tranckmore built the "Tenth Lion's Whelp" at a cost of £596 17s. 9d. His receipts for payment are preserved in the Record Office. On June 11th, 1628, Capt John Pennington wrote to Sir Edward Nicholas, Secretary to the Admiralty, requesting a warrant for John Tranckmore to take charge as master of the "Tenth Lion's Whelp," built by his brother. Nicholas Tranckmore was appointed carpenter, and John More, a native of Shoreham, boatswain, a warrant being issued by the Lord High Admiral to press seamen for her. It is curious to learn that her master-cook, after holding that office for a year, sold it to Robert Swainson "for life."

A John Tranckmore is mentioned as master of the "Shoreham" in 1634, when ten lasts of powder were delivered to him to be transported to Ireland.

In the Record Office is preserved a Certificate bearing the signature of Inigo Jones, the celebrated architect. It is dated "May ye 6, 1637," and from it we learn that the "Indeavor," of Shoreham, a barque, was to be "emploied for ye space of nine months for the carriage and transportation of stone from the Isle of Portland to London for the repair of the Cathedral Church of St. Paul." Thomas Clearke was the master of this vessel

THE STORY OF SHOREHAM

and the Cathedral mentioned in the certificate was, of course, Old St. Paul's, which was totally destroyed in the Great Fire of 1666.

During the Commonwealth and subsequently, the shipbuilders of Shoreham came into prominence as providers of vessels for the service of the State. The war-ships built here were fourth, fifth and sixth rates, sloops and fire-ships; fourth rates were 105ft., long by 32ft. beam, and were two-deckers, costing about £9,000 each; fifth rates had all their guns on one whole deck and the quarter-deck; sixth rates on one deck only.

When the "Dover" (4th rate) man-of-war was on the stocks in June, 1653, Clement Freeman wrote to the Navy Commissioners that "the building of the frigate is progressing," and asking for a general survey, stating that "he will now wait until that has been made before expecting the bill of imprest for twenty weeks pay for which he wrote previously." He adds "Robert Plumby is fit for one of the frigates building at Shoreham." In October, Captain Fraser Willoughby, having been to Shoreham and Arundel and provided 200 loads of plank and trenail for building "two great ships at Portsmouth," states that the new frigate "wants her officers," and a few days later a survey of her having been made by William Castle, the latter says "she will be ready to launch the middle of next month."

The "Dover" went off the stocks in 1654, and sailing for the West Indies in 1655, carried 160 seamen and 30 soldiers. She had a somewhat long career, and at the time of the Revolution in 1688, she was commanded by the celebrated Clowdesley Shovell, and was one of those ships in the fleet assembled to oppose the landing of William, Prince of Orange. Many of the captains were friendly disposed toward the Prince, and the commander of the "Dover" was one of those who very quickly transferred his allegiance to the new King.

It may be noted that Clowdesley Shovell rose to be Commander-in-Chief of the Fleet, and after a life spent in the service of his country, the gallant Admiral was wrecked on the Scillies in a dreadful storm on the 22nd October, 1702. His body, still living, was cast upon the shore near Porthellick Cove, and a woman who was the first to find it, coveting an emerald ring, extinguished the flickering life. This crime was at the time undiscovered. The body of the Admiral was conveyed to England, embalmed, and buried in Westminster Abbey. Some thirty years afterwards the woman on her death-bed, confessed

MEN-OF-WAR

her crime to a clergyman, delivering up the ring to him, and it passed into the possession of Sir Clowdesley Shovell's friends.

The "Dover," commanded by Edward Whitaker, in February, 1691, took a 24-gun St. Malo privateer. While in command of Andrew Douglas, she took "Revenge," (12 guns), in August, 1692; "Lion," (14 guns) in January, 1693, and "Vauban" in May, 1695. She was rebuilt at Portsmouth in 1695.

We find no further records of war-ships built at Shoreham until 1690. At this period the builders were Thomas Ellis, Nicholas Barrett, William Collins, Thomas Burgess, and Robert Chatfield. In the seven years from 1690 to 1696, seventeen men-of-war were built in the Shoreham yards. Some particulars of these ships follow :—

The "Fox" (fireship, 253 tons, 8 guns), built 1690. She had a length of 93ft. and 25ft. beam and carried a crew of 45 men. Her first commander, Andrew Leake, the son of a merchant of Lowestoft, was known from the grace and comeliness of his person, as "Queen Anne's handsome captain." His ship was in the Battle of Beachy Head. Thomas Killingworth succeeded him in command of the "Fox," and with her grappled a French line of battle-ship at La Hogue. Fire-ships were rarely successful, the Frenchman won clear, and the "Fox" was burnt in action, but Killingworth was handsomely rewarded for his brave attempt and promoted to the command of a 32-gun ship.

"Hopewell" (fireship, 253 tons, 8 guns), built 1690. After a short service in the Channel Fleet, she was burnt by accident in the Downs, 3rd June, 1690.

"Shoreham," (5th rate, 362 tons, 32 guns), built 1693. Captured "La Feroa" (10 guns) in 1695. In March or April, 1700, on the coast of Virginia, after a ten hours fight, she took a pirate ship of 20 guns and retook from her two merchantmen. During the years 1702-9, she was on the Irish Station, commanded by George—afterwards Sir George—Saunders, convoying the local trade between Whitehaven, Milford, and Bristol on the one side, and on the other from Belfast to Kinsale. While engaged in these duties, Saunders sometimes chased and captured the enemy's privateers, taking the "Francis" (8 guns) in June, 1706, and "Esperance" (12 guns) in 1709. The "Shoreham" was broken up by Admiralty order, 11th September, 1719.

THE STORY OF SHOREHAM

"Vesuvius" (fireship, 269 tons, 8 guns), built 1693, and burnt in action at St. Malo, 19th November, in the same year.

"Sorlings" (5th rate, 362 tons, 32 guns), built 1694. Took "San Salvador" (20 guns), in October, 1703, and was captured on the Dogger-Bank, 20th October, 1705, when in company with the "Pendennis" and the "Blackwall," two 44-gun ships, whose captains were killed. Captain William Coney of the "Sorlings" was tried by Court-martial, which not only acquitted him but added that it "particularly approves and recommends his conduct." The ship was retaken in February, 1711, but was not again taken into the Navy.

"Terrible" (5th rate, 253 tons, 26 guns), built 1694. Captured by a French 36-gun ship, 20th September, 1710. Her captain, Thomas Mabbot, was tried by Court-martial, but was acquitted of blame.

"Penzance" (6th rate, 246 tons, 24 guns), built 1694. Served on the Irish Station, 1697-8, and captured "Volland" (14 guns) in April, 1697. Her commander, John Aston, sold the ship's provisions and overcharged the men for clothes, for which offence he was tried in 1699. The ship was sold by Admiralty order, 24th September, 1713.

"Arundel" (5th rate, 378 tons, 32 guns), built 1695. Commanded in 1710-11, by Andrew Douglas, a former captain of the "Dover." He had been, in the interval, captain of a fourth-rate, but was dismissed the Navy for dishonesty, which the Court-martial characterised as "mean." He was restored in 1709. The "Arundel" was condemned in 1711, and sold by Admiralty order, 11th June, 1713.

"Hastings" (5th rate, 381 tons, 32 guns), built 1695. Wrecked off Waterford, 10th December, 1697, six men only being saved.

"Dunwich" (6th rate, 250 tons, 24 guns), built 1695. After about nineteen years' service convoy and cruising at home and abroad, she was sunk as a breakwater at Plymouth Dock, 14th October, 1714.

"Falcon" (6th rate, 240 tons, 24 guns), built 1695. The twelfth vessel in the Royal Navy to bear that name (the twenty-fourth "Falcon" was launched in 1899); her crew numbered 110 men. She was taken in 1695, by three 50-gun French ships off the Dodman. Her captain, Henry Middleton, was found guilty of an error of judgment in not running ashore and fined three months pay. She was retaken in 1703, by the "Romney," but not again placed in the Navy.

"Newport" (6th rate, 244 tons, 24 guns), built 1695. While on service in North America and commanded by Wentworth Paxton, taken by two French ships, 5th July, 1696, in the Bay of Fundy.

"Orford" (6th rate, 249 tons, 24 guns), built 1695, and renamed "Newport" by Admiralty order, 3rd September, 1698. In the Cadiz Expedition of 1702. Took part in the Battle of Malaga, 1704. Sold by order of the Admiralty 29th July, 1714.

"Fowey" (5th rate, 377 tons, 32 guns), built 1696. Taken by a French Squadron off the Scillies, 1st August, 1704.

"Feversham" (5th rate, 372 tons, 32 guns), built 1696. Wrecked off Cape Breton, 7th October, 1711, and her captain, Robert Paston, and most of the crew drowned.

"Gosport" (5th rate, 376 tons, 32 guns), built 1696. Taken 28th August, 1706, with 12 out of 15 merchantmen under convoy, by a squadron under Duguay Trouin. Her captain, Edward St. Lo, was acquitted and commended for his conduct on this occasion.

"Lynn" (5th rate, 380 tons, 32 guns), built 1696. In May, 1712, while in company with the "Ludlow Castle," drove ashore and destroyed a Spanish 36-gun ship and three merchantmen in Estapona Roads. Sold by Admiralty order 11th June, 1713.

The Lewes Town Records for the year 1694, inform us that "a company of vagrant showmen were taken up by the constables and conveyed to a ship at Shoreham for the sea service."

The New Shoreham Parish Registers record the burials, in 1695-6, of seamen belonging to H.M.S. "Dunwich," "Gosport," "Lynn," and "Feversham."

In 1698, when the members of the Navy Board surveyed the South Coast, the Harbour was visited and inspected, but the report they made as to its condition was not very favourable. "Shoreham admits of nothing improvable," says the report, "the haven's mouth is a very dry barr upon the ebbs of spring tides and the outsea in foul weather throws up extraordinary quantities of beach in the manner of small islands, and whether you come in or goe out you meet with great difficulty and hazard, but ships of considerable burden are built and, waiting good seasons and proper care, they get them into the sea."

THE STORY OF SHOREHAM

Defoe, in "Tour through Britain" 1724, refers to Shoreham's chief trade of ship-building, "especially West Indiamen."

In 1728, the Lords Commissioners of the Admiralty, referring to the town as eminent for building ships, state that "they are great builders because of the vast quantity of large timber which this part of England produces more plentifully than elsewhere."   A writer in the "Universal Magazine," 1760, says : "Most of the town of New Shoreham has been washed away by the sea, and yet is still a populous place and has a collector and other officers to take charge of the customs, here being a very good harbour for vessels of considerable burden.   Many ships are built both for the Navy and merchants.   The ship's carpenters and ship's chandlers, who are pretty numerous, with all the tradesmen depending on that business, seem to have settled here chiefly because of the great quantity and cheapness of the timber in the country behind them, and the river, though not navigable for large vessels, serves to bring down the floats of it from Bramber, Steyning and the adjacent country, which is, in a measure, covered with timber."

And again, in later years, the town was described as noted for shipbuilding, "in which art the inhabitants are allowed to excell."

The Shoreham builders do not appear to have built much for the Navy between the end of the seventeenth and middle of the eighteenth century, at which time the Admiralty Contractors were Stone & Bartlett, followed later, during the Napoleonic period, by Carver & Co., Hamilton & Co., and Edwardes. The following ships were built by these firms :—

"Seaford" (6th rate, 432 tons, 24 guns), built 1741.   Broken up in 1754.

"Dispatch" (sloop, 269 tons, 14 guns), built 1745.   In action 7th October, 1756, with a French sloop of greater force, and her captain, James Holbourne, was killed.   In 1762 she took "Duc de Broglie" (14 guns), and was sold 1st March, 1763.

"Hound" (sloop, 267 tons, 14 guns), built 1745.   Sold September 20th, 1773.

"Stork" (sloop, 233 tons, 14 guns), built 1756.   Captured 16th August, 1758, by a French 74-gun ship.

"Favourite" (sloop, 313 tons, 16 guns), built 1757.   In the Mediterranean from 1757 to 1762, and commanded by Tim Edwards and Philemon Pownall.   Took "Grouzard" (26 guns),

LATER BUILDERS

in 1758, "Valeur" (24 guns), in 1759, and "St. Joseph" (12 guns), in 1761. She was present at Boscawen's action with De la Clue, 18th August, 1759, and was sold in 1784.

"Matthew" (sloop, 18 guns), built 1764. An Indian ink drawing of this vessel, inscribed "The Matthew, Captain Charles Payne, built at Shoreham, Sussex, September 2nd, 1763 (Signed) T. Hood, 1764," formerly in the possession of the late Mr. John Ellman Brown, of Shoreham, is now the property of Messrs. Barclay & Co., Bankers, of North Street, Brighton.

"Conflagration" and "Vulcan" (fireships, 425 tons, 10 guns), built 1783, and both burnt at Toulon, 18th December, 1793.

"Scorpion" (sloop, 340 tons, 16 guns), built 1785. She was in the West Indies, 1793-6, and her commanders during that time were Thomas Western and Stair Douglas. She was remarkably active during the year 1795, when she captured "Victoire" (18 guns), 19th April, "L'Egalite" (16 guns), 8th August, "Sanspareil" (16 guns), 22nd July, "Republicain" (16 guns), 3rd August, and "L'Hirondelle" (16 guns), 17th August. Captured "Courier" (6 guns) while on service in the North Sea, 26th April, 1798. Sold 1802.

"Pheasant" (sloop, 365 tons, 18 guns), built 1798. Captured "Tropard" (6 guns), 8th May, 1808, "Comte de Hunebourg" (14 guns), 3rd February, 1810, and "Heros" (6 guns), 17th June, 1811. She was sold 1827.

"Spy" (sloop, 227 tons, 16 guns), built 1804. Sold 1813.

It may be of interest to record the fact that three iron cannonballs were discovered in digging out for the erection of a telephone pole, at the rear of the Star Picture Palace in Church Street. They measured from 6 to $7\frac{1}{2}$ inches in diameter, the weight of the largest being 4 lbs.

Bailey's British Directory of 1784, gives the names of three firms of shipbuilders in Shoreham, Ashman & Turner, John Edwards, and Ernest Pelham, and the Universal British Directory of 1793, gives John Edwards, and Thomas Tilstone, shipbuilders, and the names of numerous shipwrights, caulkers, blockmakers and carpenters. In the earlier directory, we find the name of Hugh Roberts, sailmaker, and Joseph Tilstone, ropemaker; the last-named being mentioned again in 1793.

The "Ropewalk" still perpetuates the memory of the industry formerly carried on by Tilstone, and later by English, and Hayman. It ceased about forty years ago with the decline of shipbuilding.

THE STORY OF SHOREHAM

The "Ropewalk" served its purpose for at least three hundred years, and it is quite probable that "Ropetackle"—more commonly "Raptackle"—the name applied to another part of the town nearer the river—is the site of a yet more ancient Ropewalk. As sail-makers the name of English has long enjoyed a world-wide reputation.

Edwards, Brown, and Olliver were building at Shoreham in 1804. About 1817, John Edwards took into partnership James Britton Balley, a native of Littlehampton, who subsequently married his daughter, and into whose hands the business eventually passed.

For many years the name of Balley, as a builder of ships, was celebrated far and wide. Many noted vessels were launched from the Old Shipyard and they did much to raise the reputation of the port to its eminence for superior coasting vessels, as well as those built for foreign service and foreign owners. A list—by no means exhaustive—of brigs, barques, and schooners, built at the Old Shipyard from the years 1823 to 1853, serves to show that they were launched at the rate of four a year. At the same time there was a great deal of repair work going on. In the early years of the century, we hear of vessels being sent from London and other ports to Messrs. Edwards & Balley's shipyard at Shoreham, "on account of the faithfulness of the work done there and the excellent oak timber which they used."

Mr. Balley died at Longcroft, Shoreham, 8th July, 1863. He left two sons, neither of whom long survived him, and the ship-building business was subsequently acquired by Mr. W. May, who continued to launch from the same yard brigs and barques, for which craft it had become so famous.

To this firm succeeded Messrs. Dyer & Son, who also carried on the traditions of the place. They were the last to build merchant-ships at Shoreham, and with the early eighties, the industry which had flourished for so many generations, ceased to be.

It was always a gala-day in the town when a ship was launched. This ceremony, performed in the orthodox style, included the christening of the ship by a lady, who dashed a bottle of wine against the bows of the vessel, at the same time naming her. The launches were witnessed by large numbers of people—shipowners, their friends, and others—and usually celebrated by a dinner or luncheon, and very frequently the day was brought to a close by a ball at the Swiss Gardens.

THE "BRITANNIA"

Our picture shows the barque "Britannia" on the stocks at the Old Shipyard. She was of about 800 tons burden and was one of the last to be launched from thence. Her bows were adorned with Britannia as a figure-head. Like many another ship of Shoreham, she sailed out from the harbour to return no more. In September, 1883, during a dense fog, she ran on to the north-east bar of Sable Island, the scene of many an ocean

The Barque "Britannia" on the stocks at the old ship-yard.

tragedy, a coast dreaded by all mariners and well-known under its sinister name of the "grave-yard of the North Atlantic." The good ship "Britannia" became a total wreck and thirteen lives were lost.

There were other shipbuilding yards on the Adur. Messrs. May & Thwaites built many brigs, barques, and schooners at Kingston, somewhat westward of the spot where the lighthouse

THE STORY OF SHOREHAM

stands. A fine oil-painting of the schooner "Kingston" built at this yard in 1838, is in the possession of Mr. E. V. Lucas, the well-known writer. Notable barques and other craft were built by Messrs. Shuttleworth at the Shoreham Canal Shipyards, Southwick, extensively used of late years as a yacht depôt by Messrs. Courtney & Birkett. Yacht-building was carried on at Shoreham by Messrs. Stow & Son, and Frank Suter up to the outbreak of the war, and we hope to see it revive again in peaceful years yet to be.

Here and there in Shoreham you will find paintings, in oil or water-colour, of the old-time sailing vessels for which the town was once so famous. The late Mrs. R. H. Penney preserved several very fine paintings of ships built for and owned by her husband. An interesting relic of one of these vessels, the "Arbutus," built at Shuttleworth's yard in 1863, for a London firm, and subsequently purchased by Mr. R. H. Penney, is preserved in the garden at "Highcroft," Brighton. This is the figure-head of the ship. A very finely executed female figure, holding in her hand an Arbutus-flower.

During the last year of the war a shipyard was started on the beach, west of the Chemical Works. This was regarded at the time as a revival of the industry, but "the old order changeth, giving place to new." Unlike the ships of other days these vessels —huge "barges" of 1,000 tons burden, were built of concrete in dry-dock. Three having been completed ready for "launching" the ceremony took place on Saturday, January 18th, 1919, in lovely weather and was performed by Mrs. Andrew Miller and other ladies, who named the ships "Creteshade," "Cretestyle," and "Cretestream." Each vessel was gaily decorated with flags and the two first-named were towed from their berths by the steam-tug "Stella" and floated on a high tide into the river. Others have since been launched, as well as the attendant tugs, also of concrete but built on stocks. The last of these, the "Cretewheel," was launched in July, 1920.

In the early part of 1918, Southwick Green was converted into a camp to accommodate the Royal Engineers. They were preparing for, and subsequently built, the two huge concrete towers or "Mystery-ships," which of late have formed so conspicuous a feature of the harbour mouth. One of the towers having been completed was towed out from the harbour on Sunday, September 12th, 1920, and successfully made her first

THE HARBOUR

and only voyage to the Solent, where she took up her final position (partly submerged) as a tower of defence near the Nab.

The cost, equipment, and endowment of the Shoreham lifeboat, "William Restall," was met by a legacy bequeathed by the gentleman after whom she was named. The present boat is the successor of an earlier one which numbered among her crew ten members of one family (Upton), a father, his six sons and three nephews.

The Harbour itself, and some account of its varying fortunes during the past one hundred and sixty years must now claim our attention for a brief space.

Owing to the bad state into which it had fallen by the middle of the eighteenth century, the prosperity of the ship-owners, merchants, and inhabitants again declined. They presented a petition to Parliament, praying that leave might be granted them to bring in a Bill to effect improvements, and Sir William Peere Williams, one of the Borough Members, introduced a Bill, which was passed on the 24th March, 1760. It appointed 51 Commissioners, who were authorised to make "a new cut through the sea-beach opposite Kingston," and to execute other necessary works "to make and maintain a new and more commodious entrance to the harbour." The first meeting of the Commissioners was held at the Star Inn, Shoreham, 24th June, 1760.

The works were carried out, but apparently with too great a desire to avoid expenditure. They quickly became undermined by the sea, and some fifteen years after their construction, the entrance began to travel eastward, forming, as the years went on, the later series of mouths before referred to. None of these remained open very long and the harbour rapidly silted up.

A most unsatisfactory state of affairs existed for a quarter of a century, during which time many surveys and suggestions for improvement were made. One of these was to reopen the old entrance opposite Shoreham; another to build extensive docks, neither of which schemes saw fruition.

An Act of Parliament, passed in 1816, resulted in the Kingston entrance being reopened. These works commenced 22nd April, 1817, by the driving in of two of the foundation piles of the new piers. The *Brighton Herald* of that time records that "a Masonic procession gave grandeur and solemnity to the occasion. The party embarked in about thirty boats, which,

THE STORY OF SHOREHAM

with flags flying and to the accompaniment of music, proceeded to the point where the ceremony of driving in the piles took place. Several thousand spectators lined the harbour, across which a bridge of boats was formed, by which means many were able to approach nearer the interesting scene of action." The ceremony included an oration delivered by a clergyman-mason.

By January, 1818, the new entrance was open to allow the passage of shipping, and at the end of the summer of 1820, an issue of the *Brighton Herald* records that :—

"By the judicious application of talent and capital, the skilful engineers, the subscribers, and the Commissioners have improved the blessings peace bestows upon a nation. They have given employment to industry in the erection of a work of which the county may be justly proud and for which they will receive the gratitude of the mercantile interest for whose vessels they have provided an asylum, and of the mariners whom they will save from shipwreck. To celebrate the happy termination of their gratuitous labours the Commissioners dined at the Star Inn, Shoreham, and there were also present M.P.'s and prominent residents of the county and of Brighton. It is intended to further improve the harbour entrance and to apply to Parliament for an Act to make a new turnpike road above the cliff from Brighton to Shoreham. It is also in contemplation to lay down an iron railway from the point at which vessels discharge their cargoes to the western extremity of Brighton, and to form a junction of the river Adur and Arun by which a navigation would be opened up between Shoreham and the Metropolis."

The turnpike road is presumably the present lower road from Shoreham to Brighton. The railway did not come until some twenty years later, while the projected communication with London, by means of a junction between the Adur and the Arun, thence to the Wey, and so to the Thames, was not destined to be realised.

The harbour entrance was finally completed in June, 1821. Good results quickly followed these improvements, and in the year, 1833 a writer describes the scene on approaching Shoreham as being of "a cheerful and active character," there being possibly no port on the south coast which displayed in those days greater activity. A great deal of the harbour's subsequent prosperity may be attributed to its proximity to the large and flourishing town of Brighton, which, with all towns and villages

TRADE OF THE PORT

between the eastern part of Rottingdean and the western part of Heene, are within the limits of the port.

The lighthouse opposite the harbour entrance was erected in 1846, and about the same period the piers were also considerably lengthened.

The canal or dock which extends from Southwick to Aldrington Basin, was opened 20th February, 1855. The harbour is therefore divided into two arms, that to the westward being deeper and leading up to Shoreham—about a mile distant from the present mouth—and to the L.B. & S.C. Railway Co.'s wharf at Kingston. The eastern arm is somewhat shallower and leads to the dock at Southwick, giving access to the canal, in which ships are enabled to lie afloat at all times of the tide.

The management of the harbour is now in the hands of a body of trustees, elected triennially by the Corporations of Brighton and Worthing, the Shoreham Urban District Council, the Steyning Justices, and the ship-owners and traders of the port of Shoreham.

The trade of the port is chiefly in coals from the North. In former years it was not an unusual event for as many as twenty colliers to enter the harbour in one day; but that was in the days of the far-famed Shoreham sailing-ships, when they traded regularly between Hartlepool and Shoreham. In the 'fifties there was a large business in fruit and eggs from Havre, Honfleur, Caen, and other French ports. Cheese, cattle, wine, and salt were among former imports. Flour and corn, timber from the Baltic and America, stone and roofing slates have been imported for many years, and the chief exports are Portland cement, chemicals, pitch, coke, and tar.

From entries in the Vestry Book of New Shoreham in 1743, and 1746, we learn that it had been customary, "time out of remembrance," for the Constable and Vicar of the Borough "to demand and receive" out of every vessel coming into port one bushel of coal, salt, or grain, according to which of these commodities the ships were laden with. Sometimes the masters of vessels resisted payment of these perquisites, but the townspeople in those days seem generally to have upheld the Vicar and Constable in exacting these dues.

The Oyster and Escallop Fishery was formerly an important and prosperous industry and gave employment to a large number of men. The dredgers, which sometimes numbered a hundred

THE STORY OF SHOREHAM

sail, usually made about three voyages a fortnight during the months from September to April inclusive ; but the other months were "fenced," and dredging was then prohibited. The beds were situated about midway between the English and French coasts and were about twenty miles in length and seven or eight in breadth.

The oysters, on being brought into Shoreham, were bought by resident merchants, who laid them down in ponds in the river and sent them thence to the markets in London, Leeds, Hull, Birmingham, Newcastle, and other parts of England. Some idea of the extent of this trade may be gathered when it is stated that, during the 'fifties, nearly 20,000 tons of oysters were sent by rail from Shoreham in one year. During the Crimean War the owners found great difficulty in manning their boats ; the war and high wages in the merchant service "having drawn a great many men from their trade." When steam vessels, built on improved lines, took the place of sailing dredgers, the industry declined. Except for a very small quantity occasionally brought in, it is a thing of the past. Such, too, is the case with escallops, which trade, though important, was not so extensive. The disused oyster-ponds are visible at low tide.

Steam packets formerly sailed between Shoreham and Dieppe, Havre, Jersey, and other ports. After the London, Brighton and South Coast Railway was opened, they ran in connection with the trains ; the Company, in the earlier days of its existence, having a passenger station at Kingston. Eventually the Steam Lines were removed to the neighbouring ports of Littlehampton and Newhaven, the Railway Company and the Harbour Commissioners being "unable to agree."

What the future may hold for Shoreham Harbour can only be a matter of speculation. During the war, the town itself enjoyed a period of prosperity never before experienced. This was owing to the presence of thousands of soldiers in camp. But the harbour was hit terribly hard : its traffic fell almost to nil and the war exacted a toll both of ships and men. We can but regret the fate of the "John Miles,"—so frequently seen in past years entering the harbour to unload her thousand tons of coal at the Gas Works—torpedoed or mined on her last voyage from the North in the early part of 1917, most of her crew perishing. Among smaller craft the defenceless "Athol" was fired on and sunk off the "Owers" at the end of April in the same year She

FATE OF THE "BRIGHTON QUEEN"

was making for Shoreham, and her small crew of five, although able to save themselves, lost their belongings. And again we recall the "Brighton Queen," a pleasure steamer so often seen leaving the harbour in those fair summer mornings of bygone years to call at the Brighton piers for her freight of light-hearted trippers. She will be seen no more, having been mined or torpedoed while on transport duty, "doing her bit" in the early days of the war, and lies somewhere beneath the waves. Who of us ever dreamed that such a fate would be hers?

It is hoped that a day will come when the traffic of the harbour will again revive and flourish as aforetime. Yet this cannot be, unless a due employment of capital and enterprise is forthcoming to make the best use of its natural advantages and possibilities, which are many and obvious.

CHAPTER XIII.

THE CHURCHES OF SHOREHAM—SCANTY DOCUMENTARY HISTORY—ST. NICHOLAS, OLD SHOREHAM—SAINTS IN A WINDOW—AN ELIZABETHAN CAPTAIN AND HIS FAMILY—"RIZPAH"—THE PARISH CLERK AND THE SAILOR KING—THE CHURCH OF ST. MARY DE HAURA—THE "ATONEMENT" OF WILLIAM DE BRAOSE—THE RUINED NAVE—CHANTRY PROPERTY—MEMORIAL INSCRIPTIONS—VICARS OF OLD AND NEW SHOREHAM—LANCING COLLEGE—THE FREE CHURCHES—THE CHURCH OF ST. PETER (R.C.).

THE earliest mention of a Church at Shoreham appears in the year 1073, when "William de Braose crossed the sea and went to Maine in the army of William, King of the English." He then gave to St. Nicholas of Bramber, "the tithes of the Church of Sorham," obviously St. Nicholas, Old Shoreham. Some two years later, when de Braose founded the Priory of Sele, he bestowed St. Nicholas, Old Shoreham, together with other churches and property in the neighbourhood, upon the Abbey of St. Florent of Saumur, near Fècamp. Domesday Book (A.D. 1086) has the usual brief notice, "there is a church."

Philip de Braose, a crusader, confirmed to the foreign Abbey, the grant made by his predecessor Returning from the Holy Land after the capture of Jerusalem in 1099, between that date and 1103, he also conceded and confirmed to the Abbey, "the Church of St. Mary de Haura, Sorham, because their right thereto existed." This is the earliest reference to the latter church.

A Bull of Pope Eugenius III., dated 14th April, 1146, one of Adrian IV., 9th February, 1157, and another of Urban III., 28th December, 1186, confer to the Abbey of St. Florent, the Church of St. Nicholas of Shoreham, "with the Chapel of St. Mary of the Port of Shoreham," but in the last-named document St. Mary is described as "the Church" of the Port of Shoreham.

The taxation of Pope Nicholas IV. (A.D. 1291), to whose predecessors in the See of Rome, the first fruits and tenths of all Ecclesiastical benefices had for a long time been paid, values the Church of Old Shoreham at £24, and New Shoreham at £10.

Although the patronage of the two churches was in the hands of the Abbot of St. Florent, it was usually exercised through

OLD SHOREHAM CHURCH

the dependent Priory of Sele, except in time of war with France when the King of England exercised the right of presentation.

By a Letter Patent, dated 21 Richard II. (1398), the Church of Old Shoreham was appropriated to the Priory of Sele and confirmation of this was given by another Letter Patent, 1 Henry IV. (1399), "provided that a competent sum from the fruits and profits of the church be yearly paid to the poor parishioners and the vicarage sufficiently endowed." In 1459 Sele Priory was granted to Magdalen College, Oxford, which thus became and still remains the Patron of both livings.

THE CHURCH OF ST. NICHOLAS, OLD SHOREHAM,
is one of the most interesting in Sussex and is well known to all who love the study of the past. It is of Saxon foundation, the masonry of that period being yet in evidence in the long-and-short quoins at the north-west angle of the nave and also in the blocked doorway in the north wall near the west end.

The Saxon building consisted of chancel, nave, and western tower. The Norman builders considerably enlarged the fabric and gave it the present cruciform plan, by erecting a tower in place of the Saxon chancel, and building north and south transepts, —with an apse to each—and an apsidal chancel in characteristic Norman style. They lengthened the nave by including in it the space formerly occupied by the Saxon tower, and the curious "off-set" in the north wall is probably due to this alteration. The very beautiful Norman doorway in the south transept is worthy of particular notice. It appears that the nave had formerly two entrances, which are now blocked up.

The tower is a very striking feature. It is a "lantern" in two stages, the lower one ornamented with Norman arcading, three arches on each side. The upper stage is pierced with eight circular openings, two on each face, and it is capped by a low pyramidal spire. It is said to resemble the towers of many churches in Picardy.

The interior affords a fine example of Norman architecture. The piers and four semi-circular arches which support the tower are very beautiful, displaying a richness of detail seldom surpassed in village churches. The arches are adorned with a variety of carvings and mouldings. You will observe the imitation of the seashore product in the limpet. The wealth of the Norman mason's art is seen in cushion capitals, square abaci

Old Shoreham Church.

NOTEWORTHY FEATURES

with hollow chamfer, chevron with pellets, beaked, cable with beads, studs, lozenge with rose, wheel-like studs, and billet mouldings. Nor should you fail to notice the portrait heads —said to be those of King Henry I. and his Queen—which adorn the north transept arch. The King has elaborately curled hair and beard.

The Norman roof-beam is still in *situ* over the east arch of the nave. It is ornamented with the alternate billet moulding in two rows. The church also contains "that very rare feature, a late 13th century rood-screen," having trefoiled arches and circular capitals and shafts. It is probably of the same date as the chancel itself, which seems to have been entirely rebuilt during that period, replacing the former Norman apse. The roof of chestnut also belongs to the same date and its tie-beams are often quoted as displaying the "dog's tooth" moulding, almost the only known instance of its occurrence in woodwork. To the late thirteenth century belongs the small low-side window in the south wall, although the outside jambs show stones bearing tool-marks from earlier work re-used. The rebate on the inside still retains one of the shutter hinge-hooks. The east and south windows of the chancel are graceful examples of the Early Decorated style. A trefoil-headed piscina and a four-centred arch of the fifteenth century—the latter probably for the Easter Sepulchre—will be noticed in the south wall.

Of the ruined chapel on the north side of the chancel very little remains, but a piscina sufficiently denotes its ancient purpose and the doorway which once gave access from the chancel to the chapel will also be noted. A modern vestry and the vault of the Bridger family now occupy the site.

The church was restored in 1840-41. According to the *Gentleman's Magazine* of that date, it was then in "a most lamentable condition." The north transept was in ruin, the soil of the churchyard was raised so high as to conceal the walls to a height of several feet above the level of the interior and the jambs of the Norman doorway in the south transept (the principal entrance to-day) were quite concealed, the arch alone being visible. A small altar-bell was found when the earth was removed from the outside. The removal of the flooring under the singers' gallery disclosed the three memorial slabs to the Blaker family, now against the west wall of the nave.

It is, perhaps, worthy of remark that the Decorated east

window of four lights, with reticulated tracery, is filled with stained glass from the Exhibition of 1851. In the four principal lights are figures of St. Nicholas, Patron of the Church, St. Mary, Patroness of New Shoreham, St. Wilfrid, the Apostle of Sussex, and St. Richard, a thirteenth-century Bishop of Chichester.

St. Nicholas was Bishop of Myra in Lycia during the fourth

In Old Shoreham Church.

century, and died about the year A.D. 352. As all should know, he is the patron saint of mariners, merchants and bakers, and it is, therefore, appropriate that this old church, so well known from the earliest times to all those "who go down to the sea in ships," should have been dedicated to one who was ever a favourite with sea-faring folk. We find another St. Nicholas at Bramber,

SAINTS IN A WINDOW

one at Portslade and yet another at Brighton—all churches of ancient foundation. This saint, we are told, was also regarded as the special protector of the young. One legend tells us that St. Nicholas miraculously restored to life, some children who had been murdered by a pork butcher, cut to pieces and placed in a tub of brine. The incident is depicted in the window at Old Shoreham, where the children are seen rising out of the tub, "safe and sound." In some countries the saint is regarded as the secret purveyor of gifts to children, after the manner of Father Christmas, whose Yule-tide visits are so welcome to the small boys and girls of our own land.

To St. Wilfrid belongs the honour of having converted the South Saxon Kingdom from Paganism to Christianity. His first attempt to accomplish this proved futile. Returning to England from Gaul, his ship had been driven by a tempest far out of her course and at length ran aground on the Sussex coast. Then, as in later centuries, the natives were barbarous wreckers, and led on by one of their priests, they made a furious attack upon the stranded vessel. "To them," says Wilfrid's chronicler, "our great Bishop spoke gently and peaceably, offering much money, wishing to redeem their souls. But they, with stern and cruel hearts, said proudly that, 'all that the sea threw on the land became as much theirs as their own property.' And the idolatrous chief priest of the heathen, standing on a lofty mound, strove like Balaam, to curse the people of God and to bind their hands by his magic arts."

The Bishop's crew and retinue numbered 120, and offered a brave resistance, while Wilfrid and his priests knelt and prayed for their success. Finally, we are told, one of the Bishop's companions "hurled, like David of old, a stone, which struck the magician and pierced his brain." Three times the heathen attacked Wilfrid's followers, thrice were they repulsed, and finally routed with great slaughter. They were collecting larger forces for a fourth attack, when the grounded vessel floated with the rising tide, and the Bishop and his party got out to sea, with the loss of only five men. They sailed away and landed in safety at Sandwich, on the shores of Christian Kent.

Such was Wilfrid's first experience of the South Saxons. Some twenty years later (A.D. 680), owing to a disagreement with the King of Northumbria, he was banished from his Archbishopric of York. He came again to Sussex, but this time as the honoured

THE STORY OF SHOREHAM

guest of King Æthelwealh and his Queen, who had been converted to Christianity. The people, however, were still heathens. The homeless prelate—one of the most renowned men of his time—soon began his work amongst these barbarians It was a time of severe distress in Sussex, for the crops had failed, and the people were reduced to such extremities of famine that many cast themselves into the sea and so ended their miserable existence. Wilfrid taught those who would learn, the art of making nets, and fishing in the open sea, of which till then, they appear to have been strangely ignorant. In such-like practical ways he won their hearts, and they were glad to listen to his words of hope and comfort. He founded the first Cathedral Church in Sussex, at Selsea, not far from the scene of his first inhospitable reception, but this has long since been swept away by the encroaching sea. Wilfrid's history need not detain us further. His connection with Sussex ended about the year 685, when the King of Northumbria, who had driven him into exile, fell in battle, and he returned to the See of York.

Richard de la Wych, or St. Richard of Chichester, was the son of a Droitwich farmer, and we first hear of him as a lad working on the land and in the orchards of Worcestershire. Having a passion for learning, he presently betook himself to Oxford, to study, and from thence went to Paris and Boulogne. He was successively Chancellor of Oxford and Canterbury, being at length nominated as Bishop of Chichester. The Chapter readily received him, but King Henry III. refused to give up the temporalities of the See, and Richard became a homeless wanderer in his own Diocese. Travelling from parish to parish, through the forests and across the Downs of Sussex, on foot, after the manner of a primitive apostle, he found refuge with one and another of his clergy, and meanwhile discharged his duties of Chief Pastor with faithfulness. His frequent abode was the house of the parish priest of Tarring—Simon by name—where, in the intervals of his journeys, he would recur to the occupation of planting, pruning and grafting, in which he excelled. The name of St. Richard should be of peculiar interest to those engaged in the fruit-growing industry for which our district has become so noted in later times. He taught the gardeners of Tarring, Sompting, Lancing and Shoreham the art of fruit-growing, as Wilfrid, nearly six hundred years before, had taught their ancestors to be successful fishers.

CAPTAIN RICHARD POOLE

When at length, King Henry had been induced, by threats of excommunication, to give up the temporalities, and Richard became prosperous in their enjoyment, he still remained faithful in the discharge of his duties, visiting all parts of his Diocese. He bountifully relieved the poor and even nursed the sick. It was but natural that after his death—in accordance with the superstitious ideas of the time—miracles of healing were commonly reported to have taken place at his tomb in Chichester Cathedral. His shrine became a noted place of pilgrimage, and so remained until the Reformation, when it was demolished.

Such are some of the incidents in the lives of the saints depicted in the window at Old Shoreham—two of them so intimately connected with our county, and another, the Patron of the church. It is equally fitting that St. Mary, the Mother of Our Lord, should be commemorated in the ancient fane of St. Nicholas, for it is the parent of the more beautiful church at New Shoreham, dedicated to her as "St. Mary of the Harbour."

The interesting memorial in the chancel to Captain Richard Poole, and Thomas, his only son, displays the Arms of the Pooles, of Poole Hall, in Cheshire:—semée de lys, a lion rampant guardant, and the crest is a mermaid in profile, holding in her hands a naval crown.

Captain Richard Poole of Old Shoreham, according to a Confirmation of Arms made to his grandson, "served our late most gracious Sovereign Lady Queen Elizabeth of famous memory, both as a captain at sea and on land, and also served our late most gracious Sovereign Lord King James."

In the reign of Charles I., he commanded a ship of war in the expedition against Cales in Spain, and the Isle of Rhee in France. In November, 1627, while in command of the "Peter" of Shoreham, he captured a barque of St. Malo or Grenville, the "Sea Horse," and brought her into Shoreham Harbour. The memorial at Old Shoreham informs us that the captain died in the year 1652, at the age of 94, and his only son Thomas in the same year, aged 60.

The above-named Thomas, purchased in the year 1623, of one Richard Awood and Agnes, his wife, an estate at Cowfold, known as Peacock Hill, and this property remained in the possession of his descendants for more than two hundred years, until sold by the trustees of the will of George Henry Hooper of Stanmore, Middlesex and New Shoreham, who died in 1863.

THE STORY OF SHOREHAM

Thomas Poole had two sons, Thomas and Richard.

Richard, the younger, was educated in France and Spain, and was subsequently, for a year and a half, lieutenant to Captain Thomas Plunkett in the "Discovery," a 400 ton ship of war, carrying 32 guns. He was afterwards, for three years, Captain

Memorial Brass in Old Shoreham Church.

of two frigates of war, during which time "he did His Majesty (Charles I.) very good service against the Irish rebels, and ever behaved himself as best suited the quality of his commands."

In the Confirmation of Arms above referred to he is described as "Captain Richard Poole, second son of Mr. Thomas Poole,

THE CAPTAIN OF THE "DRAKE"

only son and heir of Captain Richard Poole, of Sussex," and as "descended from a noble and very ancient family of that surname in Cheshire." The Grant was made from Dublin Castle by Roberts, Ulster King-at-Arms, in the year 1648, the coat being differenced in accordance with Richard Poole's profession. Azure, semée de lys or, a lion rampant guardant of the second, on a canton argent, a ship with her mainsail furled proper, and for his crest: on a helmet and wreath of his colours, a mermaid proper, holding betwixt her hands a naval crown or, mantled gules, doubled argent.

In 1665, Richard Poole was appointed Captain of the "Drake," which was launched at Deptford in 1652—the third ship of war bearing that name—a ship which has had a long line of successors in the British Navy. The 27th "Drake," a cruiser, launched at Pembroke in 1901, was torpedoed, October 2nd, 1917, off the north coast of Ireland.

In the Admiralty records (Bill Office), under date 16th March, 1666, is a payment of £13 9s. 2d. "to Captain Richard Poole, Commander of His Majesty's ship the Drake, for so much disbursed in prest and conduct money, and other charges in presting 83 men to serve his Majesty."

CAPTAIN RICHARD POOLE.
(the younger).
ARMS.— *Azure, semee de lys or, a lion rampant guardant of the second, on a canton argent, a ship with her mainsail furled proper.*
CREST.— *A mermaid proper, holding betwixt her hands a naval crown or, mantled gules, doubled argent.*

While in command of this vessel, Richard Poole was remarkably successful in capturing a number of French ships in the Channel, immediately after the declaration of War against France and Holland; among them the "Frances" of Bordeaux, which he took in March, 1666, and brought into Shoreham Harbour.

We find no record of Captain Richard Poole's death, but from an Admiralty Bill, dated 30th October, 1678, it is apparent that he died some time between 15th April and 18th September in that

173

THE STORY OF SHOREHAM

year. Possibly he was killed in action. The Bill refers to a contract, made 15th April, 1678, with Richard Poole, master and part-owner of "ye Richard and Thomas" (a small ship which seems to have been so named after himself and his elder brother). "According to Mr. Thomas Lewsley's certificate," so runs the document, "we pray you to pay unto Mr. Thomas Poole, brother and administrator to ye above said Richard Poole, deceased, for ye use of himself and ye rest of ye owners, for hire and freight of the vessel for ye space of five calendar months and four days, from 15th April, '78, which day she entered into his Majesty's service to ye 18th September following, ye day of her discharge, being employed for the use of a war, and to attend upon his Majesty's ship the . . . (word illegible) at £5 per tunn for each tunn of her burthen. Ditto the sum of £80 15s. 7d." There were two small abatements for stores and victualling, but the nett amount paid to Thomas Poole for the services of this ship appears to have amounted to £392 9s. 10d.

Thomas, elder son of Thomas and grandson of Captain Richard Poole (commemorated on the tablet at Old Shoreham), Administrator to his brother Richard's estate, in the Admiralty Bill just quoted, was baptised at New Shoreham, in June, 1617. He married in 1648, Faith, second daughter of William Merlott of Itchingfield, Sussex, by his wife Faith Newman, widow, daughter of John Killingworth, of London. She was baptised "Faith" at Itchingfield in October, 1626. This lady assumed the Puritan name of "Faint-not." In the Baptismal Registers of New Shoreham in 1649 we read "Helen or Ellen daughter," and in 1652, "Thomas, son of Thomas and Faint-not Poole." Two other sons of the marriage were Richard, born 1655, and William, 1659. Strange though it may seem, we find the memorial to the above-named lady, which is in the choir pavement of New Shoreham Church, worded thus : " Here underneath lieth buried Fanny Poole, the wife of Thomas Poole, of Shoreham, gent., and the second daughter of William Merlott, of Hitchingfield, who ended this life Feb., 1665."

Thomas Poole was one of the Overseers to the will of his father-in-law, William Merlott, of Itchingfield, proved 17th May, 1653, in which the testator refers to "my lining (linen) at Shoreham, in ye cheste in ye possession of my sonne Poole."

He was one of the assessors and collectors in the Borough of Shoreham for the tax raised by Act of Parliament, April, 1649, for

POOLE FAMILY

Army purposes. By his will, dated 1672, he makes his son Thomas residuary legatee; to his son Richard, he leaves "the mault house and Duke's," to his daughter, Ellen, £300, and to his son William, some fields and orchards in the occupation of William Power.

The three sons—Thomas, died in 1699, in which year his burial as "Captain Thomas Poole," is recorded in New Shoreham Registers ; Richard, of Old Shoreham, buried there as " Richard Poole, gentleman," 8th April, 1685, and William, described as "of Cowfold," in a Poll for Knights of the Shire, taken at Lewes, 24th May, 1705. His burial is recorded in the Registers of Old Shoreham—"Mr. William Poole, February 6th, 1714/5." He left no issue, his only sister, Ellen or Helen, widow of Richard Geere, being sole heiress. This lady had married, June 26th, 1675, at Southwick, Richard Geere, of Ovingdean. The marriage licence is entered in the books of the Archdeaconry of Lewes, and therein she is described as "Eleanor Poole, of New Shoreham." She was buried in the chancel at Old Shoreham, November 22nd, 1737, the registers describing her as "Eleanor Geere, widow gentlewoman from Portsmouth," and left an only daughter, Elizabeth, the wife of John Poole.

This John Poole, whose immediate ancestors were of Plymouth and Portsmouth, was probably related to his wife's family, though in what degree is not clear. His descent is recorded in an old Bible now in possession of the Hooper family. It is known as the "Poole Bible," and records that "John was the grandson of Lodovick Poole and his wife Elizabeth, who, with other issue, had John, born September 15th, 1635." He was Mastmaker of Portsmouth, and married Rachel Mason, their eldest son being the John Poole before-mentioned as the husband of Elizabeth Geere. John Poole, sen., surrendered to his son and his heirs for ever, the ground on which the houses on Portsmouth (*i.e.*, Southsea) Common, were subsequently erected.

It is a matter of regret that the interesting series of memorial inscriptions to John and Elizabeth Poole and their family, formerly in the chancel at Old Shoreham, are no longer to be found there. They must have been removed by the hand of the "restorer," working "not wisely, but too well." They are, however, recorded in the pages of Cartwright and Dallaway's Rape of Bramber :

" John Poole, Esq., died July 5th, 1751, aged 68. Master Shipwright of H.M. Dockyard at Sheerness."

THE STORY OF SHOREHAM

"Elizabeth, his wife, only child of Hellen Geere, her mother."
"This Hellen was only sister and heiress to William Poole, gent., and lies next to the bodies of Thomas and Richard Poole, mentioned on the brass plate in the niche opposite this stone."
"Mary, the wife of Captain John Fawler, died December 19th, 1757, aged 40, fourth daughter of John and Elizabeth Poole."
"Eleanor Poole, daughter of John Poole, Esq., and Elizabeth, his wife, died, January 6th, 1778."
"Rachel, second daughter of John Poole, Esq., and wife of Siderik Elgar, gent., died June 1st, 1775."
"Elizabeth Poole, died October 8th, 1762, eldest daughter of John Poole, Esq., and Elizabeth."
"Thomas Poole, Esq., of New Shoreham, died November 4th, 1778."
"Susan, youngest daughter of John and Elizabeth Poole, wife of Captain James O'Hara, R.N., 1779."

The residence of the Poole family at Old Shoreham was a good specimen of ancient domestic architecture. It stood in a large garden near to the village, and quite close to the river, and was latterly used as the Parish Workhouse and demolished when no longer needed for this purpose, by the erection of the Union Workhouse at New Shoreham.

The family Mansion at New Shoreham was in the High Street, on the site of the present Town Hall and premises adjoining. Its situation is described in the Court Rolls of the Manor, as "lying at the south part of the highway in New Shoreham, on the west side of the Old George Inn." Both Mansion and Inn are shown in the *frontispiece*, the Inn being the further building. The Mansion appears to have been a very fine example of Elizabethan or earlier style having richly carved barge boards and a handsome porch. The entrance hall and principal apartments are said to have been very spacious and elaborate in decoration. Here Thomas Poole, a bachelor, the last of the Shoreham Pooles, and his un-married sister, known locally as "Miss Nelly Poole," lived in good style; "keeping their carriage, the livery of the coachman and footman being of scarlet plush." Many years later, the same style was adopted by their grand-nephew, Dr. Robert Hooper, of Saville Row and Stanmore, Middlesex.

Tradition had long handed down in the Poole family a story of treasure hidden somewhere in this old Mansion, and when it

FAWLER FAMILY

was dismantled and finally demolished to make room for the Custom House (now the Town Hall), it was quite expected that this would be found. An old inhabitant of the town and friend of the family, Mr. Richard Roberts, was anxious that care should be taken in the work of pulling down, and careful search was made, but in vain. From what this idea of hidden treasure arose, is not clear. Possibly it had its origin in the troublous times of the Civil War.

The above Thomas Poole, who was churchwarden of New Shoreham and whose name was inscribed on one of the bells, re-cast in 1767 (not the present peal), died in 1778, as before noted; his sister Eleanor having pre-deceased him in January of that year. He left an only sister, Susan or Susannah, the wife of Captain James O'Hara, and she died in the following year.

The family property in Old and New Shoreham then descended to the issue of Captain John Fawler and Mary, his wife, fourth daughter of John and Elizabeth Poole. This marriage was solemnized at St. Peter's Cornhill, 18th October, 1743. They had three children—John, Thomas, and Mary. Of John Fawler little appears to be known beyond the fact that he was in the army, that he went to "the Indies" and was not again heard of, but is supposed to have died there. Thomas, the younger son, was a medical practitioner at Clapham, Surrey. He married Anna Blisset but had no family, and died and was buried at Clapham, 1st September, 1784. His widow had a life interest in the Poole estate, and it then passed to his sister Mary and her husband, John Hooper, ancestors of the present owners.

The situation of Old Shoreham Church is both picturesque and romantic. The delightful view of the old bridge and the church from the Lancing side of the river never fails to arrest the eye of the artist, and more than once has found a fitting place on the walls of the Royal Academy. Nor is the view from the churchyard, across the river to Lancing Downs, less pleasing, and possesses an added interest, when it is said that the late Lord Salisbury and his Countess, with this prospect before them, plighted their troth beneath the shadow of the old church walls.

Not long since, the writer observed, growing from between the joints of some stonework at Old Shoreham a specimen of the starry clover (Trifolium Stellatum), a plant said to be peculiar to the immediate neighbourhood. It is a native of Mediterranean shores.

THE STORY OF SHOREHAM

The tragic and perhaps somewhat gruesome story of a mother's devotion is told in connection with the churchyard.

John Stephenson, a lad who carried the mails between Brighton and Shoreham, set out as usual on the night of November 1st, 1792. He rode horse-back, and on this occasion carried one letter only, containing half a sovereign. At Goldstone Bottom, Hove, he was waylaid and robbed by James Rook and Edward Howell, of Old Shoreham—the former, a young man of twenty-four, is said to have been the dupe of his companion, a man of forty. No violence was used, and after sharing the trifling booty, the two robbers returned to Old Shoreham—Howell went to the mill, and Rook to join some companions at the "Red Lion," at that time kept by a man named Penton.

A frequent visitor to the Inn in those days was an old woman named Phoebe Hessel—a well-known character in her day. As was often her custom she called for some refreshment while Rook and his companions were making merry, and overheard their conversation. Satisfied that Rook was concerned in the crime she informed the constable, Bartholomew Roberts, and the arrest quickly followed. Howell was taken at the mill, where at the time, he was reading a pamphlet to the miller. Both robbers were subsequently identified by the mail-boy, and were committed from the "Fountain Inn," at New Shoreham, for trial at the Spring Assizes at Horsham. Thither they were conveyed on horseback, handcuffed and pinioned with strong cords, and each had his legs roped together under the horse's belly. In addition to the constable who accompanied them, there was a military escort of four cavalry.

Sentenced to be executed at the spot where the robbery had been committed, we are told that "an immense concourse of people" witnessed the hanging of these two unfortunate men on the 26th April, 1793. The bodies, in accordance with the barbarous custom of those days, were afterwards each enclosed in a skeleton dress and hung upon the gibbet, where they remained some time decaying, a terror to the timid. "Gibbet Barn" long indicated the spot where this ghastly sight—a fairly common one in days gone by—had been. It was near where the Dyke Railway crosses the Old Shoreham Road.

But the pathetic part of the story has yet to be told. Rook's mother lost her reason, but the love she bore her dead son never left her. As time went by, and wind and rain had caused the

RIZPAH

clothes and flesh to decay and the bones to fall to the ground, she nightly sought the ghastly gibbet and gathered these relics, bringing them away with her and conveying them to her cottage at Old Shoreham. When at length the elements had done their work and the gibbet was stripped of its burden, the devoted mother deposited the bones which she had collected, in a chest, and buried them in the churchyard.

Lord Tennyson's poem "Rizpah" is founded on this tragedy. In those lines the poor old dying woman tells how, "in the loud black nights" she was "led by the creak of the chains to grovel and grope" for the objects of her search and how she had buried them all "in holy ground."

It is perhaps worthy of remark that a Primitive Methodist was recently sexton at Old Shoreham. It is presumed to be somewhat unusual for a Nonconformist to hold this office in the Church of England, and so we note it.

Many years ago, the host of the "Red Lion" was also parish clerk, and did all the church singing. He would read out the psalm or hymn, verse by verse, and then gravely sing it. But at length he grew old and infirm, and one Sunday astonished the parson and congregation, by giving out, instead of the first verse of the psalm, the following, spoken of course in the broadest "Sussex" : "This is to give notice that I shan't sing any more alone in this 'ere church."

William IV. and Queen Adelaide chanced to be passing through from Chichester to Lewes one Sunday morning. Perhaps it was the same parish clerk, who caught sight through the church window of the approaching cavalcade, and, leaping to his feet, stopped the service by announcing : "it is my solemn duty to inform you that their Majesties the King and Queen are just now crossing the bridge." Thereupon, the whole congregation jumped up and ran out to show their loyalty.

The Sailor King was already well acquainted with Shoreham and the loyalty of its people. Many years before his accession to the throne, he is known to have visited the town He was then Duke of Clarence, and to celebrate his 28th birthday (21st August, 1789) Shoreham gave a firework display which included a representation of the Siege of Gibraltar. From a newspaper of the day we learn that "the red-hot balls from the garrison had a most striking effect, and the whole display was under the direction of Captain Roberts, of Shoreham." So pleased

CHURCH OF
SAINT MARY DE HAURA
NEW SHOREHAM

ST. MARY DE HAURA

was the Royal Duke with the compliment paid him, that he called the next day on Captain Roberts and afterwards went on board his packet, "amidst the acclamations of a vast concourse of the sons of Neptune." Captain Roberts, it may be added, had twice circumnavigated the world with Captain Cook, and in October, 1790, it was arranged that there should be another expedition to the South Seas for fresh discoveries and of this he was to have the sole command.

The Sailor King's successor, Queen Victoria (then Princess), when on visits to the Royal Pavilion at Brighton, was often seen passing through the town taking equestrian exercise. On several occasions while staying at Hove, King Edward motored through Shoreham, and once at least while on a journey westward, alighted from his car and took walking exercise on the Beach Green. The visits of His Majesty King George V., during the dark days of the war are detailed elsewhere in these pages.

The Church of St. Mary de Haura or St. Mary of the Harbour, New Shoreham.

"The hoary grey church, whose story silence utters and age makes great," is the successor of an earlier building, erected on the same site presumably between the dates 1097 and 1103, and referred to by Philip de Braose in the deed by which he confirmed to the monks of Sele the right which they already had thereto.

It is presumed that this earlier edifice gave place to another, erected about the year 1130, which is the date assigned to that portion of Norman work still remaining. The church as then built consisted of a nave of five bays—the greater part of which is now in ruin, although enough is standing to show the Norman details which graced it—the present tower up to the first stage; then probably capped by a low pyramidal spire, as at Old Shoreham; north and south transepts, which yet remain; and a chancel with semi-circular apse. Both transepts had apsidal chapels.

Some time between the dates 1175—1210, the Norman chancel and transept chapels were removed to make room for a choir of five bays, and there is a tradition that this part of the church, which is exceedingly beautiful, owes its foundation to William de Braose who seems to have been somewhat of a bold, bad baron, before he turned his attention to church-building.

William de Braose enjoyed the favour of Kings Henry II.,

THE STORY OF SHOREHAM

Richard I., and John, and into his keeping the first-named gave the Castle of Abergavenny. Possessing the spirit of his Norman ancestors he resolved to subdue the whole of Gwent, and in 1176, with this aim in view, invited the Welsh chieftains and others of distinction to a grand banquet in Abergavenny Castle. When mirth was at its zenith and the feasters had quaffed the foaming tankard and rich wine freely, and to their heart's content, de Braose proposed that all the Welsh present should bind themselves by an oath, in accordance with the king's orders, henceforth to travel unarmed through the country. They were not to carry bows and arrows, javelins, spears or swords. This proposal met with indignant refusal, two of the most powerful chieftains—Sesyllt ap Dynswald and Jenan ap Rhiryd, declaring that they would not go unarmed on the orders of the King of England or any of his barons. Then, at a special signal from de Braose, the banqueting hall was instantly crowded with English soldiers. The unfortunate Welshmen had laid aside their bows and arrows, and being thus totally undefended, the soldiers fell upon them, and massacred them to a man. Not content with having turned his festive hall into a shambles, de Braose hastened away with all possible speed to the house of Sesyllt, and entering by force, murdered Cadwaladyr, the chief's son, and seizing the lad's mother carried her off a prisoner to his fortress.

De Braose was with Richard I. in Normandy in 1196, and we have already seen that he was the powerful adherent of King John, while history further records the sinister fact that he was in close attendance on that monarch at the time of Prince Arthur's death.

Revenge for the Welsh murders, though slow in coming, came suddenly and certainly. The sons of the slain chieftains, rose and marched to Abergavenny Castle, scaled the walls, took possession of the fortress and razed it to the ground. De Braose, the object of their hatred was absent, but the Welsh followed him to Monmouthshire, where he was wounded, but not slain. Thenceforward, misfortune dogged his footsteps. Failing to make payment due to the Crown for Munster and Limerick, which had been bequeathed him by his brother, he fell into disfavour with King John, who demanded hostages in the persons of his children, these being refused he was outlawed, and the former friend and favourite of kings disguised himself as a beggar and fled from Shoreham—which town had once

A BEAUTIFUL CHURCH

owned him as lord and master—to France, where he spent his last years in begging from door to door. Nevertheless, history records that he was buried in St. Victor's Abbey.

The wife of de Braose was Maud de Valerie, daughter of Fitz-Walter, Earl of Hereford. She was a reputed witch, who for many years had been regarded as a student of occult mysteries and one who "did at unholy hours practise magic arts to the annoyance of her neighbours." However as this may be, she seems to have been a most affectionate mother, for upon the King's demand that her children should be given up, she refused, declaring that she would not trust her family "to one who had so cruelly murdered his own nephew." Thereupon the King ordered Maud and her children to be taken by force, and, under a strong escort, conveyed to Windsor, where—so the story goes— they were imprisoned in the castle dungeons and slowly starved to death.

But to return. You will be loth to think that so fair a piece of architecture as this rich choir-end at New Shoreham owes its inception to one whose hands—as we have seen—were so foully stained with blood, but such is the legend, and whether erected as an "atonement" or otherwise, the choir is certainly a very beautiful piece of work. It belongs to the Transitional period, that is, as far as the string-course of quaterfoils on a level with the triforium floor.

When the building had reached this stage, it was probably roofed over; for the style of the triforium and clerestory is of the Early English period, erected when the roof was removed and the building carried up and vaulted; the massive flying buttresses being added to support the outward thrust, and the choir presenting in its finished state much the same appearance as at the present day. About the same time another storey was added to the tower, giving it a height of 83ft. to the top of the parapet.

A remarkable similarity of style, and especially of foliage, has been observed to exist between the work in Tynemouth Church and the choir of New Shoreham; and this resemblance is at once so special and individualistic that, as far apart as the places are, it has been conjectured that the same hand and brain must have designed both. New Shoreham is said to be the only instance in which the choir aisles of a parish church are continued at an early date as far as the east end.

Interior
of the
Church
Arthur D Packham,
1920.

THE RUINED NAVE

It is, however, the opinion of some that this building was designed and intended to serve for something more than the parish church of a rapidly rising sea-port ; for, not only was the church—even as at first built—a grand cruciform structure, but the original Norman aisless choir was taken down and rebuilt on a greatly enlarged scale and in the most sumptuous style.

Although all direct historical reference is wanting, it is not improbable to assume that the monks, settled by de Braose at Sele Priory, were designed to be removed to Shoreham.

This idea seems to receive some confirmation from the fact that William, son of Philip de Braose, gave to the monks of Florent, " the land at Shoreham of Ulnare the clerk," which the deed states " Saracenus formerly held." This gift he and his brother Philip made at the altar of St. Peter in the Church of Sele possession being given to David, a monk of St. Florent in the presence of his court. De Braose also gave to the monks of Sele Priory, " in honour of the Blessed Mother of God, a house situated on the north side of the Church of St. Mary at Shoreham, free from all customary payments."

The description of the position of this house seems to apply to "The Cottage"—formerly St. Mary's Cottage—a building of considerable antiquity, whose walls may well have been standing at the time when de Braose gave his monks " a house situated on the north side of the Church of St. Mary." Possibly the land of Ulnare the clerk may have been the garden-land adjoining to the west, on which it was designed to erect conventual buildings. In recent years the cottage has received very careful restoration at the hands of the owner.

The foundations of the ruined Norman nave of the Church were excavated and examined during the summer of 1915, when some interesting discoveries were made. These included a south porch of spacious dimensions—apparently erected during the fifteenth century—and some of the original floor tiling. At the same time, part of the choir pavement was taken up and the foundations of the original semi-circular apse disclosed.

At what period the nave fell to ruin is uncertain. The tradition —long accepted—that this took place during the fifteenth century, is now a matter of doubt. It was believed that the present west end comprising one bay of the nave, was built up at that time ; and the doorway which has Norman details, constructed into a pointed arch from stones brought from the former western entrance.

THE STORY OF SHOREHAM

Another theory is, that the church was partly destroyed during the Reformation, but there seems to be no proof of this, and small reason to suppose that such should have been the case, seeing that the edifice was neither an Abbey nor a Priory Church—although it may have been intended for such—and Henry VIII.'s minister, Thomas Cromwell, had therefore no reason to include it in his destruction of monastic buildings. Yet another tradition tries to fasten the cause of its ruin on Oliver Cromwell, but again proof is wanting.

If you will examine the old carved oak chimney-piece before referred to, you will observe, in addition to the interesting details in connection with the shipwrights' craft, that one panel is devoted to what we may reasonably presume to be intended for a representation of the Church of New Shoreham as it appeared when the carving was executed—probably early in the 17th century. Crude as it is, it apparently depicts the original nave having a large Decorated west window and a spacious south porch such as would have appeared over the foundations recently uncovered. The tower is also shown surmounted by a spire—now lacking. The evidence afforded by this old relic cannot be passed over in silence. It seems to go far to prove that the nave did not become altogether ruinous until late in the 17th century, and that possibly the present west end was not closed up in its somewhat "patchy" form until the beginning of the 18th century.

In these pages no attempt will be made to give a full description of this noble fragment of antiquity, whose details are so beautiful and so varied. Swinburne, in sweet song, tells us that this shrine has seen "eight hundred waxing and waning years." It is "bright with riches of radiant niches, and pillars smooth as a straight stem grows." Its tower is "set square to the storms of air," and "stately stands it, the work of hands unknown."

Often as you may enter its doors, you will not leave without noting something in its beauty which had before escaped you. You will pause to admire the handiwork of those skilled artizans who carved the stone into such cunning patterns—sometimes so delicate, at times so fantastic, and in places even grotesque. As we stand in this ancient vaulted choir and note its arcades, study its wealth of conventional carving in imitation of foliage, fruit, and flowers, its deep round and hollow mouldings which catch the light and shade so wonderfully, the work of those old-time masons, centuries ago, can but remind us that we have

AN ANCIENT BRASS

added little to the delicate beauty of architecture since their day, and the stones which they carved with such consummate skill seem to cry out to us, that what they created we can only feebly imitate.

It is seldom that one has the opportunity of viewing the interior of a church devoid of its pew or chairs, and so obtaining some idea of the appearance of the building in mediaeval times, when the whole of the service was rendered by the worshippers, standing and kneeling. The only seats provided were usually against the walls and were intended for the comfort of the aged and infirm. Hence "the weakest must go to the wall," and at Shoreham a seat of stone was provided for their use. In these days we often hear the old saying quoted as above, though it has quite lost its original meaning.

Shoreham people are justly proud of this heritage of the past. It speaks to them with no uncertain voice, of centuries when their town was wealthy and its merchants and citizens were prosperous.

Possibly the memorial to one of these merchants is to be found in the ancient brass in the choir pavement. It depicts a civilian and his lady, attired in the costume of about the year 1450, but is without inscription, and therefore these notable townsfolk are nameless.

This is the most ancient memorial—if such it may be called—which the church possesses, and in this respect possibly it may be found somewhat disappointing. In a church of such noble proportions one would fain behold the sculptured "knyghte and fayre ladye," lying side by side, on tombs displaying all the glory of heraldic devices. No such monuments will be found at New Shoreham. Possibly some members of the de Braose and de Mowbray families may have found sepulture in the nave, but if so, doubtless their memorials became desecrated with its decay and ruin.

Of "the chantry scituate in the parisshe church of Newe Shorham" a few particulars have been preserved but the name of the founder is unknown.

It may be mentioned, that a chantry was an endowment for the maintenance of one or more priests to sing daily mass for the souls of the founders or others specified by them. Usually the priests who served these chantries were quite independent of the vicar or parish priest (Shoreham seems to have been an

*Memorial Brass to an unknown Civilian and Lady in the Church of
St. Mary de Haura, New Shoreham (circa 1450).*

THE CHANTRY

exception to this rule), and sang their office at a particular chapel, altar, or part of the church other than the High Altar, specially set apart for the purpose. Thus Shakespeare represents King Henry V. as saying, in his prayer to the God of Battles, on the eve of Agincourt :—

. and I have built
Two chantries, where the sad and solemn priests
Sing still for Richard's soul.

It appears from the returns made in the reign of Edward VI. that the income derived from the chantry in New Shoreham Church was more than that from the parsonage, and hence the vicar in times past had usually also filled the office of chantry priest. Thomas Mylles, "of the age of 70 years," was then incumbent, and the return further stated, "without the said chantry the cure cannot be well served."

The chantry property included one toft with the close adjoining, and four acres of land in "le Millhouse" in New Shoreham, worth per annum 20s., also the profits of 18 acres "in Ledham quarter," 13 acres in the South field, 5 rods next Northbourne, 4 acres fresh marsh and 5 acres in Old Shoreham, in the tenure of John Shelder, worth 50s. The farm of eight acres in Southwick, and common of pasture for eight oxen, four cows and one horse in the common fields of New Shoreham, Old Shoreham and Southwick were worth 16s. 8d., making a total income of £4 6s. 8d. "The premises be letten by indenture bearing date the 6th day of May, 31st year of King Henry th'aythe (1539) unto Margaret Lewknor, widow, for the term of 40 years for the rent aforesaide." The profits of the parsonage were worth £3 6s. 8d.

Some further information as to the chantry lands is to be found in the will of Owen Holmare, of New Shoreham, dated 3rd July, 1553, and proved 22nd November, 1555. Therein he says : " I bequeathe to Henry Wilson all my lands I purchased of Master Henry Polstede, Esq., belonging to the chantry of New Shoreham, lying and being in the parish of New Shoreham, Old Shoreham, and Southwick, willing him to give my brother Edward Holmare, £10. After the death of Henry Wilson, I bequeath the said premises to Owen Wilson, son of the said Henry, and his heirs for ever." The testator also made a bequest of his "bark and her apparel" to his three brothers, William, Thomas, and Edward Holmare.

THE STORY OF SHOREHAM

A later Owen Holmare, whose will is dated 5th August, 1588, desired "to be buried in the Parish church of New Shoreham" and left 20s. to the poor. He bequeathes to his son John "all my freehold lands, houses, and tenements in New Shoreham to

him and his issue—for lack of issue then to my daughter Margaret Holmare and her issue—in default, to my next heir male." He left to his daughter Margaret "£50, at her age of 20, and my best gold ring and a piece of gold 15s." To Alice Holmare "my supposed sister" 15s. To his god-children 5s. each. There is

WILLS

no signature or witnesses to this will, and on 12th August, 1588, commission was issued to William Holmare, next-of-kin, to administer the goods of the deceased during the minority of John and Margaret his children, no executor being named.

Thomas Jackson (will dated 2nd September, 1603) desired to be buried in the Church of New Shoreham and bequeathed to the reparation of the said Church 10s. "To my now wife Elizabeth all my houses, lands, etc., in New Shoreham for life, with remainder to my eldest son Richard and his heirs for ever. To my said son, my half of the bark called the Bartholomew and half her apparel at his age of 20, and 6 yards of Yarmouth fishing nets and ropes. To my son Robert, my half part of the bark called the Mary of Shoreham, with her apparel, etc., at his age of 20." The testator made other bequests, and there was a nuncupative codicil, dated 12th September, in the presence of Thomas Freland and John Eightaker, of Brightelmestone, at Yarmouth, to the effect that "as this voyage to Yarmouth is like to prove very chargeable," he gave his "two half parts of the said barks" to his wife instead of his sons. The will was proved 7th February, 1603-4.

Richard Goulde of New Shoreham, yeoman, by will dated 16th December, 1618, desired to be buried in the Parish Church and left 20s. towards its repair. To his son Richard Goulde, he left all his lands and tenements in New and Old Shoreham, "except a house where Edward Mercer and William Smyth now dwell, which shall be sold to pay my daughters legacies, and also a new house where John Parsons now dwells and a croft of land in New Shoreham, called the "Long Croft" which my wife Joan shall have for life, and after her death my son Richard and his heirs for ever." To his daughter Sara, he left £60 at age 21, and to each of his other daughters, Cicely, Margery, and Jane Goulde £60 at age 18, or "if my daughters marry before the said ages the legacies shall be paid then." Other small bequests follow and the will was proved 29th June, 1620, by the relict.

Repentance Avis, of New Shoreham (will dated 16th December, 1622 and proved 4th March 1623-4), "to be buried in the churchyard of New Shoreham and I give to that church 10s. and to the poor of the said town 10s. To my son William Avis £250. To my daughter Sara Avis £66 13s. 4d. at her age of 21 or day of marriage. To my brother John Avis my best suit of apparel and 20s." To brothers Thomas and Robert Avis 20s., and other

THE STORY OF SHOREHAM

small bequests to kinsfolk and servants. Robert Tranckmore, of New Shoreham, shipwright, is named as one of the overseers of this will.

The numerous memorial inscriptions in the church, excepting those of quite recent date have been recorded in Vol. 52 of the Sussex Archæological Collections, and therefore need not here be quoted at length. The low platform at the east end of the choir hides from view an inscription to Walter West, of Woodmancote, who died in 1648 and whose wife was Elizabeth, eldest daughter of Thomas Shirley, of Preston Place (Brighton). In the north transept will be noticed memorials to the family of Hooper, of Stanmore, Middlesex and New Shoreham, some of whom rest beneath the east end of the choir and others in the churchyard. The Arms of the family are emblazoned on several of the memorials—Or, on a fesse between three boar's passant az, as many annulets of the first. Crest—a boar's head erased at the neck az, bezante ar, and crined or.

By her marriage with John Hooper, esquire—a descendant of the Hoopers of Sarum, Wilts, and Boveridge, Dorset, through a branch which settled at Kelso on the borders of Scotland—Mary, daughter of Captain John Fawler and Mary, his wife (née Poole), carried the Poole inheritance to her husband. Both John and Mary Hooper are commemorated in the north transept, he died in 1820 and his wife pre-deceased him in 1802. They had five sons to the memory of whom are tablets in this part of the church —John Benjamin Hooper, died in 1808, James Hooper of Bentinck Street, Manchester Square, died 1832.

Robert Hooper, M.A., M.D., the celebrated Physician of Saville Row and Stanmore, Middlesex, who lectured on the Practice of Medicine to large classes in London and made a special study of Pathology. Dr. Hooper was a most industrious writer—the author of numerous works on Medical Science many of which have been translated into Continental languages and numerous editions issued from time to time in England, in America, and on the Continent. Dr. Hooper made a considerable fortune and retired to Stanmore. He died in London, 6th May, 1835, and rests beneath the choir of this church.

Thomas Poole Hooper, M.A., for sixteen years Vicar of New Shoreham, Rector of Kingston-by-Sea, and for twenty-two years Vicar of Sompting, where he died in 1837.

George Henry Hooper " of this place and Stanmore, Middlesex "

A LONG-LIVED FAMILY

who died 15th June, 1863, aged 83 years. There is also a memorial tablet with Arms and Crest—Hooper (as above) quartering Ross of Morinchie, Scotland—Gules 3 lions rampant, accompanied with as many stars argent—to "Mrs. Margaret Brewse Hooper, wife of George Henry Hooper" who died in 1838. This lady was the daughter of Alexander Ross, esquire (Chief of the Ordnance Department at Gibraltar) by his first wife Margaret Clunas, and was grand-daughter of Alexander, son of John Ross of Tain, in the county of Ross, where the family had been settled for many generations.

Two sons and four daughters were the issue of this marriage—George Henry Hooper who died in 1904, aged 89 years and was buried in Kensal Green Cemetery; the Rev. Robert Poole Hooper, M.A., who died in 1918, aged 92 years, and was buried in Hove Cemetery; Esther who died in 1844, aged 7 years; Margaret who died in 1883, aged 69 years; Helen who died in 1891, aged 78; and Mary Fawler, widow of the Rev. Joseph Maude who died in 1913, aged 93 years and 9 months.

The combined ages of the three daughters and two sons of George Henry Hooper, who lived to old age, give the somewhat remarkable total of 421 years, being an average of 84 years to each life; while, from the birth of George Henry Hooper in 1780, to the death of his son, the Rev. Robert Poole Hooper in 1918, the long period of 138 years had elapsed.

The clock in the church tower was given in 1896 by the last-named gentleman in memory of his wife Harriett Brereton, who died February 22nd, 1886, and of Randle Brereton their son, killed in action, in South Africa, January 4th, 1881. This clock replaced an older one presented by Mr. John Perry, who was elected M.P. for the Borough in 1689, 1695, 1698, and 1702.

In the choir pavement will be noticed the grave of "Captain Cornelius Smith, of Dover, who served his King, country, and friend faithfully and honourably" and died in 1727. It would no doubt be of interest if we could learn something more of the connection of this gallant captain with the town of Shoreham There is a memorial to Abraham Aldersey, described as "of London, gent.," who died in 1711, and the Registers inform us that he was Collector of Her Majesty's Customs during the reign of Queen Anne. Formerly there was a memorial to Henry Medley Kilvington, who died in 1808, and to his wife. This has quite disappeared, but its interest lies in the fact that thereon he

THE STORY OF SHOREHAM

was described as "Barrack Master of this place," which seems to bring Shoreham of a century ago curiously in touch with recent years.

The Rev. C. M. A. Tower, writing in the Parish Magazine, November, 1914, says : "The presence of soldiers, whether encamped or as old inhabitants have "heard say" in barracks in Shoreham is no new event. Our Registers of just one hundred years ago betray the presence of West Essex Militia, 5th and 44th Regiment of Foot, 10th Battery of Artillery, 10th Dragoons, Marines, and others in Shoreham."

A history of Brighton, dated 1824, mentions Military Barracks situated here at that time, "but," says the writer "not of great magnitude." They were in fact, situated on the site of Buckingham Gardens, and there was also—or had been previously—an encampment on Ravenscroft, the land now occupied by the villas in Southdown Road and Ravens Road.

The church tower contains a fine peal of eight bells, cast at Messrs. Mear's foundry in 1898, and were hung after the restoration of the tower itself in that year. They replaced six which had been in a defective condition for some years past. These older bells had been recast by voluntary subscription in 1767 by Lester & Pack, of Whitechapel, and two bore the inscription often found on the bells of that firm :

> "Our voices shall with joyful sound
> Make hills and valleys echo round."

and the Tenor :

> "In wedlock's bands all ye who join,
> With hands your hearts unite.
> So shall our tuneful tongues combine
> To laud the nuptial rite."

Number 5 bell was inscribed with the names of Thomas Poole, and John Butcher, Churchwardens.

Although the ascent is somewhat tiresome owing to the narrow stairway, the view from the summit of the tower is worth the climb for those who can endure it ; but the parapet is a low one and care should be observed, especially on a windy day. From this point of vantage there is an extensive and pleasant prospect of sea and shore, and the town presents a certain quaintness of detail not otherwise obtained and perhaps not generally known.

The choir was formerly roofed with cast lead slabs. One

VICARS OF OLD SHOREHAM

of these has been preserved and bears in raised letters the names of Richard Herring and William Harfill, and the date 1677. A sundial on the south transept was placed there in 1813 by J. Edwards and T. Tate, Churchwardens.

The Vicars of Old Shoreham.

Anciently, the Vicar of Old Shoreham, besides the vicarage house was entitled to receive all the tithes of grass, hemp, flax, wool, milk, lambs, calves, and pigs of the whole parish, and all the bread offered in the church. All other tithes and oblations were divided into three parts, of which the Prior and Monks of Sele took two and the Vicar one. The oblations made on the vigil and day of the Exaltation of the Holy Cross, were not included in this division but belonged wholly to the Prior and Monks.

Circa, 1150, Anfred, Priest of Sorham is mentioned—1190, Jocelin, Presbyter of Old Sorham. He had a dispute with the monks of Sele about the division of the tithes of the parish. It was finally agreed that for the future, instead of the usual division, there should be granted to the Vicar for the term of his life, a lease of the portion belonging to the monks, except the tithes of cheese, lambs, and wool of Erryngham, also 3s. paid from a mill and a like sum from the gabel of the lord of the same manor, for which he was to pay them 5½ marks per annum.

1242, Simon de Offenham—1249, William, Chaplain of Sorham—1252, Sir Ralph Middleton, Vicar.—Florentius.—1263, Robert de Bletchington of whom frequent references are found in the Assize Rolls of the period, in one of which his predecessor Florentius is mentioned. Robert de Bletchington held two other benefices as well as that of Old Shoreham (Papal Letters).

Circa 1295-6, John de Brewose, who was doubtless of the family of the Lord of Bramber. He is described in an Assize Roll 23 and 24 Edward I., as "parson of the Church of Old Shoreham," and as making complaint that Edmund Earl of Cornwall, Gilbert de Mulsham and eight other persons had unjustly deprived him of a plot of ground containing 60ft. in length and 31ft. in width. The jurors said that "Gilbert and all the others except the Earl, unjustly disseised John de Brewose of the tenement he claims, therefore it is agreed that John recover possession

THE STORY OF SHOREHAM

thereof and his damages. Gilbert and the others in mercy, and John de Brewose in mercy, for a false claim against the Earl, pardoned."

1299, Thomas de Brantyngham—ante 1312 Bertrand Grycardi, ex-Rector of Shoreham. He was Canon of Liege in 1312.—1318, Nigel de la Falayse " parson of Old Shoreham." In the year named he purchased of John Benet of New Shoreham, and Agnes, his wife, for 100 marks, 16 acres and 3 roods arable land.

1341, Thomas de Brembre. It is possible that he was the same individual who was appointed Dean of Wimborne, August 5th, 1350. He founded a chantry in the north transept of Wimborne Minster and was buried there in 1361.

March 4th, 1353, Thomas de Brantyngham presented to the Church of Old Shoreham in the King's gift, " by reason of the Priory of La Sele being in his hands on account of the war with France."—April 12th, 1353, Peter Cook of Halsted. Ratification as parson of Old Shorham and revocation of the King's late presentation of the church to Thomas de Brantyngham. The latter became Bishop of Exeter in 1370. He was appointed Lord High Treasurer in 1378, but was succeeded in the following year by Richard Fitzalan, Earl of Arundel and Surrey. Thomas de Brantyngham again received the appointment in 1380, and held it until 1389, in which year he was succeeded by John Gilbert, Bishop of St. Davids. Brantyngham held the Bishopric of Exeter until his death, 23rd December, 1394, his successor being Edmund Stafford, Lord High Chancellor. (Hadyn's Book of Dignities).

1360-1367, William Gategangs (De Banco Rolls). He exchanged in 1383, with John Larke, parson of Milham, Norfolk.— 1391, John de Melton presented by the King. He is again mentioned in 1394.—September 3rd, 1397, Thomas Yokeflete presented by the Priory, but the presentation disputed by John Inglewood who was presented by the King. A commission appointed by the Bishop determined in favour of the former, January 10th, 1397-8.

Where known, the date of Institution is given in the list which follows : July 16th, 1403, John Horsham.—September 29th, 1410, William Elys.—1478, Walter Gosse, mentioned in Bishop's Visitation.—John Rogers.—September 20th, 1504, John Hornbye who was also Vicar of New Shoreham.—January 22nd, 1532-3, John Smyth.—May 29th, 1556, John Heppe.—April 13th, 1561,

A SKILFUL HORSEMAN

John Godman.—May 30th, 1575, Richard Sysson (also Vicar of New Shoreham).—January 2nd, 1607-8, James Wrenche
John Fowkes (B.A., 1607-8, M.A., 1609), Vicar of Old Shoreham and of Bolney. Instituted to Old Shoreham 15th February, 1609-10, and to Bolney 15th October, 1627. Is mentioned (1612) together with Robert Wood, Vicar of New Shoreham and John Bridge, Vicar of Portslade as furnishing a corselet towards the Nation's armoury. He was buried at Bolney, 16th January, 1640-1, and was succeeded at Old Shoreham by John Johnson.

February 9th, 1663-4, Francis Smith, M.A., of Magdalen College, Oxon. He was also appointed in 1677, Rector of Clayton-cum-Keymer, which he held with Old Shoreham until his death in 1683, being succeeded April 16th in that year by Simon Winch who was also Curate and Sequestrator of New Shoreham.

The living of Old Shoreham was sequestrated March 9th, 1685-6, and the following Curates were licensed : September 24th, 1695, John Gray (also Rector of Southwick).—July 25th, 1751, Montague Cholmley, who resigned 1752, and was succeeded by Thomas Waldegrave who was also Vicar of Washington.—Robert Norton the Rector of Southwick was deputy Curate 1755 to 1761, and Mathew Nicholas, Rector of Beeding, deputy Curate 1756 to 1771.—John Morgan was Curate, 1770 to 1818.

1784-1828, Thomas Hatch also Vicar of Washington. In his obituary notice which appears in the *Gentleman's Magazine* it is recorded that he died 15th April, 1828, at Washington, Sussex, aged 84. He took the degree of M.A. in 1769, "but as his prospect of succeeding to a fellowship was very remote he accepted a commission in the East India Company's service and served as Captain in a regiment of sepoys. Returning to England in 1782, he was ordained, proceeded B.D. in 1783, and in 1784, was presented by his College to the livings of Old Shoreham and Washington. He was in his youth distinguished for his skill in horsemanship, so much so, that, in company with two of his fellow collegians (who were afterwards Doctors of Divinity) he exhibited, during a long vacation at some provincial towns, several equestrian feats which are now confined to Astley's. During the last war (Napoleonic) he served as Lieutenant in the corps of Yeomanry Cavalry commanded by Sir Cecil Bisshop. For the 44 years of his Incumbency he was strictly resident on his living." However, we find John Evans was Curate of Shoreham, 1816 to 1828.

THE STORY OF SHOREHAM

September 4th, 1828, Zacharias Henry Biddulph. Second son of Rev. T. T. Biddulph, minister of St. James', Bristol, and brother of Rev. Theophilus Biddulph. Fellow of Magdalen College, Oxon., where he graduated B.A. 1813, and M.A. 1815, B.D. 1823. Presented to the livings of Old and New Shoreham 1828, and to the Vicarage of Backwell, Somerset in 1831. Died, 21st November, 1842.

May 19th, 1843, William Wheeler, B.D., Vicar of Old and New Shoreham. Old Shoreham Vicarage House was built during his Incumbency and was afterwards the residence of his successors at Old Shoreham until the preferment of the late Vicar to Ashurst. A volume entitled "Sermon's preached in the Parish Churches of Old and New Shoreham, Sussex," by William Wheeler, B.D., Vicar, was published at Brighton in 1847, the preface is dated "Old Shoreham, Advent, 1846." The Rev. William Wheeler was received into the Roman Catholic Church on Saturday, December 17th, 1855, by Dr. Manning, the eminent Cardinal who was formerly Archdeacon of Chichester.

April 24th, 1856, James Bowling Mozley, B.D. A man of letters. Among other writings, he published in 1865, his Bampton Lectures, on "Miracles," recognized as a valuable and important work. It reached a fifth edition in 1880, and by some has been thought worthy of being numbered among the "Best Hundred Books." The Rev. J. B. Mozley took an active part in favour of Mr. Gladstone, when he was elected M.P. for the University of Oxford, in 1847, and in 1869, when Prime Minister, Mr. Gladstone made him a Canon of Worcester which preferment was exchanged in 1871, for the position of Regius Professor of Divinity at Oxford, and Canon of Christchurch.

Dean Church calls Dr. Mozley "after Mr. Newman, the most forcible and impressive of the Oxford writers," and as "having a mind of great and rare power, though only recognized for what he was, much later in life." He also speaks of "the sweetness, the affectionateness, the modesty and the generosity of Canon Mozley, behind an outside, that to strangers might seem impassive." A memorial to Canon Mozley and his wife is to be seen in the chancel at Old Shoreham.

July 15th, 1878, Henry Cadwallader Adams. Boys of a generation ago delighted in reading stories from the pen of the Rev. H. C. Adams and his books are still read by the youth of to-day. Most of them deal with school-boy life, and perhaps one

VICARS OF NEW SHOREHAM

of the most interesting is that entitled "For James or George." This is a story of the Stuart Rebellion of 1745, wherein the adventures of the Young Pretender and his adherents on the march from Scotland to Derby, and the subsequent retreat to the North, are related in a very entertaining manner. The story first appeared in the pages of the *Boys' Own Paper* and was afterwards published in book form. The Rev. H. C. Adams resigned his vicarage in 1897, when the livings of Old and New Shoreham were united, the then Vicar of New Shoreham taking charge of both parishes. The Rev. H. C. Adams died at Guildford and was buried in the Cemetery of that town.

The Vicars of New Shoreham.

A document preserved at Magdalen College, dated 11th July, 1261, records the admission of "John the Chaplain" to the Vicarage of New Shoreham, and among other matters it is specified that he is to have " the house which Ralph the late Vicar had."

1274, Robert.—1293, John de Grey.—Thomas de Renham, Vicar of the Church of New Shoreham figures in an Assize Roll of 29 Edward I. (1301) as having with Thomas Selide unjustly disseised Ralph Boltere and Maude, his wife, of their free tenement in New Shoreham. The Vicar pleaded that he entered the tenement in question only as tenant of a certain Reginald Kenewood and Hodiena his wife, and not by disseisin. Ralph and Maud recovered seisin of the premises but were "in mercy" for a false claim against the Vicar.

Ante 1356, Thomas.—John Avenell (1381) exchanged with Reginald Catigo, "Parson of Akeset" (Exceit, on the River Cuckmere). The latter only retained his benefice a very short time as in the same year Thomas de Bradfield exchanged the living with John Long, Vicar of Youngemonteney, in the Diocese of London who, 12th January, 1383-4, exchanged with Thomas de Kent, Chaplain of the Chantry of St. Katherine in the Church of Edburton, Sussex. This was the Chantry which William de Northo had founded in the reign of Edward II., when he assigned certain lands and rents in Edburton, Southwick, New Shoreham, and Woodmancote, to a priest to celebrate divine service daily for ever in the Church of St. Andrew, Edburton "for the health of the souls of himself and Christine his wife, during their lives and after their deaths, and for the soul of Olyve, his former wife."

THE STORY OF SHOREHAM

June 3rd, 1388, Henry Woolston exchanged with John Marescall.—"Thomas Brydham, Vicar of New Shoreham" is one of the witnesses to the will of Ralph Double in 1392.—July 30th, 1401, John Clark.—October 11th, 1405, John Cook.—September 30th, 1439, Thomas Shawe.—October 1st, 1440, Robert Cornewell.—June 26th, 1441, John Philip.—"Giles," Vicar of New Shoreham, is cited to appear at the Bishop's Visitation in 1478.—December 15th, 1479, John Penteney.—June 29th, 1484, Andrew Parke. William Benett (resigned 1502).—August 5th, 1502, John Hornby (also Vicar of Old Shoreham).—Richard Tede.—July 5th, 1513, William Clarke.—William Balenden.—March 30th, 1517, Thomas Wygyn.—May 14th, 1533, John Smyth.—John Tomson.—John Atkinson.—June 16th, 1545, Thomas Mylles, mentioned both as Vicar and Chantry Priest in the returns made of the Chantry lands in the reign of Edward VI.

Richard Sysson, Vicar of Old and New Shoreham. Ordained Priest by Richard Curteys, Bishop of Chichester 31st March, 1574. Instituted to former living 30th May, 1575, on presentation of Magdalen Coll., Oxon., and to the latter, 19th October, 1577. Adam Cartwright, presented by Queen Elizabeth, was instituted in 1579, but Richard Sysson retained the benefice. He was buried at New Shoreham 24th September, 1607.

Robert Woods, M.A., ordained Deacon and Priest by John, Bishop of Norwich, 26th May, 1605. Instituted 19th September, 1608, on Collation by Bishop of Chichester through lapse and inducted 23rd September following.—July 5th, 1615, William Greenhill.—(John Draper, Curate 1630, to December 31st 1633).—John Nurth, B.A. of Magdalen Coll., Ordained Deacon by George Carleton, Bishop of Chichester 24th September, 1626. Instituted 31st December, 1633, on presentation of his College, and inducted 9th January, 1633-4.—Daniel Harcourt, Curate licensed May, 1633.—In 1649, Richard Bonner and in 1651, Thomas Hallett were Ministers under the Commonwealth. As such they were intruders, having no status in the English Church. They were, of course, followers of the Directory of Public Worship instead of the Book of Common Prayer and any ordination they might have had would be non-episcopal. Richard Bonner, however, was ordained by the Bishop of Chichester after the Restoration, and ultimately became Rector of Maresfield in 1651, which benefice he retained until his death in 1693.

Circa 1662, the living was sequestrated and thereafter the

VICARS OF NEW SHOREHAM

following were Curates-in-charge: Peter Wynn (Rector of Southwick), 1670-72.—Edward Lowe (Vicar of Brightelmeston), 1673-79.—Robert Sparrow (Rector of Newtimber, 1631), 1679-83. —Simon Winch (Vicar of Old Shoreham), 1683-86.—Isaac Boardman (Rector of Coombes), 1687-90.—John Webb, 1692.—John Gray (Curate and Sequestrator of Old Shoreham), 1695-1713.

Rice Williams, B.A., ordained Deacon by William, Bishop of Llandaff, 21st September, 1690, and Priest by same 29th July, 1693. Instituted 3rd July, 1713, on presentation of Queen Anne by reason of lapse, and inducted 25th August following. He is mentioned (10 George I.) as receiving tithes in New Shoreham in respect of "Hayler's Mill" and Glasspool's public houses— the "King's Arms" and "The Ship." He was buried at New Shoreham, 22nd May, 1727.

Edward Martin, ordained Deacon by Thomas Bowers, Bishop of Chichester, 22nd December, 1722, and Priest by Thomas, Bishop of Ely, 1st March, 1723-4. Vicar of New Shoreham, November 27th, 1728. He married at Pyecombe, 7th July, 1737, with Mrs. Elizabeth Temple of that place and died 13th April, 1766.—August 27th, 1766, William Marchant.

Thomas Poole Hooper. Third son of John Hooper, Esq., by his wife Mary, daughter of Capt. John and Mary Fawler (née Poole). Born in London. Matriculated at Pembroke Coll., Oxon., 1791. B.A. 1797, M.A. 1800. Vicar of New Shoreham, February 25th 1802 and Rector of Kingston-by-Sea, 1809. Resigned the living of New Shoreham (1815) on presentation to Sompting, which living he retained as well as Kingston till his death at Sompting in 1837. He was buried in New Shoreham Church where there is a tablet to his memory.

August 7th, 1815, John Gould.—September 10th, 1819, Richard William Hutchins.—September 4th, 1828, Zacharias Henry Biddulph (also Vicar of Old Shoreham).—June 19th, 1843, William Wheeler (also Vicar of Old Shoreham).—April 26th, 1856, Harris Smith, D.D.—March 7th, 1889, Edmund Francis Guise Tyndale. It was the great ambition of this gentleman to restore the ruined nave of the church back to its mediæval beauty, but his sudden and premature death after only seven months' residence in the town prevented the fulfilment of this desire.

April 9th, 1890, Charles Edward Steward (whose son, John Manwaring Steward, after many years Missionary work, was consecrated 5th Bishop of Melanesia in 1919).

THE STORY OF SHOREHAM

June 2nd, 1894, Charles Marsh Ainslie Tower, who, February 14th, 1897, on the resignation of the Rev. H. C. Adams, became also Vicar of Old Shoreham and took up his residence in Old Shoreham Vicarage. On his preferment to the living of Ashurst early in 1920, Mr. Tower's long vicariate of the two Shorehams terminated, greatly to the regret of his congregation and the townspeople generally, by whom he was, and is, deservedly esteemed.

Gerald Holmes-Gore, inducted Vicar of New Shoreham February 5th, 1920 and of Old Shoreham, June 6th, 1920.

Lancing College.

It was in 1847 that the Rev. Nathaniel Woodard (afterwards Canon of Manchester) became Curate of New Shoreham. He occupied the Vicarage and it was there that he entered on his great scheme of education, at first by devoting part and eventually the whole of the vicarage house to the purpose upon which he had set his heart.

"Here he opened a day school for boys, and from this tiny acorn sprang the mighty oak which was to spread its ramifications throughout the country."

Soon afterwards, additional accommodation being required, houses adjacent to the vicarage were taken as well as others in Church Street and the buildings erected south of the churchyard. In the latter, the College of St. Saviour was founded and remained until 1870, when the collegians migrated to Ardingly, but their first home was for many years known as St. Saviour's Hall, and the name lingers even yet.

It is beyond our purpose to trace the development of the great movement known as the Woodard Schools. Let it suffice that from so small a beginning it has grown to its present proportions. In addition to the three great Colleges of Lancing, Hurstpierpoint, and Ardingly in Sussex, there are numerous others of the Woodard foundation elsewhere in England and Wales.

On the adjacent hillside overlooking the Adur Valley, stands St. Nicholas College, Lancing—the most important of them all. The first stone of these buildings was laid 21st March, 1854, by the founder, and, in 1868, Bishop Gilbert of Chichester laid the first stone of the Chapel.

THE REALIZATION OF A VISION

More than fifty years have passed since that day, and the fabric has slowly assumed the proportions and beauty of a stately Cathedral, and services have been held in it for some years.

So far as the exterior is concerned it is yet unfinished. A lofty tower of such imposing height and dimensions as to require a foundation of sixty feet in depth—already laid—will one day rise at the north-west angle. At its summit, the founder, possibly having in mind St. Nicholas of old, planned that there should be a chamber where a light could always be burned at night for the guidance of mariners far out at sea. May it be so.

The interior of the Chapel, majestic and beautiful with clustered columns, acutely pointed arches, and slender shafts soaring upward to the vaulting, is somewhat reminiscent of Westminster Abbey. In this Cathedral of the South Downs we see the realization of the founder's vision "after years of work and waiting, and the slow progress of a scheme which, in its early days, to many seemed too vast to be possible of fulfilment."

The spirit of mediæval times has surely breathed here, for one cannot but feel that the handiwork of the craftsmen has been a real joy to them. More than one mason has spent the greater part of his life putting the best of his work into this exquisite poem in stone, and one at least is known to have been engaged continuously on the Chapel for a period of over forty years.

One learns with interest of the cargo of stone intended for another port, wrecked years ago at the mouth of the Adur, and bought up by Canon Woodard for " a mere song," then barged up the river to Lancing to be wrought by the masons and find a suitable place in the building. But such luck was of rare occurrence, great difficulties had to be met and overcome, vast sums of money have been needed, and have been lavished with unsparing hand, and great statesmen such as the late Lord Salisbury and Mr. Gladstone have been interested in the work.

In the Crypt beneath the Chapel is the tomb of the founder, who passed to his rest on the 25th April, 1891, and long before the Chapel had attained its present beauty.

When at length the dedication service took place, with all the imposing and stately ceremonial appropriate to such an occasion, the Archbishop of Canterbury was assisted by fourteen other Bishops, all of whom were, or had been in the past, connected with the Woodard Schools.

Lancing College from the river

THE FREE CHURCHES

A Chapel of the Countess of Huntingdon's Connexion was founded at Shoreham in the year 1800, but the ground on which the building stands was not made over to the Trustees until 1812, when they acquired the site for £75.

"Star Lane Chapel," as this place of worship was popularly named, became, at a time when the anti-High Church agitation was somewhat strong in the town, a sort of opposition to the Parish Church. In those days it was known as the "Protestant Free Church," and the minister was the Rev. J. E. Goode, a man who preached in a somewhat prosy style, "sermons so lengthy that few of his most zealous followers could sit them out."

It is of interest to note the fact that the Rev. J. E. Goode successfully prosecuted his claim to the Dunmow Flitch in 1859. This is believed to be the only recorded instance of that award being made to a Sussex claimant.

In more recent years, the Congregationalists worshipped in Star Lane Chapel until their removal to the Church in Gordon Road, which is still in course of erection.* Meanwhile, the old Chapel after serving for some years as a public hall for lectures, concerts, and other entertainments was turned to its present use as a Cinema Theatre.

The Baptists held their first meetings in the town, in a room over a butcher's shop and in a sail-maker's loft, until an iron chapel was erected in Western Road, to be superseded later by the permanent Chapel and Schoolroom, erected in 1880. Their first settled minister at Shoreham was the Rev. Joseph W. Harrald who baptized several of the early members of his church in the River Adur. Mr. Harrald was afterwards, for many years, the devoted friend and private secretary of Charles Haddon Spurgeon, who was wont to refer to him as his "Armour Bearer." With Mrs. Spurgeon, he compiled an autobiography of the celebrated preacher's life which appeared in four volumes in 1897-8.

The Particular Baptist Chapel in John Street was erected in 1867, and the Primitive Methodist Chapel in the High Street in 1879. The Wesleyan Chapel in Brunswick Road was built in

*This place of worship still retains the early traditions of its parent in Church Street. Mr. G. F. Harker, representing its congregation, was in 1912, at the Annual Conference at Ebley, chosen President of the Countess of Huntingdon's Connexion.

THE STORY OF SHOREHAM

1900, succeeding the older Chapel in New Road, now the meeting place of the Salvation Army.

The late General Booth received a very cordial reception from the members of the Urban District Council and inhabitants of the town when he passed through Shoreham a few years ago. Some who were present in the crowded High Street on that occasion may have recalled the earlier days of the Salvation Army in Shoreham. In former times a somewhat rough element, known as the "skeleton army," often molested those who were followers of the General's teaching.

The Catholic Church of St. Peter

is an edifice of flint with stone dressings in the style of the 13th century. It was erected at a cost of £5,000 defrayed by the Duchess of Norfolk and the Rev. William Wheeler. The Church was opened in August, 1875, and consists of nave and chancel with a Lady chapel on the north side. The interior is replete with those accessories of worship required for the ornate and elaborate ritual of the Roman Communion. The Presbytery adjoining was completed in 1877. There is a small convent in West Street.

CHAPTER XIV.

PARLIAMENTARY HISTORY—PAYMENT TO MEMBERS IN EARLY TIMES —EIGHTEENTH CENTURY BRIBERY AND CORRUPTION—EXTRAVAGANCE AT ELECTIONS—LIST OF THE MEMBERS FOR NEW SHOREHAM—BIOGRAPHICAL NOTES.

In the 23rd year of the reign of Edward I., Roger de Beauchamp and Thomas Pontoyse were summoned to represent the town of New Shoreham in the great Council of the Nation.

During the Edwardian period there existed a system of payment to Members for their services. In the case of a Borough the sum of two shillings daily was chargeable upon the inhabitants for each burgess who represented it. Thus, in 1335, when Robert Puffare, by order of the King, " came to London in Mid-Lent to inform the King and his Council on the state of the shipping," the bailiffs of Shoreham were ordered to pay the expenses of his journey to and from London and during his sojourn in the City at the rate of two shillings per day. On November 30th, 1355, there was a writ for the same rate of payment per day for nineteen days, for the expenses of John Bernard and Walter Bailiff of Shoreham, and in May, 1357, the same rate of payment for Walter Woxebrugg and Thomas Fynyan. Two shillings per day seems to be little enough, and one is inclined to marvel how they were able to " do themselves " on so small a sum, but it should be borne in mind that the purchasing power of money becomes less as the centuries advance, a fact which has become patent to most of us during recent years.

In the early days of Parliamentary representation the Members were chosen from among the townsmen themselves, and you will notice in glancing through the list, the names of many who have figured in the history of the town and who have been mentioned in previous pages. Later on, we find the names of Lewkenor, Covert, Shirley, Morley, Stapley, Springett, Fagge, Shelley, Bishopp, Goring, Burrell and Loder—Sussex families whose names are as household words to all who study the history of the County. Something will be said of most of these, as well as of those notable men who, although not natives of Sussex, were eminent public servants.

THE STORY OF SHOREHAM

During the 18th century the town attained an un-enviable notoriety for bribery and corruption. The representation was eagerly sought for by contending parties, more especially as a return might be expected for the outlay incurred consequent on contested elections. Successful candidates were able to exercise a degree of patronage in favour of their supporters, and those whom they wished to advance by obtaining from the Government of the day, the appointments connected with the Customs, Tide-waiters, and other offices, supposed to be "in the gift" of the Members representing the Borough.

In Shoreham this sort of patronage was made use of to the fullest extent possible—"not that we consider it in this respect worse than its more fortunate neighbours," says one writer, "but it had the misfortune to have its delinquencies discovered."

Doubtless, for many years, this system of bribery and corruption had flourished in the town, but its first glaring example is afforded in the account of a visit paid to Shoreham by Mr. Nathaniel Gould, who arrived pending an Election.

"*The Crier went through the Town.*"

Mr. Gould, certainly seems to have come to the town with the intention of making himself popular. Shortly after his arrival the public crier went through the streets with his bell, giving notice to all the voters to repair to the "King's Arms," to receive a guinea per man and to "drink Mr. Gould's health."

Such an invitation was too good to be resisted. Most of the voters went to the Inn, drank Mr. Gould's health, received

BRIBERY

the promised guineas, and shortly after elected and returned him as their Member.

But Mr. John Perry, the defeated Member had yet to be reckoned with. On the 3rd January, 1701, this gentleman petitioned Parliament, as did some of the inhabitants on the 26th February following, " that Thomas Edwards had corruptly returned Mr. Gould," and the whole story connected with the visit of that gentleman to Shoreham and the subsequent Election came out.

On the 13th March, Mr. Gould petitioned the House in reply. He pleaded " mistaken apprehension of the Law, acknowledged his error, and with the greatest humility, submitted himself to the justice and favour of the House."

The House expelled him and directed that no new writ should be issued that session, but when it was, the Shoreham voters re-elected him.

A number of petitions followed. On 2nd November, 1705, Mr. John Perry petitioned against the return of Mr. Wicker. On 25th November, 1708, some of the inhabitants against the return of Mr. Richard Lloyd. At a Bye-election, 18th December, 1708, Gregory Page was returned and on the 22nd of the same month, Mr. Gould petitioned against his return. None of these petitions were proceeded with.

On the 16th November, 1709, the return of Mr. Richard Lloyd was petitioned against by some of the inhabitants on the ground of "treating and undue practice," but on the matter being investigated by a Committee of the House of Commons, Mr. Lloyd was declared duly elected. Again, in 1710, the defeated candidates petitioned against the return of Messrs. Page and Gould, but it came to nothing and the elected Members retained their seats.

These particulars are sufficient to show us the unsatisfactory state of Political affairs in the Borough, and it is matter for small surprise that we find Dr. Burton, the Greek scholar, after having visited Shoreham, writing in 1751, that "they (the townspeople) get rich every seven years by pocketing gifts for their votes." It is on record that during the reign of George II., more money was spent at Shoreham and Bramber Elections than all the lands in the parishes were worth at twenty years' purchase. On one occasion the landlord of the "Star Inn" boasted that, during an Election, then just over, he made £300 of one pipe of canary !

THE STORY OF SHOREHAM

It appears that a majority of the freemen of the Borough formed themselves into a club under the name of the " Christian Society." The date of its formation has not been ascertained, but it flourished for many years, and under the cloak of piety and religion the members carried on what they called " burgessing business," setting the Borough for sale to the highest bidder while the rest of the freemen who " were not of this flock " were deprived of the benefit of their votes.

The Christian Society's usual place of meeting was the "Star Inn," over which hostelry it was customary to hoist a flag whenever it was desirable to call the members together. None but voters for representatives in Parliament were ever admitted into the Society, but most of the voters were members. They employed a constant clerk and held regular monthly and occasional meetings, and the members took an oath of secrecy and entered into a bond, under a penalty of £500, to bind them together with regard to " burgessing."

The traffic was carried on by means of a " Select Committee," whose members made the pretence of scruples of conscience their reason for never appearing or voting at any Election themselves, but who, having sold the Borough to the highest bidder and received the stipulated price, gave directions to the rest how to vote, and shared the money as soon as the Election was over.

In February, 1770, a report of the death of Sir Samuel Cornish reached Shoreham. At once the flag was hoisted over the "Star Inn," and the members of the Christian Society assembled. Many of them declared that they would support the highest bidder, but some, and among them Hugh Roberts, the High Constable, who by virtue of his office was Returning Officer, expressed themselves offended at such a declaration and, saying that the Society was " nothing but a heap of bribery," withdrew.

The report of the Member's decease proved to be false, he did not die until late in the year. Five candidates then offered themselves for election. Three of them—Thomas Rumbold, John Purling, and William James went to the poll, which took place on the 26th November, resulting in the following number of votes being recorded : Rumbold, 87 ; Purling, 37 ; James, 4.

Hugh Roberts queried 76 of Rumbold's votes and returned Purling. The former petitioned. A Select Committee of fifteen was appointed to deal with the matter, and the corrupt practices of the Christian Society were then made public.

AT THE BAR OF THE HOUSE

On the 8th February following, Hugh Roberts was called to the Bar of the House of Commons and charged with having made a false return to Parliament. During his examination and defence some further interesting facts came to light.

He stated that on the death of Sir Samuel Cornish, five candidates for the vacant seat came down from London, and that the agent of one of them, inadvertently "mentioned in company " that the Christian Society had appointed a committee of five to make terms with the candidates, that General Smith had offered for the seat £3,000 and to build 600 tons of shipping at Shoreham, but that Mr. Rumbold "had bid more." Further, that at the last Election an affidavit was made and read, that Mr. Rumbold's agent had agreed with the members of the society to give them £35 for each vote, and for these reasons Roberts had disqualified these electors although they had taken the bribery oath.

Hugh Roberts pleaded that if he had done wrong it was without intent, and submitted himself to the decision of the House. On the 12th February he brought up witnesses in his favour, but the House, judging that this assumption of such power by a Returning Officer, upon whatever principle it was based, would be a most dangerous precedent, ordered him to be taken into custody by the Sergeant-at-Arms.

The next day, with all humility, he acknowledged the offence by which he had incurred the displeasure of the House, their justice in punishing him, begged pardon and implored to be discharged from confinement. In consideration of the circumstances in his favour and of his having exposed so corrupt an organization he was discharged, after having received, kneeling at the Bar of the House of Commons, a severe reprimand from the Speaker, Sir Fletcher Norton.

The Shoreham Election of 1770, became the talk of the country. A full enquiry into the practices of the Christian Society was made, and a Bill was brought in to disfranchise the eighty-one freemen who were its members. The Bill met with " some opposition " but finally received the Royal Assent, 8th May, 1771.

This Act, after reciting that " a wicked and corrupt society, calling itself the Christian Society," existed in Shoreham, incapacitated and disabled by name 68 of its members from voting at Parliamentary Elections. By this, a sufficient number was not left to enable the Borough to continue to exercise the right of sending two representatives. Its limits were therefore extended so that every freeholder above the age of one-and-twenty, having, within the Rape of Bramber, a freehold of the clear yearly value of 40s., was allowed to give his vote at every Election of a burgess or burgesses to serve in Parliament for the Borough of New Shoreham. The number of voters became about 1,200 residing in 48 parishes comprising the Rape of Bramber, but excepting the Borough of Horsham.

At every subsequent Parliamentary Election in the town, the Act of Disfranchisement was required to be read before the writ and the laws against bribery and corruption. In former times this duty was performed by an official who had the unpleasant task of naming—with others—himself as a voter disfranchised for bribery, concluding with the loyal response "God Save the King."

The Election of 1774, was the first which took place after the right of voting was extended to the Rape of Bramber.

Sir John Shelley, Bart., of Michelgrove, and James Butler, Esq., of Warminghurst, who had previously represented Arundel, were proposed as candidates in the Tory interest, while Charles Goring, Esq., of Wiston, was proposed in the interest of the Liberals. John Aldridge, Esq., of New Place, also offered himself. There were thus four candidates, all of whom were gentlemen living within the Rape.

To make a union of interests, Sir John Shelley and Mr. Butler, in the early part of September, coalesced and published an address, being supported by the Government. Upon this, Messrs. Goring and Aldridge also coalesced, and, in their address, stated that "they scorned to be the corruptors of the people and were anxious to be their free-chosen agents."

The canvass was carried on with great activity on both sides. The Election took place on the 13th October and two following days and was held in the north transept of the church, a practice begun in 1770—the year notorious, as we have seen, for the exposure of the "Christian Society."

Under date October 14th, 1774, the diary of Mr. John Baker, of Horsham, records a visit of that gentleman to Shoreham while this Election was in progress and informs us that he "went to the 'Dolphin Inn' and then walked up to church, where polling candidates, Sir John Shelley, Mr. Goring, Mr. James Butler and Mr. Aldridge. Mr. Goring ahead a good deal. The three others doubtful."

ELECTIONS

At the close of the poll on the 15th, the numbers were declared to be : Charles Goring, Esq., 372 ; Sir John Shelley, Bart., 320 ; James Butler, Esq., 245 ; John Aldridge, Esq., 199—the result being the return of one member in each interest.

In 1780, Sir Cecil Bishopp was returned unopposed in conjunction with John Peachey, Esq., for the Borough of New Shoreham. At the next Dissolution in 1784, their return was opposed by the Earl of Surrey and John Aldridge, Esq., in the Liberal interest. Previously, however, to the 7th April—the day of Election—the Earl of Surrey withdrew, but Mr. Aldridge carried the contest to a poll, which lasted three days and resulted in the return of the old Members, thus : John Peachey, Esq. (C) 411 ; Sir Cecil Bishopp, Bart. (C) 313 ; John Aldridge, Esq. (W) 272.

During the debate in the House of Commons, March 13th, 1782, on the Bill "for regulating the future Elections at Cricklade, in Wiltshire," a good deal of reference was made to the Shoreham Bill on a like subject (11th Geo. III., cap. 55) and its consequences variously stated to the House.   Mr. F. Montague who closed the debate, referring to this Bill, said : " Lord Camden highly approved of the conduct of Parliament on that occasion, as he said 'by it, Shoreham was taken out of Bengal.'   Indeed, the consequences of the Bill proved his Lordship's opinion to be well-founded, for that Borough which had been for a long time before, the occasional seat of occasional nabobs, now returned two English country gentlemen and thus was Shoreham at last brought back to its original county, that of Sussex."

In 1790, the return of Mr. John Peachey and Sir Cecil Bishopp, was again opposed by Mr. Aldridge in conjunction with Sir Harry Goring, Bart., and John Challen Esq., of Shermanbury. On the 20th June, Mr. Peachey finding the opposition too strong for him, retired. The poll commenced on the 24th June and at its close on the evening of Saturday, 26th, the numbers were : John Aldridge, Esq., 331 ; Sir Cecil Bishopp, Bart., 319 ; Sir Harry Goring, Bart., 331 ; John Challen, Esq., 151. In the course of Sunday, the 27th, Sir Cecil Bishopp also retired and the poll continued open on Monday and at its final close the numbers were : Sir Harry Goring, Bart. (L) 379 ; John Aldridge, Esq. (L) 379 ; Sir Cecil Bishopp, Bart. (C) 320 ; John Challen, Esq. (C) 153.

Mr. John Aldridge died in May, 1795, and the Hon. Charles William Wyndham and Sir Cecil Bishopp offered themselves, but

THE STORY OF SHOREHAM

before the Election Sir Cecil withdrew and the Hon. C. W. Wyndham was returned.

At the General Election in 1796, Sir Cecil Bishopp again offered himself in opposition to Sir Harry Goring, who retiring previously to the day of Election, Sir Cecil was returned in his place.

In 1802, Sir Cecil was again returned with Sir Timothy Shelley, Bart., who succeeded Mr. Wyndham. At the next Election, in 1806, Sir Cecil again came forward; Sir Charles Merrik Burrell, Bart. also offered himself, and, on the 30th October, Sir Cecil retired and Sir Charles Merrik Burrell and Sir Timothy Shelley became the Members.

The Election of June, 1826, for the Rape of Bramber and the Borough of Shoreham, with its record of extravagant and lavish payments, shows that although bribery by direct money payment had presumably been abolished, indirectly it was still rampant.

At this Election, Sir Charles Merrik Burrell, Bart., Henry Howard, Esq., and E. Burtenshaw Sugden, Esq., were the three candidates for the two seats. The last-named gentleman was an eminent lawyer. The result at the close of the poll was: Burrell, 865; Howard, 545; Sugden, 483—being the return of one Conservative and one Liberal.

The Election cost these gentlemen nearly £6,000. Of this sum £707 found its way to the "Fountain Inn," and in addition, an item of £44 18s. 11d. "previous to election" and £32 10s. for the "waiters and ostlers of the 'Fountain.'" The "Royal George" netted £384, the "King's Head" £215, and "The Schooner" £120. There was also an item of £65 "for hire of band."

The list of bills incurred at Worthing on account of this Shoreham Election came to over £1,000; while the amount paid for counsel, agents, and hustings, was but a few pounds short of £2,800.

This outpouring of money is referred to in a letter dated December 8th, 1826, requesting payment of £139 "for wines supplied during the Election." The writer of the letter says: " as the period for petitioning has expired, I presume it will not be long before the bills are paid, *they begin to be very clamourous at Shoreham.*"

The practice of holding the Elections in the Church was discontinued after 1826, mainly through the influence of the Rev. Z. H. Biddulph, Vicar, who doubtless felt that such proceedings were quite unsuited to the sacred character of the building. At

THE MEMBERS FOR NEW SHOREHAM

subsequent Elections hustings were erected, sometimes in East Street near the churchyard, and more latterly in the High Street. On one occasion this work had been performed in a somewhat "jerry-built" manner and gave the mischievous shipyard apprentices a good opportunity for practical joking. Having passed some stout ropes round the erection they gave a "long pull and a strong pull," with the result that polling-clerk, voters, and others were shortly struggling together, sorting themselves out from the wreckage.

Formerly it was the custom for the newly-elected Members to stand with head uncovered, on *the stone*, while the result of the poll was declared. This stone is let into the pavement at the eastern end of the Market Place in front of "Stone House" —probably so named from this circumstance—and, although used for the ceremony at Election time, it was not, we think, placed there for that express purpose, and an element of mystery surrounds its origin.

On account of the electors being so scattered, Shoreham with four other constituencies, was made an exception to the clause in the Reform Act of 1832, which provides, "it shall not be lawful to pay any money on account of the conveyance of any voter to the poll." At the same time the places for polling were fixed at New Shoreham and Cowfold. By the Redistribution of Seats Act, 1885, Shoreham, after returning members to Parliament for 590 years, lost the direct representation altogether and became merged in the Mid or Lewes Division of the County of Sussex. This arrangement has recently been revised. The town is now included in the Horsham and Worthing Parliamentary Division and so voted at the late General Election.

THE MEMBERS OF PARLIAMENT FOR NEW SHOREHAM.

23	Edward I.	1295	Roger de Beauchamp	Thomas Pontoyse
26	,,	1298	Godfrey atte Curt	Roger le Wake
29	,,	1300-1	Roger de Beauchamp	Richard de Bokyngeham
30	,,	1302	Henry de Burne	Roger de Beauchamp
33	,,	1304-5	Richard Serle	Simon Iveny
1	Edward II.	1307	Richard Must	Richard Serle
2	,,	1309	John Virley	John Frewyn
5	,,	1311	John Virley	John Frewyn
7	,,	1313	Henry de Bourne	William de Pevense
12	,,	1319	John Loute	John Baudefait
19	,,	1325	William Vyvyan	Thomas Moraunt

THE STORY OF SHOREHAM

MEMBERS OF PARLIAMENT (contd.)

2	Edward III.	1327-8	Ralph Bovet	John le Blake
2	,,	1328	Henry de Whitewei	John Swele
2	,,	1328	Anselm atte Putte	John Swele
3	,,	1328-9	Anselm atte Putte	John Swele
4	,,	1329-30	Robert Apetot	Robert le Kenne
6	,,	1331-2	John de Beauchamp	Anselm atte Putte
6	,,	1332	Anselm atte Putte	Richard Moust
6	,,	1332	Anselm atte Putte	John atte Grene
8	,,	1333-4	Anselm atte Putte	David Fynian
8	,,	1334	John Beauchamp	Germanus Hobelyt
10	,,	1335-6	Robert le Puffare	John Beauchamp
10	,,	1336	John de Beauchamp	John atte Grene
10	,,	1336-7	Robert Puffer Simon l'houte	Thomas Fynian
12	,,	1337-8	John Beauchamp	John Bernard
13	,,	1339	Robert Puffare	John Bernard
13	,,	1339-40	Robert le Puffare	John Bernard
14	,,	1340	John Beauchanp	Robert le Puffare
15	,,	1341	John Beauchamp	Hugo de Coumbes
18	,,	1344	John Beauchamp	Robert Puffere
20	,,	1346	Robert Puffere	William L. . . .
22	,,	1348	John Beauchamp	Henry le Poffare
25	,,	1350-1	John Bernard	Thomas Fynian
28	,,	1354	Walter Woxebrugge	Thomas Finyan
29	,,	1355	John Bernard	Walter Bailiff
31	,,	1357	Walter Woxebrugg	Thomas Fynyan
32	,,	1357-8	Thomas Bokyngham	William Snellyng
34	,,	1360	John Bernard	Walter Bailiff
34	,,	1360-1	John Bernard	Walter Woxebrugge
36	,,	1362	Thomas Fynyan	Thomas Bokyngham
37	,,	1363	John Bernard	William Snellyng
40	,,	1366	Ralph Iver	William Snellyng
42	,,	1368	John Bernard	John Barbour
43	,,	1369	Richard Combe	John Barbour
45	,,	1371	William Snellyng	
46	,,	1372	William Snellyng	John Barbour
47	,,	1373	William Taillour	Ralph Frere
51	,,	1376-7	William Taillour	Ralph Frere
1	Richard II.	1377	Richard Bernard	John Barbour
2	,,	1378	John Barbour	William Taillo (ur)
3	,,	1379-80	John Barbour	Gregory Fromond
5	,,	1381	Richard Bernard	Simon Benefelde
5	,,	1382	William Shirford	Richard Bernard
6	,,	1382	John Barbour	John Skully
6	,,	1382-3	John Lynton	Simon Banfeld
7	,,	1383	John Lynton	Simon Banefeld
7	,,	1384	Simon Benfeld	John Lynton
8	,,	1384	Simon Benfeld	Richard Bernard
9	,,	1385	Robert Frye	John Lenton
10	,,	1386	William Corveyser	Richard Bernard

SIR RICHARD LEWKENOR

MEMBERS OF PARLIAMENT (contd.)

11	Richard II.	1387-8	Simon Benefeld	Richard Bernard
12	,,	1388	Richard Bernard	John Skolley
13	,,	1389-90	Simon Benfeld	Richard Bernard
15	,,	1391	John Scully	Robert Frye
16	,,	1392-3	John Scully	Richard Bernard
18	,,	1394-5	Simon Benfeld	Richard Bernard
20	,,	1396-7	Simon Benfeld	Robert Frye
21	,,	1397 & 1397-8	William atte Hulle	Gregory Fromond
1	Henry IV.	1399	Robert Frye	John Sopere
3	,,	1402	William Ede	Roger Farncombe
7	,,	1405-6	William Hokere	William Peke
9	,,	1407	John Skully	John atte Gate
1	Henry V.	1413	William Ede	John Draper
2	,,	1414	Robert Benefeld	William Ede
5	,,	1417	Richard Dammere	Adam Feret
9	,,	1421	John Fyndon	Richard Roger
2	Henry VI.	1423	Richard Dammere	William Langlegh
4	,,	1425-6	Richard Roger	Adam Feret
6	,,	1427	John Wrythere	John Waleys
8	,,	1429	William Snellyng	William Yongge
9	,,	1430-1	Adam Feret	John Furly
10	,,	1432	Richard Jay	Richard Daunvere
11	,,	1433	Thomas Hille	John Ham
14	,,	1435	Richard Jay	John Furly
15	,,	1436-7	Richard Jay	John Kempe
20	,,	1441-2	Richard Jay	Thomas Grevet
25	,,	1446-7	John Veske	John Weston
27	,,	1448-9	William Redston	John Beckwith
28	,,	1449	William Bury	John Gloucestre
29	,,	1450	Thomas Gynnour	Edward Raf
31	,,	1452-3	Edward Raffe	William Say
38	,,	1459	Hugo Mill	Richard Awger
39	,,	1460	Robert Spert	Nicholas Morley
7	Edward IV.	1467	Richard Lewkenor	William Brandon

The above-named Sir Richard Lewkenor is supposed to have built the original Brambletye House, near Forest Row, of which mansion the gateway only remains, the other existing ruins being of later date. Sir Richard was M.P. for Horsham, Shoreham, and East Grinstead ; was Sheriff of Sussex in 1495 and died 13th February, 1503. He was twice married, his first wife being Elizabeth, daughter and co-heiress of Thomas St. Clere, and his second, Katharine, daughter of Lord Scales and widow of Sir Thomas Grey, Knt. She was one of the ladies to the Queens of Edward IV. and Henry VII., and held Brambletye till her death, 9th June, 1505. She was buried at East Grinstead.

THE STORY OF SHOREHAM

| 12 Edward IV. | 1472 | Peter Veske | Richard Farnefold |
| 17 ,, | 1477-8 | Peter Veske | John Cookson. |

From 22 Edward IV. (1482-3) to 14 Henry VIII. (1523) no returns for Shoreham have been found and it is possible that during that period the town was not represented.

| 21 Henry VIII. | 1529 | John Covert | John Mitchell |

John Covert was the elder son of Richard Covert by his fourth wife, Blanche, daughter of John Vaughan of Burgenne, Esq. Fined for Knighthood in 1533. He sat for the County in 1553 and was Sheriff of Sussex in 1555. He is said, in the Visitation, to have " commanded at the siege of Bullen," 1544. He married (first) Elizabeth, daughter of John Cooke of Rustington, and had by her, Richard and William (and second) Ann Beard of Cowfold.

37 Henry VIII.	1544-5	John Gates	Henry Gates
1 Edward VI.	1547	William Fewyllames, or Fitzwilliams	Anthony Bourchier
7 ,,	1552-3	Master John Fowler, one of the King's Majestie's Privy Chamber	Master Thomas Harvey, Esq.
1 Mary	1553	Thomas Roper, Esq.	Thomas Elderington, Esq.
1 ,,	1554	Leonard West, Esq.	William Modye, gent.
1 & 2 Philip & Mary	1554	Simon Lowe, " of the cytie of London, gent."	William Modye, gent.
2 & 3 ,,	1555	Francis Shirley, Esq.	Thomas Huggen, Esq.

Francis Shirley was son of Sir Thomas Shirley of West Grinstead (second son of Ralph Shirley, of Wiston, who died 1545) by his wife, Elizabeth, daughter and heiress of Marmaduke Georges *alias* Russell, of Gloucestershire. The Manor of West Grinstead was granted to him in 1549 on the attainder of Thomas Seymour, Baron Seymour of Sudley, to whom it had been granted in fee farm in the first year of Edward VI. He was Sheriff of Surrey and Sussex in 1574. Little else has been preserved concerning him, but it appears in Edward the VI.'s reign he had a difficulty with Lord la Warre concerning certain land called Estcourt, said to be parcel of the Manor of Kneppe, but really belonging to West Grinstead. In the reign of Elizabeth we find him Lessee of the " Chappil House or Seller " on the south side of Bramber Bridge, with the land adjoining, granted to him by the College of St. Mary Magdalene at Oxford, for a term of 50 years.

SIR EDWARD LEWKENOR

He married Barbara, second daughter of Sir Richard Blount, of Mapledurham, Oxon, Knt., Lieutenant of the Tower of London, by Elizabeth, daughter of Sir Richard Lyster, Lord Chief Justice, King's Bench. Francis Shirley died March 1577, seized of Boddington, Howe Court, and West Grinstead in Sussex, and of Hatherley in Somerset; and left a son, Thomas, then 22 years of age. He was buried at West Grinstead, 24th March, 1577, by the side of his wife, Barbara, who pre-deceased him and was buried 28th February, 1563, both burials being recorded in the Registers. (Shirley Stemmata).

4 & 5 Philip and Mary	1557-8	Anthony Hussey	Richard Baker
1 Elizabeth	1558-9	Richard Lestrange	Nicholas M(yn ?)
5 ,,	1562-3	Henry Knowles, Esq.	Nicholas Myn
13 ,,	1571	William Dix	John Bowles

(No returns for this Parliament have been found. The above names are given by Browne Willis in "Notitia Parliamentaria")

14 Elizabeth	1572	Edward Lewkenor, Esq.	Edward Fenner, Esq.

Sir Edward Lewkenor, of Kingston-Bowsey (Kingston-by-Sea), Sussex and Denham Hall, Suffolk. Aged 11, on the death of his father (Inq. P.M.) who was Groom Porter to Edward VI. and died in the Tower 25th June, 1556 (Machin's Diary) but whose four sons and six daughters were restored in Blood. Sir Edward married Susan, daughter and co-heir of Thomas Hyham, of Hyham Hall, Suffolk. "Funeral verses on the death of Sir Edward (19th September, 1605) and Lady Susan, his wife, and death's apology and a rejoynder to the same" were printed in 1606.

27 Elizabeth	1584	William Necton, Esq.	Thomas Fenner, gent.
28 ,,	1586	,,	John Yonge, gent.
30 & 31 ,,	1588 & 88-9.	,,	(John) Yonge, gent.
35 ,,	1592-3	,,	Herbert Morley, Esq.
39 ,,	1597	,,	John Yonge, Esq.
43 ,,	1601	John Morley, Esq.	Robert Bristowe, Esq
1 James I.	1603-4	Sir Bernard Whitstones, Knt., of Hangleton, Sx.	Sir Hugh Beeston, Knt.
12 ,,	1614	Sir Charles Howard, Knt.	Thomas Shelley, Esq.

No returns for this Parliament have been found. The names given are from a list found among the Duke of Manchester's papers. Browne Willis in his "Notitia Parliamentaria" gives the names of John Morley, Knt., and Hugh Beeston, Knt.

THE STORY OF SHOREHAM

18 James I.   1620-1 Sir John Morley, Knt. Sir John Leedes, Knt.

Sir John Leedes, of Wappingthorne. Eldest son of Thomas Leedes (born 1566, and created Knight of the Bath, 25th July, 1603) by his wife, Mary, daughter and heiress of Sir Thomas Monson, of North Melford, Yorks.

Sir John was knighted 8th January, 1610-11. He married Bridget, daughter of Thomas Monson, of Burton, Lincolnshire. On his election as Member for Shoreham, he sat in the House for a week but without taking the oath, and this being found out he was adjudged incapable of sitting during that Parliament and a new writ was issued. He had sat in previous Parliaments so could not profess ignorance. His friends pleaded in his excuse that it was negligence and not presumption, but he was censured and discharged. Not being a very wise man we find him in the same year committed to custody for " idle words " or, as another account has it, " for prattling " and expressing discontent with the King and Government. (Sussex Archæological Collections, Vol. 54). Sir John Leedes died in 1656 and his will was proved in 1658. His son Thomas who was M.P. for Steyning in 1640, was slain near Oxford, in 1645.

16 Feb. 1620-1. Inigo Jones, Esq. (*vice* Sir John Leedes, expelled from the House).

Inigo Jones a celebrated architect. Son of Inigo Jones, a clothworker of London. Born 15th July, 1573. In his youth travelled on the Continent. Designed shifting scenery, machines and dresses for many masques which were performed at Court. Surveyor of Works to Henry, Prince of Wales (eldest son of James I.), 1610-1612. In Italy, 1613-1615, and purchased works of art for the Earl of Arundel, the Earl of Pembroke and Lord Danvers. Surveyor-General of Works 1615. Designed the Queen's House at Greenwich (1617-35), Lincoln's Inn Chapel (1617-23) west side of Lincoln's Inn Fields. The Banqueting House at Whitehall, begun in 1619 and completed in 1622 at a cost of £15,653 3s. 3d. and still standing, was intended by Jones to form part of an immense Palace, which was to take the place of Old Whitehall, but was never completed. It was from one of the windows of this Banqueting House that Charles I. stepped out on to the scaffold for execution in January, 1648-9. As Surveyor, Jones directed extensive repairs to Old St. Paul's Cathedral (see also a reference to a Shoreham ship which he chartered for the conveyance of stone for this work).

ANTHONY STAPLEY

During the Civil War, Jones took refuge with the Marquis of Winchester in Basing House. He was there during the siege which lasted from August, 1643 until 14th October, 1645, when Cromwell took the place by storm and the inhabitants were made prisoners. Jones' estate was sequestrated, but on payment of a fine he recovered it. He died unmarried 21st June, 1652, and was buried by the side of his father and mother in the Church of St. Benet. His monument, for the erection of which he left £100, was carved with reliefs of St. Paul's Cathedral and the church in Covent Garden. It was injured in the Great Fire and destroyed when the church was rebuilt by Wren. Large collections of his drawings are at Worcester College, Oxford, and at Chatsworth.

21 James I.   1623-4 Anthony Stapley,Esq. William Marlott, Esq.
1 Charles I. 1625   ,,   ,,

Anthony Stapley (1590-1655) Regicide. Baptised at Framfield, 30th August, 1590. Son of Anthony Stapley, of Framfield, Sussex, by his third wife, Ann, daughter of John Thatcher, of Priesthawes, Sussex. The Stapley family removed about 1615 from Framfield to Patcham. Anthony represented the Borough of New Shoreham in two Parliaments, 21 Jac. I., 1623-4 and 1 Chas. I., 1625; and Lewes, 1628 (elected 26th February, 1627-8) having unseated Sir George Rivers on petition. Returned, both for Lewes and the County in the short Parliament of 1639-40, but sat for the County and represented it in the Parliaments of 1653 and 1654. In January, 1639-40, Stapley was reported to Dr. William Bray, Archbishop Laud's chaplain, as causing trouble to the Church by his Puritan leanings. On the outbreak of the Civil War he received a Colonel's Commission in the Parliamentary Army and was present at the siege of Chichester, December, 1642, with Sir William Waller. He was left as Governor of the town and garrison when Waller moved on to the siege of Arundel. Took the Covenant, 22nd September, 1643. At the beginning of 1644 took exception to the quartering in the town of some of Waller's horse ; the dispute was referred to the Committee of the House of Commons and finally to the Committee of both Kingdoms, 22nd February. He was ordered by both bodies to obey Waller's commands. While detained in London he was exonerated from all blame in case of disaster occurring at Chichester during his absence. He resumed command of the town and garrison at the termination of the proceedings,

THE STORY OF SHOREHAM

early in March, and retained his governorship till 1645, when he was succeeded by Col. Algernon Sidney. Stapley was one of the judges of Charles I. and was present in Westminster Hall, 27th January, 1648-9, when sentence was pronounced and signed the death warrant 29th January. He was elected a member of the first Council of State of the Commonwealth, 17th February 1648-9, (when he signed the engagement) and re-elected 17th February, 1649-50, 25th November, 1651, 30th November, 1652, and 9th July, 1653. One of Cromwell's immediate Council of thirteen, 29th April to 14th July, 1653, and of the Supreme Assembly called 6th June, 1653. He had joined the Admiralty Committee of the Committee of both Kingdoms 6th June, 1649, was nominated Vice-Admiral for the County of Sussex, 22nd February, 1650, and took the oath of secrecy the following day. He died early in 1655, and was buried at Patcham. At the Restoration he was one of the Regicides notified as dead and excepted from the Act of pardon and oblivion, 6th June, 1660. Stapley married Ann, daughter of George Goring, of Danny, and sister of George, Lord Goring. She was buried at Patcham 11th November, 1637, and left three sons and two daughters. Stapley married a second wife—Dame Anne Clark—who pre-deceased him, May 15th, 1654.

1	Charles I.	1625-6	John Alford, Esq.	William Marlott, Gent.
3	,,	1627-8	Robert Morley, Esq.	,,
16	,,	1640	John Alford, Esq.	,,
16	,,	1640	,,	,,

John Alford, Esq., J.P., Sussex. Eldest son of John Alford, Esq., of Offington, by his wife, Judith, daughter of Sir Edward Downing, Knt. Sat for New Shoreham as above and for Arundel 3 Charles I., 1627-8. He married (18 Jac. I.) Frances, younger daughter of Sir Thomas Bishopp, 1st Baronet, of Parham, Sussex, M.P., and by her had two daughters. He died 5th January, 1648-9, and was buried at Broadwater. (Foster's Members of Parliament).

William Marlott (or Merlott) of Shoreham. Baptised 30th May, 1574. On a call of the House, 5th February 1644, William Marlott was absent, as being on service of the Parliament. He took the Covenant 27th March, 1644. Buried at Shoreham, 8th February, 1646. Administration of his estate granted to Mary Marlott, relict July 15th, 1646 (S.A.C. v.-102, xli.-107-113).

      Herbert Springate, Esq. (probably elected *vice* William Marlott, deceased)

EDWARD BLAKER

Richard Cromwell	1658-9	Edward Blaker, Esq.	John Whalley, Esq.
12 Charles II.	1660	,,	Herbert Springate, Esq.
13 ,,	1661	,,	Sir Herbert Springate, Bart.

Edward Blaker, Esq., of Buckingham in Old Shoreham, son of Edward Blaker, of Portslade, by his second wife Susanna, daughter of Tuppen Scrase, of Blatchington. Baptised 10th January, 1629-30, admitted Student of the Inner Temple November, 1647, then described as "son and heir of Edward Blaker" and as "of Portslade." Sheriff of Sussex, 1657. M.P. for New Shoreham 1658, till his death 13th September, 1678. Buried at Old Shoreham (see notes on Buckingham House).

Sir Herbert Springett (or Springate) of Broyle Place, Ringmer, Sussex, created a Baronet 8th January, 1660, was the eldest son of Sir Thomas Springett, Knt., by May, daughter of John Bellingham, of Erringham, Esq., Married Barbara, eldest daughter of Sir William Campion, Knt., by Elizabeth his wife, eldest daughter and co-heir of Sir William Stone, Knt., of London, and by her (who died 1696, aged 85) had issue—May, married Sir John Stapley, Bart., of Patcham, and died in 1708, having had issue. Elizabeth married John Whalley, Esq., of Ringmer. Charity died unmarried. Sir Herbert died 5th January, 1661-2, aged 49, and the baronetcy became extinct. His decease occasioned a New Election at Shoreham. (Burke's Extinct Baronetcies. S.A.C. viii.-45).

20 Jan. 1661-2. William Quartermain, Esq., M.D., *vice* Sir Herbert Springett, deceased.

William Quartermain. Son of Walter Quartermain, of Stubbington, Bucks., gent. Brasenose College, Oxon. Matriculated 10th October, 1634, aged 16. B.A. from Magdalene Hall 4th June 1635, M.A. 9th April, 1638, Doc. Med. Pembroke Coll. 23rd June, 1657. A Physician in the Navy. Physician in Ordinary to Charles II. F.C.P. 1661, F.R.S. At the Royal Coll. of Physicians he came before the Censor's Board for examination 4th December, 1657, and 8th January, 1657-8 and was approved on both occasions. He did not appear on the third examination and was never admitted a member of the College. This was probably due to his being engaged in his professional capacity with the Fleet.

THE STORY OF SHOREHAM

When the Earl of Ormonde, during the Protectorate, paid a visit to England in 1658 with the object of preparing for the return of Charles II., he was accompanied through Suffolk by Dr. Quartermain and hearing that " Cromwell was on his track " he was conducted into Sussex and to Shoreham by the Doctor. Thence he embarked and returned to the King.

Pepys, under date 24th May, 1660, writes : " Up and made myself as fine as I could with the lining stockings and wide canons that I bought the other day at Hague. Extraordinary press of noble company and great mirth all the day. There dined with me in my cabin, Dr. Earle and Mr. Hollis, the King's Chaplains, Dr. Scarborough, Dr. Quartermain and Dr. Clarke, Physicians ; Mr. Darcy and Mr. Fox (both very fine gentlemen) the King's servants, where we had brave discourse."

On the decease of Sir Herbert Springett, William Quartermain was elected Member for New Shoreham, 13 Charles II., 1661.

The Doctor seems to have been the unlucky possessor of sea-washed lands, for the State Papers for 6th November, 1664, contain a petition from him stating that 300 acres of land called Gatcombe Haven near Portsmouth had been recovered from the sea at too great a cost and asking for another grant of land, the cultivation of which would enable him to re-imburse himself for his loss.

He seems to have been twice married, his second wife (whom he married either at St. Margaret's, Westminster, or in the Abbey itself, in 1662) being Mary, daughter of Sir Thomas Dyke, of Horeham, co. Sussex. Dr. Quartermain was buried in St. Martin's in the Fields, 11th June, 1667. His decease occasioned a New Election at Shoreham 24th October, 1667, when John Fagge, Esq., was elected. (Foster's Alumni, Ox. (1500-1714) 111, 1225. Notes and Queries 11 S. viii. 370-470).

24 Oct.,	1667	John Fagge, Esq., *vice* William Quartermain, Esq., M.D., deceased.
11 Feb.,	1672-3	Henry Goreing, junr., Esq., *vice* John Fagge, Esq., deceased.
24 Oct.	1678	Sir Anthony Deane, Knt., *vice* Edward Blaker, Esq., deceased.

The descent and date of birth of Sir Anthony Deane, Knt., one of the most accomplished ship-builders of his time and an eminent public servant, are still a matter of doubt. A writer in the Dictionary of National Biography states that he was

SIR ANTHONY DEANE

born circa 1638 and was elder son of Anthony Deane, mariner of Harwich, whose will (P.C.C. 227 Pell) was proved 1659. But in an exemplification of arms and grant of a crest made to Sir Anthony, 1683, he is described as "son of Anthony Deane, of London, gent., and grandson of Anthony Deane of Gloucester." (East Anglian N.S., iii -147).

An Anthony Deane of Gloucester (presumably the same as above matriculated as poor scholar at Bradgates Hall, Oxford, 18th June, 1610, aged 14, and was described as "son of Edward Deane, of Pinnock, Gloucester."

Richard Deane (1610-1653), the Regicide, was also a son of Edward Deane, of Pinnock (see Memorial to Anne, widow of Edward Deane, in Buckingham Church) and used the same arms as his name-sake, Sir Richard Deane, Lord Mayor of London, 1628, and is presumed to have been a relation—possibly a grand-nephew. The Lord Mayor was a son of George Deane, of Dunmow, Essex. The Regicide had some connection with Essex for he left his estate at Hornchurch in that county to his sister Mary, widow of Dru Sparrow, Secretary to the Generals at sea, killed in action, 18th February, 1652.

Sir Anthony appears to have borne the same arms with but a slight difference of tincture (the chevron being sable instead of gules) as Sir Richard Deane, the Lord Mayor—Argent, on a chevron sable, between three Cornish choughs ppr. as many crosses pattee or, and his crest was—on a wreath argent and sable, the stern of one of His Majesty's first-rate ships called the "Royal Charter" in natural colours, viz., lower counter and buttocks sable, sternpost proper, second counter, galleries, uprights, and taffrail or.

This crest was evidently an allusion to Sir Anthony's eminence as a ship-builder. He began life in the dockyard at Woolwich and with the assistance of his friend, Samuel Pepys, the Diarist, obtained 15th October, 1664, the appointment of master shipwright of Harwich, and of Portsmouth, 1668. In connection with the duties of his office, we find him writing June 6th, 1669, to the Navy Commissioners that he "had been to Shoreham, Arundel, and Pulborough, about timber." Both Pepys and Evelyn bear testimony to the beauty of his draughtsmanship and modelling, and the former was never weary of acknowledging his obligation to Deane for initiating him into the many mysteries of "shipwrightry." He was the inventor of a cannon

THE STORY OF SHOREHAM

"which, from its shortness and bigness, they do call Punchinello." He received a commission 20th April, 1667, as Captain of a company which he was to raise, train, and exercise from amongst the workmen at Harwich yard for defence of the port in case of foreign invasion, so Pepys speaks of him in his diary as "Captain Deane." By his industry he rose to be Surveyor-General of the Royal Shipyards and a Commissioner of the Navy 1675, and was knighted on board ship about the same time.

On the death of Edward Blaker (of Buckingham House, Old Shoreham) in 1678, the Duke of Monmouth wrote to Capt. Goring in the following terms—"understanding that a considerable part of the Corporation of Shoreham, on a vacancy of one of their burgesses in Parliament, had invited Sir Anthony Deane to succeed him and knowing him to be a person very well qualified I was early persuaded to recommend him and to desire you would not let him want your assistance." This assistance was apparently given and Sir Anthony was returned for New Shoreham 24th October, 1678

He represented the town but a short time. In the next Parliament, 31 Charles II., 1678-9, he sat for Harwich, and for the same place, 1 James II., 1685. He was Mayor of Harwich in 1676 and 1682. In 1679 he built yachts for Louis XIV.

Sir Anthony Deane did not escape persecution and a joint charge of betraying the secrets of the British Navy was made against himself and Pepys in 1675. They were accused on the depositions of Col. John Scott, of sending particulars to the French Government and also of a design to dethrone the King, and extirpate the Protestant Religion. Both were committed to the Tower under the Speaker's warrant, May 22nd, and were brought to the Bar of the King's Bench, June 2nd following and refused bail, but were afterwards allowed to find bail for £30,000. At length, after several months' delay, it was found that Col. Scott refused to acknowledge the truth of the original depositions, and the prisoners were relieved from their bail, February 12th, 1679-80. James, a butler, at one time in Pepys' service, confessed on his death-bed, 1680, that he had trumped up a story relating to a change of Religion which his former master was supposed to have made and that he had done this at the instigation of Mr. Harbord, M.P. for Launceston, an enemy of Pepys.

Sir Anthony Deane resigned his post as Commissioner of the Navy in 1680, but in the following year he again formed one

SIR ROBERT FAGGE

of the New Board appointed by the Duke of York (afterwards James II.) to help in improving the condition of the Navy which was then in a very reduced state. After the Revolution he sought retirement in Worcestershire and corresponded with Pepys. He died at his house in Charterhouse Square, London, at an advanced age (Holman, in MS. History of Essex, says he was over 90) in 1721, and was buried in the Church of the Crutched Friars. He was twice married, his second wife being Christian, daughter of Robert Hawkins of Lyons, in Bocking, widow of Sir John Dawes, Knt., of Putney, whom he married at St. Martin Outwich, London, July, 1678

31 Charles II.	1678-9	Robert Fagge, Esq.	John Cheale, Senr., Gent.
31 ,,	1679	John Hales, Esq.	,,
33 ,,	1680-1	Robert Fagge, Esq.	John Hales, Esq.

Sir Robert Fagge, 2nd Bart., of Wiston (son of Sir John Fagge, 1st Bart., who received his title on the return of Charles II.). Born about 1649. Married 21st September, 1671, at Wiston (with the consent of Mary Beard, her aunt), Elizabeth—then sixteen years of age—orphan daughter of Benjamin Culpeper of Lindfield, Sussex. Also sat for Steyning, 1690-5 and 1701-2. Succeeded to the baronetcy 18th January, 1700-1. Died, 26th August, 1715, and was buried at Albourne, Sussex. His will proved September, 1715. Succeeded by his second but only surviving son and heir, who was baptised 9th August, 1763, Robert.

It is to Sir Robert Fagge that James Bramstone, who was Rector of Harting, Sussex, alludes when he writes in his " Art of Politics " in connection with the Parliamentary Representation of Steyning and Bramber, that worthy electors will

" Leave you of mighty interest to brag
And poll two voices like Sir Robert Fagge."

| 1 James II. | 1685 | Sir Edward Hungerford, K.B. | Sir Richard Haddock Knt. |

Sir Richard Haddock greatly distinguished himself in the Dutch Wars in the reign of Charles II. In the Battle of Solebay, 28th May, 1672, he was in command of the " Royal James," which was closely engaged and grappled by two of the enemy's ships. According to Haddock's own account, " about 12 o'clock, I was shot in the foot with a small shot, I supposed out of Van Ghent's maintop, which pressed me after a small time to go down to be dressed." Then describing how they got loose from the ships

THE STORY OF SHOREHAM

that had grappled them, he concludes, " at that time the surgeon was cutting off the shattered flesh and tendons of my toe, and immediately after we were boarded by the fatal fire-ships that burnt us." The " Royal James " blew up, only some half-dozen of her crew, among whom were Haddock and his lieutenant, Thomas Mayo, being saved. On his return to London, Haddock was presented to the King, who took off the cap he was wearing and placed it on the gallant commander's head. This cap was still preserved in the family at the end of the 18th century.

Convention　　　1688-9　Sir Edward Hungerford　John Monk, Esq.
2 Wm. & Mary　1689-90　　　,,　　　John Perry, Esq.

Sir Edward Hungerford (1632-1711). Son and heir of Anthony Hungerford, a Royalist (who represented Chippenham in the House of Commons in 1620, and Bath in the Long Parliament, and died 1657), his mother was Rachel (died January, 1679-80), daughter of Rice Jones, of Astall, Oxon. He was born 20th October, 1632, and baptised at Blada Bourton, Oxon. He was a K.B. at the Coronation of Charles II., 23rd April, 1661.

In April, 1669, Sir Edward's town residence, Hungerford House, Charing Cross, was destroyed by fire and he settled in 1681 in Spring Gardens. He obtained some reputation as a patron of archery and was Lieut.-Col. of the regiment of Archers, 1661, and Col., 1682.

In January, 1679-80, he presented a petition for the summoning of a Parliament, and his avowed opposition to the Court led to his removal from the Lieutenancy of his county, May, 1681. But Sir Edward was best known for his reckless extravagance. He is said to have disposed of thirty manors in all. By way of restoring his waning fortunes he obtained permission, 1679, to hold a Market on Mondays, Wednesdays, and Saturdays, on the site of the demolished Hungerford House and grounds. In 1682 the Market House was erected there, apparently from Sir Christopher Wren's design. A bust of Sir Edward was placed on the north front with an inscription, stating that the Market House had been built at his expense with the King's sanction. In 1685 Sir Stephen Fox and Sir Christopher Wren purchased the Market and received the tolls. The Market House was rebuilt in 1833, and removed in 1860, when Charing Cross Railway Station was built on the site.

Hungerford sold the Manor and Castle of Farleigh to Henry Baynton, of Spye, Berks, for £50,000, in 1686, but about 1700 it

CAPTAIN HENRY PRIESTMAN

was purchased by Joseph Honoton of Troubridge, in whose descendants possession it remained till July, 1891, when it was bought by Lord Donnington. In his old age, Hungerford is said to have been a poor Knight of Windsor. He died in 1711, and was buried in the Church of St. Martin-in-the-Fields.

Sir Edward Hungerford married thrice. By his first wife, Jane, daugher of Sir John Hele, of Devonshire (died 18th May, 1664), and who was buried at Farleigh, he had an only son Edward, who married in 1680 at the age of nineteen, Lady Alathea Compton, and died September, 1681. By his second wife, Jane Culme (died 1674), and by his third wife, Jane Digby—perhaps the Lady Hungerford buried 23rd November, 1692—he also left issue. A daughter of the first marriage married in March, 1684, Clotworthy Skeffington, second Viscount Massarene, and died 2nd February, 1731-2, and left to her eldest son portraits of her father and grandfather and of other relatives. In her will she mentions a brother and sister then living. With the death of Sir Edward, the history of the Farleigh family of Hungerford practically ceases.

Sir Edward Hungerford represented New Shoreham in Parliament, 1 James II. 1685, Convention, 1688-9, and 2 William and Mary, 1689-90. He afterwards sat for Stevning, 7 William III., 1695, 10 William III., 1698, 12 William III., 1700-1, and 1 Anne, 1702.*

7 William III.   1695   John Perry, Esq.   Capt. Henry Priestman.

Captain Henry Priestman's first command was to the "Antelope" in 1672, and in the following year he was promoted to the command of the "Richmond." Sent in 1675 to the Mediterranean in command of the "Lark," in 1677-8 appointed to the "Swan," and, in the same year, to his first ship the "Antelope," with instructions to guard the fishing at Yarmouth. In 1681, commanded "Reserve," in 1683 "Bonaventure" in the Mediterranean and appointed Commodore in the Straits. He was sent in 1684 to Tetuan to treat with the Emperor of Morocco In 1688, he was placed in command of the "Hampton Court," and succeeded Sir William Booth, in 1689, as Comptroller of the Storekeeper's accounts, quitting that office on being nominated a Commissioner for executing the office of Lord High Admiral.

* (Hare's Hungerfordiana, 1823. Jackson's Guide to Farleigh, Gent's Magazine, 1832, II., 113-115. Notes and Queries 5, Series II., 293. Burke's Extinct Peerage—Hungerford of Heytesbury. Burke's Vicissitudes of Families, First Series).

Luttrell mentions a report of his appointment as Governor of Greenwich Hospital in 1710 in place of Sir William Gifford. He died August 20th, 1712, aged 65, and was buried in Westminster Abbey.

His memorial in the Abbey is a fine medallion, suspended by a knot of ribbons fastened to a pyramid of various coloured marbles. Round the head and underneath are naval trophies and sea instruments. The inscription is to "Henry Priestman, Esq." and describes him as Commander of a squadron of ships of war in the reign of Charles II., a Commissioner of the Navy, and one of the Commissioners for executing the office of Lord High Admiral of England, in the reign of William III.

10 William III.	1698	John Perry, Esq.	Charles Sergison, Esq.
12 ,,	1700-1	Nathaniel Gould, Esq.	,,
13 ,,	1701	Charles Sergison, Esq.	Nathaniel Gould, Esq.

Charles Sergison. Born 1654. Entered the service of the Crown as a dockyard clerk in 1671 and was Clerk of the Acts for thirty years. During this period, which included the War of Spanish Succession, the work of the Navy Board was excessively heavy and Sergison won the highest opinion of the several administrations with whom he acted. The emoluments of the office were large, though rather by perquisites and fees, than pay, and, in 1691, Sergison was able to purchase Cuckfield Park, in Sussex. During the reign of Anne he more than once asked for permission to retire but was told that he could not be spared. Afterwards, when he was suspended at the age of 65, in 1719, he seems to have felt it an undeserved insult. During the remainder of his life he lived at Cuckfield Park, where he died worth £150,000, 26th November, 1732. There is a monument to him in Cuckfield Church and a good portrait of him at Cuckfield Place. His wife was Anne, daughter of Mr. Crawley of the Navy Office. She pre-deceased him and on his death, without children, the estate passed to his grand-nephew, Thomas Warden, who took the name of Sergison. He also died leaving no children, and was succeeded by his brother Richard, who assumed the name of Sergison. In his family the Cuckfield estate remains. Charles Sergison formed a large collection of MSS. relating to the Navy, and although some of these have been dispersed many are still at Cuckfield Place. He had also a fine collection of models which has been preserved entire and in beautiful condition at Cuckfield.

SILVER-TONGUED HAMMOND

| 1 Anne | 1702 | John Perry, Esq. | Nathaniel Gould, Esq. |
| 4 Anne | 1705 | Nathaniel Gould, Esq. | John Wicker, Esq. |

John Wicker, Esq. Previously to his election as Member for New Shoreham, represented Horsham in four Parliaments. He possessed at the beginning of the 18th century a very extensive property in Horsham and adjoining parishes. He rebuilt or enlarged the house at Horsham Park, which, upon his death in 1767, descended with the rest of his extensive property to his only child and heiress.

| 7 Anne | 1708 | Anthony Hammond, Esq. | Richard Lloyd, Esq. |

Sir Anthony Hammond. Elected Member for New Shoreham in 1708, but under date 7th December, 1708, Luttrell (Diary vi. 281) has this entry—" This day the Commons carried it by 18—134 against 116—that Anthony Hammond being a Commissioner of the Navy and employed in the out-posts was incapable of being elected a Member of Parliament by an Act passed 6 Queen Anne, so 'tis expected a writ will be ordered for a new election at Shoreham." At the Election 18th December in that year, Gregory Page was returned for the Borough. Although Hammond was celebrated as a Politician and wit and as an eloquent and graceful speaker, so much so that Bolingbroke styled him the " Silver-tongued Hammond," his want of tact led Chesterfield to say that " he had all the senses but common-sense."

18 Dec.	1708	Gregory Page, Esq. (vice Anthony Hammond, disabled to sit).	
9 Anne	1710	Gregory Page, Esq.	Nathaniel Gould, Esq
12 ,,	1713	Nathaniel Gould, Esq.	Francis Chamberlayne Esq.
1 Geo. I.	1714-15	,,	Sir Gregory Page, Bart.

Sir Gregory Page, Bart., of Greenwich. The eldest son of Gregory Page a considerable merchant of London, and a Director of the East India Company. He was created a baronet by George I., 3rd December, 1714. Sir Gregory, like his father, was an eminent merchant and for many years an East India Director. He married Mary, daughter of Thomas Trotman, citizen of London, and had issue, two sons and two daughters. Sir Gregory died 25th May, 1720. His decease caused a Bye-election at Shoreham.

THE STORY OF SHOREHAM

11 June	1720	Francis Chamberlayne, Esq. (*vice* Sir Gregory Page, deceased).
8 Geo. I.	1722	Sir Nathaniel Gould Francis Chamberlayne, Esq.
1 Geo. II.	1727	,, ,,

Sir Nathaniel Gould, of Fleetwood House, Stoke Newington, the residence of Lt.-Gen. Fleetwood, son-in-law of Oliver Cromwell. He married Frances, daughter of Sir John Hartopp by his wife Eliza, daughter of Lt.-Gen. Fleetwood by his first wife. With his father-in-law, Sir John Hartopp, Bart., and two others he was trustee of the will of Lt.-Gen. Fleetwood. First elected for New Shoreham 7th January, 1700-1, but un-seated (as before described) on the petition of some of the inhabitants that his election had been procured by bribery. Re-elected 1701 (13 William III.) and represented the town in seven subsequent Parliaments. At the Election in 1722 (8 George I.) he was described as Sir Nathaniel Gould, Knt. He was a Director of the Bank. He died 20th July, 1728, and in his will dated 6th June 1724, and proved 23rd July, 1728, by John Gould, Esq., he mentions his " houses and lands, etc., in New Shoreham, Sussex " which he bequeathed to " my nephew John Gould to whom my daughter Elizabeth Cooke is to resign any claim she may have."

Francis Chamberlayne. Eldest son of Travies Chamberlayne, of the Ryes, Essex (who died at Thorpe, co. Warwick, 1695) M.P. for New Shoreham, 12 Anne, 1713. Defeated 1715, but chosen at a Bye-election 11th June, 1720, *vice* Sir Gregory Page, deceased, and with Sir Nathaniel Gould, sat for the town in the two following Parliaments. Died 26th September, 1728, then described as of Thorpe, co. Warwick. The decease of both Members occasioned a Bye-election in Shoreham.

29 Jan.   1728-9 Samuel Ongley, Esq.   John Gould, jr., Esq.
(*vice* Sir Nathaniel Gould and Francis Chamberlayne, deceased).

Samuel Ongley, Esq., of Old Warden, co. Bedford. Son of Samuel Ongley, of St. Michael's, Cornhill, London. Born 1697. Matric. St. John's College, Oxford, 13th December, 1716. Married Anne (who died 2nd February, 1761) only daughter of John Harvey, of Ickwell Priory, co. Bedford (who was M.P. co. Beds., 1713-15) nephew of Sir Samuel Ongley, Knt., of Old Warden (a linen draper in Cornhill, whose income was said to be £10,000 per annum and who died 25th August, 1726) and heir to his Kent estates. Sat for New Shoreham 1728 till 1734 and

THE FREDERICKS

for Bedford from 1734 till his death s.p. 15th June, 1747. Under Sir Samuel Ongley's will the estate (on the death of Samuel Ongley, M.P.) descended to his great-nephew, Robert Henly Ongley, of Old Warden, who was M.P. for Bedford, 1754-61, and for the County of Bedford 1761-80 and July, 1784-5, and was created Lord Ongley in the Peerage of Ireland, 1776.

John Gould, jr., Esq., nephew of Sir Nathaniel Gould. A Director of the East India Company   Died 25th July, 1740.

| 8 Geo. II. | 1734 | Thomas Frederick, Esq. John Phillipson, Esq. |

Thomas Frederick, Esq., of Walton, Surrey. Eldest son of Sir Thomas Frederick, Knt., of Westminster (Governor of Fort St. David, East India) who died 1730. He was born 25th October, 1707. Matric. New College, Oxford, 19th March, 1725. A Trustee for Georgia. M.P. for New Shoreham, 1734, till his death (un-married) 21st August, 1740.

| 28 May | 1739 | John Phillipson, Esq., re-elected after appointment as one of the Commissioners of the Navy. |
| 24 Nov. | 1740 | John Frederick, Esq. (*vice* Thomas Frederick deceased). |

John Frederick, Esq., of Bur Hill, Walton, Surrey. Second son of Sir Thomas Frederick, Knt. Born 1708. Matric. New College, Oxford, 19th March, 1725. Married (22nd October, 1741) Susannah, daughter of Sir Roger Hudson, Knt. Elected M.P. New Shoreham as above. West Looe, Dec., 1743-61. Defeated at Chippenham, 1741, and at Colchester, 1761. A Commissioner of the Customs, March 1761, to March, 1782. Succeeded his cousin, Sir Thomas Frederick as 4th Baronet, 16th December, 1770, and died 4th April, 1783.

| 15 Geo. II. | 1741 | Charles Frederick, Esq. Thomas Brand. |

Thomas Brand, of the Hoo in the parish of Kimpton, Herts, only son and heir of Thomas Brand by his wife, Margaret Nicholls, of St. Andrew's, Holborn, daughter and heiress of John Nicholls, of Chipping Barnet and Edgware, in Middlesex. She purchased (1732) the Manors of Kimpton, Great Bibbesworth and the Hoo from Sir Henry Hoo Keate, 3rd Baronet, whose father had rebuilt the mansion. M.P. for New Shoreham as above and also sat for Tavistock, 1747, Gatton, 1754 and 1761 and Okehampton, 1768, till his death 22nd August, 1770.

THE STORY OF SHOREHAM

He married 9th January, 1748-9, Lady Caroline Pierrepoint, eldest daughter of Evelyn (Pierrepoint) 1st Duke of Kingston, by his second wife, Lady Isabella Bentinck. She died 9th June, 1753, and was buried at Kingston, leaving one son, Thomas, who married the Hon. Gertrude Roper who succeeded her brother as Baroness Dacre and on her death 3rd October, 1819, her eldest son, Thomas, became 20th Lord Dacre, whose second son was the Rt. Hon. Henry Bouverie Brand, of Glynde Place, Sussex, Speaker of the House of Commons, afterwards Lord Hampden. (Sup. Vol. Victoria History of Herts).

21 April	1746	Charles Frederick, Esq., re-elected after appointment as Clerk of the Deliveries of the Ordnance.
21 Geo. II.	1747	Charles Frederick, Esq. Robert Bristow, Esq.
10 April	1750	Charles Frederick, Esq., re-elected after appointment as Surveyor-General of the Ordnance.

Charles Frederick, Esq. Third son of Sir Thomas Frederick, Knt. Born 21st December, 1709. Matric. New College, Oxford, 19th March, 1725. Admitted to the Middle Temple, 1728. Married, firstly (20th August, 1741) the youngest daughter of Sir Roger Hudson, of Sunbury, Middlesex, and secondly (18th August, 1746) the Hon. Lucy Boscawen, daughter of the 1st Viscount Falmouth. M.P. for New Shoreham 1741-54, Queenborough, Kent, 1754-80. Installed as Knight of the Bath, 26th May, 1761. Clerk of the Deliveries of the Ordnance, April, 1746-50. Surveyor-General of the Ordnance, April, 1750—March 1782. Comptroller of H.M. Laboratory at Woolwich from before 1749 to 1782. F.R.S. and F.S.A. 1731. Director of the Society of Antiquaries, 1735-6 and 1737. Died near Hammersmith, 18th December, 1785.

27 Geo. II.	1754	Robert Bristow, Esq.	Richard Stratton, Esq.
27 Dec., 1758.		Sir William Peere Williams, Bart. (*vice* Richard Stratton, Esq., deceased).	
1 Geo. III.	1761	George Broderick, Viscount Middleton	Sir William Peere Williams, Bart.

George, Viscount Middleton, in the Peerage of Ireland. Eldest son of Alan, second Viscount, one of the Commissioners of the Customs in England, by his wife Lady Mary Capel (married 7th May, 1729) youngest daughter of Algernon, 2nd Earl of Essex. Born 3rd October, 1730, and married 1st May, 1752, Albinia, eldest daughter of the Hon. Thomas Townshend, and sister of the

SIR WILLIAM PEERE WILLIAMS

first Viscount Sydney, by whom (who died 18th September, 1808) he had six sons and one daughter. Died 22nd August, 1765, and was succeeded in the title by his eldest son George, who married, 3rd December, 1778, Frances, daughter of the Rt. Hon. Thomas, Lord Pelham, of Stanmer, in Sussex. Lord Middleton's decease occasioned a Bye-election at Shoreham.

Sir William Peere Williams, Bart. Grandson of William Peere Williams, Law Reporter of Gray's Inn. (His father, Sir Hutchins Williams was created a baronet, and died 4th November, 1758). First elected M.P. for New Shoreham 27th December, 1758, *vice* Richard Stratton, deceased, and again 1 George III., 1761. In 1760 he introduced a Bill into Parliament for the improvement of Shoreham Harbour, which resulted in an entrance being formed at Kingston and the carrying out of other necessary works. He was one of the first Harbour Commissioners.

Sir William was a Captain in Burgoyne's Dragoons (now the 16th Lancers) and was killed in 1761 at the siege of St. Cas, in the Island of Belleisle, situated off the coast of France in the north of the Bay of Biscay.

"In the recklessness of a desponding mind he approached too near the enemy's sentinels and was shot through the body." The exact date of his death is not known but it was probably during the last week in April, 1761. The sum of £250 in bank notes was found in his pockets and, with the body, was honourably returned by the French Government.

Walpole, writing to George Montague, Esq., under date 5th May, 1761, says : " We have lost a young genius, Sir William Williams. An express from Belleisle arrived this morning, brings nothing but his death. He was shot—very unnecessarily riding too near a battery ; in sum, he is a sacrifice to his own rashness and ours." The citadel capitulated 7th June, 1761.

A letter of Gray, the poet, to Mason in August, 1761, contains the following remarks : " Mr. Montague (as I guess at your instigation) has earnestly desired me to write some lines to be put on a monument which he means to erect at Belleisle. It is a task I do not love, knowing Sir William Williams so slightly as I did ; but he (Mr. Montague) is so friendly a person and his affliction seemed to me so real that I could not refuse him. I have sent him the following verses which I neither like myself nor will he I doubt : however, I have showed him that I wished to oblige him."

THE STORY OF SHOREHAM

The following is the epitaph composed by Gray, and is still to be seen in the Church of La Palais :

> Here foremost in the dangerous paths of fame,
>   Young Williams fought for England's fair renown ;
> His mind each Muse, each Grace adorned his frame,
>   Nor envy dared to view him with a frown.
>
> At Aix his voluntary sword he drew
>   There first in blood his infant honour sealed
> From fortune, pleasure, science, love, he flew,
>   And scorned repose when Britain took the field.
>
> With eyes of flame, and cool undaunted breast
>   Victor he stood on Belleisle's rocky steeps—
> Ah ! gallant youth : this marble tells the rest,
>   Where melancholy friendship bends, and weeps.

In the expedition to Aix, referred to in the fifth line, Sir William Peere Williams was on board the " Magnanime " with Lord Howe and was deputed to receive the Capitulation.

Although Belleisle, at the time Sir William was killed, had not surrendered, Gray calls him " Victor" in the sense that he belonged to the side which was ultimately victorious.

Dying un-married, his brother, Sir Booth Williams, succeeded him in the baronetcy which became extinct 2nd February, 1784.

4 Dec.	1761	John, Lord Pollington, Baron of Longford in the Kingdom of Ireland (created Earl of Mexborough), *vice* Sir William Peere Williams, deceased.
	1765	Samuel Cornish, Esq. (*vice* Lord Middleton, deceased)
8 Geo. III.	1768	Sir Samuel Cornish, Peregrine Cust, Esq. Bart.

Sir Samuel Cornish, Bart., of Sharnbrook, co Berks. Vice-Admiral of the Red, F.R.S., etc. Created a Baronet 29th January, 1766. He purchased from Sir Philip Boteler, Baronet, of Teston, Kent, the Manors of Sharnbrook, Tofte, and Temple Hills in the county of Berks. Died s.p. 30th October, 1770, when the baronetcy became extinct. His estates devolved under Sir Samuel's will on his nephew, Admiral Samuel Pitchford who assumed the name of Cornish.

Peregrine Cust, Esq., of Wanstead, Essex. Fourth son of Sir Richard Cust, 2nd Bart. He was baptised at Leasingham,

SIR JOHN SHELLEY

19th May, 1722, and educated at Eton. A London Merchant and Director of the East India Company, 1767-9. Died, 2nd January, 1785.

26 Nov.   1770   Thomas Rumbold, Esq.   (*vice* Sir Samuel Cornish, deceased).

THE CONSTITUENCY EXTENDED TO INCLUDE THE WHOLE RAPE OF BRAMBER.

15 Geo. III.   1774   Charles Goring, Esq.   Sir John Shelley, Bt.

Sir John Shelley, 5th Bart. Married firstly Wilhelmina, daughter of John Newnham, Esq., of Maresfield Park, co. Sussex, by whom (who died in 1772) he had an only son, John, his heir; and secondly, in 1775, Elizabeth, daughter of Edward Woodcock, Esq., by whom he had three daughters who all died un-married. Sir John was Keeper of the Records in the Tower and Clerk of the Pipe. He was also (for some time) Treasurer of the Household and a Privy Councillor. He died 11th September, 1783.

21 Geo. III.   1780   Sir Cecil Bishopp, Bart.   John Peachey, Esq.

John Peachey, Esq. Eldest son of James Peachey, 1st Lord Selsey. Born, 16th March, 1749. Married 19th January, 1784, Hester Elizabeth, daughter of George Jennings, Esq., of Newsells, co. Herts, by whom he had issue, three sons and one daughter. He succeeded his father in the title, February, 1808. Died, 27th June, 1816, and was succeeded by his second son, Henry John, at whose death, without issue, in 1838, the title became extinct.

24 Geo. III.   1784   John Peachey, Esq.   Sir Cecil Bishopp, Bt.
30 Geo. III.   1790   Sir Harry Goring, of Highden, Bart.   John Aldridge, Esq.

John Aldridge, Esq., of St. Leonard's Forest, Sussex, which he inherited from Captain William Powlett, of St. Leonard's Forest and West Grinstead. M.P. New Shoreham, 1790, till his death, 16th May, 1795. He married Henrietta, daughter of J. Clater, Esq., and relict of J. Tomlinson Busby, Esq. She died in 1806, leaving issue, two sons and two daughters. (Foster's Members of Parliament).

30 May   1795   Charles William Wyndham, Esq., of Bignor Park (*vice* John Aldridge, Esq., deceased).
36 Geo. III.   1796   Chas. Wm. Wyndham,   Sir Cecil Bishopp, Bart., Esq.
41 Geo. III.   1801   Sir Cecil Bishopp, Bt.   Timothy Shelley, Esq.

THE STORY OF SHOREHAM

Sir Cecil Bishopp, 8th Bart., F.R.S. Eldest son of Sir Cecil, 7th Baronet, by his wife Susannah, eldest daughter and eventually sole heiress of Charles Hedges, Esq., of Finchley, co. Middlesex. Born 20th December, 1753, and married 27th June, 1782, Harriett Anne, only daughter and heiress of William Southwell, Esq., of Frampton, co. Gloucester, of the same family as Lord de Clifford. Sir Cecil sat for New Shoreham in four Parliaments as set forth above.

Sir Cecil preferred a claim to the ancient Barony of De la Zouche, in right of his mother and was eventually summoned to Parliament in the dignity originally created in 1272, when William la Zouche was called to Parliament as Baron de la Zouch or Souche. From him the Barony came in regular succession to the 11th Baron, Edward la Zouche, who, dying in 1625, left two daughters—Elizabeth, wife of Sir William Tate of De la Pre Abbet, in Northamptonshire, M.P., and Mary, wife, first of Thomas Leighton, Esq., and secondly of William Connard, Esq., between whom and their descendants the Barony fell into abeyance until called out by the Crown 27th August, 1815, in favour of Sir Cecil, whose mother, Susannah Hedges, was maternally great-great-great-granddaughter of Sir William Tate by Elizabeth Zouche, eldest daughter and co-heiress of the last Baron.

Lord de la Zouche died 11th November, 1828, when the Baronetcy passed to his kinsman Sir George Bishopp, and the Barony fell into abeyance between his two daughters, but was terminated by the Crown in favour of the elder. Lord de la Zouche's eldest son who was a Lieut.-Col. in the Army, died without issue in 1813 from wounds received in Upper Canada, and his second son, who was in the Navy, died un-married in 1808.

46 Geo. III.	1806	Timothy Shelley, Esq.	Sir Charles Merrik Burrell, Bart.
47 ,,	1807	Sir C. M. Burrell.	Timothy Shelley, Esq.
53 ,,	1812	,,	,,

Sir Timothy Shelley, 2nd Baronet. Eldest son of Sir Bysshe Shelley of Castle Goring, co. Sussex (created a Baronet 3rd March, 1806) by his first wife (married, 1752) Mary Catherine, only child of the Rev. Theobald Mitchell, of Horsham, by Mary, daughter of Nathaniel Tredcroft, Esq.

Sir Timothy was born in Red Lion Square, Middlesex, September, 1753, and baptised at the Church of St. George the Martyr

THE GORINGS

on the 20th of the same month. Married at West Grinstead, October, 1791, Elizabeth, daughter of Charles Pilfold, Esq., of Effingham, co. Surrey, by whom he had issue, Percy Bysshe the Poet, John, and four daughters.

Sir Timothy sat for Horsham 30 George III. (1790) and for New Shoreham in four Parliaments as above. On the 18th June, 1804, we find his name in a minority on "the additional force bill" and in a majority on Mr. Whitbread's motion against Lord Melville, late Treasurer of the Navy, April 8th, 1805. Sir Timothy died 24th April, 1844, and was succeeded in the Baronetcy by his grandson, Percy Florence, the son of the Poet. (Eminent English Statesmen).

58 Geo. III.	1818	Sir C. M. Burrell.	James Martin Lloyd, Esq., of Lancing.
1 Geo. IV.	1820	James M. Lloyd, Esq.	Sir C. M. Burrell.
7 ,,	1827	Sir C. M. Burrell.	Henry Howard, Esq., of Aldingbourne.
1 William IV.	1830	,,	,,
1 ,,	1831	,,	,,
3 ,,	1833	,,	Henry Dent Goring, Esq., of Yapton Place.
5 ,,	1835	,,	,,
1 Victoria	1837	Henry Dent Goring, Esq.	Sir C. M. Burrell.

Henry Dent Goring, Esq., better known as Sir Harry Dent Goring, 8th Baronet, was the eldest son of Sir Charles Forster Goring, 7th Baronet. Born 30th December, 1801, and succeeded to the title on the death of his father, 26th March, 1844. He married firstly, 2nd August, 1827, Augusta, daughter of John Harvey of Thorp Lodge, near Norwich (from whom he was divorced by Act of Parliament, 21st June, 1841) and had issue, one son and one daughter. Secondly, 11th May, 1842, Mary Elizabeth, daughter and heiress of John Griffiths Lewis, of Llanddyfian, co. Anglesey and widow of James Panton of Plas Gwyn in that county, and by her (who died October, 1871) had issue four daughters.

Sir Harry was great-great-grandson of Sir Henry Goring, 4th Baronet (fourth son of Sir Henry Goring, of Wappingthorne, in Steyning) who on the 22nd January, 1722, was created by "James III. of England and VIII. of Scotland" Baron Bullinghel and Viscount Goring, with remainder to the heirs male of his body. Sir

THE STORY OF SHOREHAM

Henry was succeeded by his eldest son Charles Matthew Goring, 2nd Vis., 5th Bart., who died August, 1769. He was succeeded by his elder son and heir, Harry Goring, 3rd Vis., 6th Bart., born 26th April, 1739, and died December, 1824, succeeded by his elder son and heir, Charles Forster Goring, 4th Vis., 7th Bart., born 11th July, 1768, and died 26th March, 1844, succeeded by his eldest son and heir, Sir Harry Dent Goring, 5th Vis., 8th Bart., the subject of these notes.

Sir Harry Dent Goring died in Paris, 19th April, 1859, and was succeeded by his only son and heir, Charles Goring, 6th Vis., 9th Bart., born 1828 and died s.p. 3rd November, 1884.

The titles then devolved on Craven Charles Goring, 7th Vis., 10th Bart., cousin and heir male, elder son of the Rev. the Hon. Charles Goring, next younger brother to the fifth Viscount Born 24th October, 1841, and died 16th March, 1897, leaving no issue. He was succeeded by Harry Yelverton Goring, 8th Vis., 11th Bart., cousin and heir male, being the eldest son of the Hon. Forster Goring, fourth son of the fourth Viscount. Born July, 1840. Married, 19th July, 1875, Sarah Ann, daughter of John Hickin, Esq., and has issue.

| 5 Victoria | 1841 | Sir C. M. Burrell, Bart. | Charles Goring, Esq. |
| 11 ,, | 1847 | ,, | ,, |

Charles Goring, Esq., son of Charles Goring, Esq., of Wiston, co. Sussex, by his third wife, Mary, daughter of the Rev. John Ballard, Fellow of Winchester (married 7th May, 1812—died, November, 1845) and grandson of Sir Charles Matthew Goring, 2nd Vis., 5th Bart., through his second wife, Elizabeth, sister and co-heiress of Sir Robert Fagge, Bart., of Wiston. Born July, 1817. Married, 19th September, 1849, Juliana Mary Caroline, daughter of Sir Willoughby Woolston Dixie, Bart., of Market Bosworth, co. Leicester. Mr. Charles Goring succeeded his cousin, Sir Harry Dent Goring, as Member for Shoreham, July, 1841, defeating Lord Edward Howard, the poll at that Election being : Sir Charles Merrik Burrell (C), 959 ; Charles Goring, Esq. (C), 856 ; Lord Edward Howard (L), 673.

Politically, Mr. Charles Goring was a Conservative and Protectionist. In August, 1847 (11 Victoria) Sir Charles Merrik Burrell and Charles Goring, Esq., were returned without opposition, both being described as " Peelites." Mr. Goring died 17th November, 1849. His large estates were inherited by his

SIR CHARLES MERRIK BURRELL

brother the (late) Rev. John Goring, of Wiston. His widow married secondly, Henry Townshend Boultbee, Esq., of Springfield, co. Warwick.

28 Dec.—1849, Lord Alexander Francis Charles Gordon-Lennox (vice Charles Goring, Esq., deceased).
16 Victoria   1852   Sir C. M. Burrell.   Lord A. F. C. Gordon-Lennox.
20   ,,   1857   ,,   ,,

Alexander Francis Charles Gordon-Lennox. Commonly called Lord Alexander Lennox. Fourth son of Charles, 5th Duke, of Richmond, K.G., by his wife, Lady Caroline Paget, eldest daughter of Henry William, 1st Marquis of Anglesey. Born 14th June, 1825. Entered the Royal Horse Guards in 1842, and became Captain, 1847. M.P. for New Shoreham, 1849-59. Married 6th August, 1863, Emily Frances, second daughter and co-heiress of the late Col. Towneley, of Towneley, Lancashire, and had issue, a son, born 17th August, 1868. Died January, 1892, at his residence in Pont Street, after a protracted illness and buried 26th January, 1892, in the Roman Catholic Cemetery of the Church of St. Thomas of Canterbury, at Fulham.

22 Victoria   1859   Sir C. M. Burrell.   Stephen Cave, Esq.

Sir Charles Merrik Burrell, 3rd Bart. Eldest son of Sir William Burrell, Bart., L.L.D., F.R.S., and S.A., M.P., by his wife, Sophia, daughter and co-heiress of Sir Charles Raymond, Bart., of Valentine House, Essex. (Mr. Raymond, the father-in-law of Dr. Burrell, was created a Baronet 3rd May, 1774, with remainder to his son-in-law, who became in consequence at the decease of Sir Charles Raymond, Sir William Burrell, 2nd Baronet). Sir Charles Merrik was born in 1774 and married, 8th May, 1808, Frances O'Brien, sister of the first Lord Leconfield, and by her had issue—Charles Wyndham (died 1827), Percy, 4th Bart., Walter Wyndham, 5th Bart., and Caroline Julia.

Sir Charles Merrik built Knepp Castle on the estate purchased by his grandfather, Sir Charles Raymond for £18,900 and left by him to his daughters—Sophia, Lady Burrell, and Juliana Boulton. Sir C. M. Burrell bought the Boulton moiety and became possessed of the whole. He had a house in Richmond Terrace which gave occasion to a famous trial in 1833. He contended that as it was on the site of the old Palace of Whitehall, it was not liable to the poor rate of St. Margaret's, Westminster.

THE STORY OF SHOREHAM

The trial involved antiquarian evidence of a most interesting nature. "The Beadle" won the day.

Sir Charles Merrik Burrell was M.P. for New Shoreham in sixteen consecutive Parliaments, being first elected 46 George III. (1806) and at his death in 1862, was "Father of the House." His portrait was painted by R. Reinagle, R.A., and engraved. Sir Charles died 4th January, 1862. Lady Burrell died 28th September, 1848.

5 Feb.—1862, Sir Percy Burrell, Bart. (*vice* Sir C. M. Burrell, Bart., deceased).
28 Victoria   1865   Stephen Cave, Esq.   Sir Percy Burrell, Bt.
16 July—1866, Stephen Cave, Esq., re-elected.
32 Victoria   1868   Stephen Cave, Esq.,   Sir Percy Burrell.
37   „   1874   Sir Percy Burrell.   Stephen Cave, Esq.

Sir Percy Burrell, 4th Bart. Second son of Sir Charles Merrik Burrell, 3rd Bart., M.P. Born, 1812. Educated at Westminster, and Christ Church, Oxford. Married 26th August, 1856, Henrietta Catherine, daughter of the late Vice-Admiral Sir George Brooke Pechell, M.P. for Brighton. Succeeded to the Baronetcy on the death of his father in 1862. He was a J.P. for Sussex and patron of three Church livings. Died s.p. 19th July, 1876, and was succeeded in the title by his brother Walter Wyndham.

13 March.—1874, Stephen Cave, Esq., re-elected.

Sir Stephen Cave. Eldest son of Daniel Cave, of Cleve Hill, near Bristol, by his marriage on 15th April, 1820, with Frances, only daughter of Henry Locock, M.D., of London. Born at Clifton, 28th December, 1820, and educated at Harrow and Balliol College, Oxon., where he graduated B.A., 1843, and M.A., 1846. Called to the Bar of the Inner Temple 20th November, 1846. On 29th April, 1859, he entered Parliament in the Conservative interest for Shoreham and retained his seat for that constituency to 24th March, 1880. Sworn a member of the Privy Council, 10th July, 1866. Served as Paymaster-General and Vice-President of the Board of Trade from that date to December, 1868. In 1866 appointed Chief Commissioner for negotiating a fishery convention in Paris. As Judge Advocate and Paymaster-General he acted from 25th February, 1874 to November, 1875, and from that date to 24th March, 1880, as Paymaster-General only. In December, 1875, sent on a special mission to Egypt, charged by Lord Beaconsfield to report on the financial condition

SIR WALTER WYNDHAM BURRELL

of that country. Returned in March, 1876, and was nominated G.C.B., 20th April, 1880. Fellow of the Society of Antiquaries, of the Zoological Society and of other learned Societies. Chairman of the West India Committee and a Director of the Bank of England and the London Dock Company. Married 7th September, 1852, Emma Jane, eldest daughter of the Rev. William Smyth of Ellington Hall, Lincolnshire. He died at Chambery, Savoy, 6th June, 1880

5 Aug.—1876, Sir Walter Wyndham Burrell, Bart. (*vice* Sir Percy Burrell, Bart., deceased).
43 Victoria 1880 Sir Walter Wyndham Burrell. Robert Loder, Esq.

This was the last Election for New Shoreham, as by the Reform Bill of 1885 the Borough was disfranchised after returning Members to Parliament for 590 years.

Sir Walter Wyndham Burrell, 5th Bart., was the third son of Sir Charles Merrik Burrell, 3rd Bart., M.P. Born 26th October, 1814. Married, 10th June, 1847, Dorothea, daughter of the Rev. John A. Jones, late Rector of Burly-on-the-Hill, co. Rutland, and had issue. Succeeded his brother, Sir Percy, as 5th Bart., 19th July, 1876.

Sir Walter Wyndham Burrell was called to the Bar at Lincoln's Inn, 1840, was a J.P., for Sussex and served the office of High Sheriff in 1871. In 1877, on the resignation through ill-health of Lord Pelham, Sir Walter was chosen to succeed him as Provincial Grand Master of Freemasons for the Province of Sussex, a post which he held till his death. Elected M.P. for New Shoreham, July, 1876, at the Bye-Election occasioned by the death of his brother Sir Percy, and again 43 Victoria, 1880 (the last Parliament to which Members were sent from Shoreham). Sir Walter retained his seat till 1885, when the Borough was disfranchised under the Redistribution of Seats Act. The name of Burrell had appeared as Member for Shoreham for a period of 79 years, the third, fourth and fifth baronets having in succession sat for the Borough.

Sir Walter died at West Grinstead Park, 24th January, 1886. He was succeeded in the Baronetcy by his eldest son, Charles Raymond, 6th Baronet. He also left one other son and four daughters. Sir Charles Raymond Burrell died 6th September, 1899.

THE STORY OF SHOREHAM

Knepp Castle, the family seat of the Burrells, was destroyed by fire in January, 1904. The large and valuable library, many priceless manuscripts, and nearly the whole of the collection of pictures—several by old masters and including some by Holbein—perished in the flames. The Castle was afterwards re-built.

Sir Robert Loder, Bart , J.P., D.L. Born 7th August, 1823. Married (1847) Maria Georgiana, fourth daughter of Hans Busk and grand-daughter of Sir Hans Busk. High Sheriff, 1877. Elected M.P. for New Shoreham, 1880. Created a baronet 27th July, 1887. Died at Beach House, Worthing, 27th May, 1888. Succeeded by his eldest son, Sir Edmund Giles Loder, 2nd Bart., of Leonardslee, Horsham, who died 14th April, 1920. Sir Edmund's only son was killed in the Great War, and the title therefore passed to his grandson, a child of six years of age.

Sir Robert Loder's fifth son, Gerald Walter Erskine Loder, Esq., represented Brighton in the Conservative interest from 1889 till 1905.

CHAPTER XV.

COACHING DAYS—THE CARRIER AND HIS CART—OPENING OF THE RAILWAY—SHOREHAM IN THE 'FIFTIES—THE SWISS GARDENS—SOME OLD CUSTOMS.

LESS than two hundred years ago, a journey to London or any distant city was a slow and painful process, especially in winter time, when the roads were almost impassable, and going, to say the least of it, was "heavy." It is on record that the Shoreham to London coach, "frequently made use of a pair of oxen to drag it over some of the worst stretches of the road."

According to an advertisement which appeared in the *Times* of August 22nd, 1793, a coach left London for Shoreham twice a week, and there was a coach from Bath and Bristol every day.

In the year 1800, the Bath, Bristol, Chichester and Portsmouth Post Coach set out from the Old Ship, Brighton, every Tuesday, Thursday and Saturday morning at 8 o'clock, passing through Shoreham, Arundel, Southampton, Salisbury, &c., and returned on Mondays, Wednesdays and Fridays. At this time and subsequently, the Shoreham Mail, though made up at Brighton—every evening before 7 o'clock, did not "set out" till early the next morning, with letters for Shoreham and Worthing; but in 1805, it "set out" from Brighton, "after the arrival of the London Mail."

About the year 1815 an accident at the Sussex Pad, by which a gentleman lost his life, was solely attributable to the racing of two coaches. One of the coachmen admitted at the inquest that he had received orders "to get in first, though he should lose a horse."

The great snowstorm of Christmas, 1836, sadly interfered with coaching. The Gloucester Mail, instead of reaching Brighton on Sunday, was not heard of until after noon on Monday, and then could get no further than Shoreham, the bags being sent on by the Worthing Mail Cart.

Both the Fountain and Star Inns were well-known posting houses. In the 'fifties the Star was conducted by George Cross, a survivor of the old coaching days. He had been a coachman,

THE STORY OF SHOREHAM

"and looked it, every inch." He might have sat for the portrait of Tony Weller, and in his dogmatic fashion of letting all outsiders realise their hopeless ignorance of horseflesh and the art of driving, was looked up to as a species of man who "knew everything."

During the early years of the nineteenth century, the "Shoreham Cart" was the only public means of conveying goods between Shoreham and Brighton. Its owner and driver

HIGH ST. SHOREHAM.
EAST END. (From Sketch made Sept. 1897.)

was John Moorey, who sometimes carried a passenger or two in his vehicle. He "set out" every morning from Shoreham at nine, reaching the King's Head in West Street, Brighton, at twelve, and leaving again for Shoreham at three, "in weather foul or fine."

A somewhat remarkable man in his day and generation, old John Moorey combined with the business of country carrier the art of quackery, and his cures of ague, colic, dyspepsia, lumbago and tic, are said to have been most wonderful. "Nurses and grandams," we are told, "knew full well he could concoct most wholesome."

A local rhyme credits him with extensive knowledge and peculiar gifts, including prophecy and second sight, but like all prophets, he found some who lacked faith in his powers.

Doubtless a good sort of fellow, John took the world as he found it. He was fond of his glass of grog, and so after the day's work was done, having fed his horse and put his cart in the shed, he would repair in the evening to the Star, and, from the comfortable settle's snug embrace and before a blazing fire, hold forth to those "who did believe." Amongst the assembled company on these occasions, the rhyme informs us that :—

> There was Harry Hather and "Canab"
> "Calibogus" and Tom Puzzy,
> Caleb Burrows and "Old Slab,"
> With others quite as muzzy.
>
> Still, there were many, most profound—
> Such as the sexton and the crier—
> Who looked with solemn gestures, round,
> Their souls being all on fire.
>
> While John described the sights he saw
> As he did drive along ;
> Which quickly struck these friends with awe
> Whom he did mix among.
>
> Strange sights on earth, strange sights at sea,
> And stranger still in sky ;
> Which unto him did oft appear,
> And sometimes very nigh.
>
> I do remember well, a tale
> John Moorey once did tell
> Of scores of ships all in full sail
> That in the clouds did dwell.
>
> And which he saw so wondrous clear
> As he did pass "Bo-peep,"
> With smoke of guns, and as it were
> Ships sinking in the deep.
>
> Then John, said he, "a battle's fought
> By Nelson on the sea,
> Some ships he sunk, and some he caught,
> And some from him did flee."

THE STORY OF SHOREHAM

And true as he did then declare,
Brave Nelson on the Main
That very day at Trafalgar
A great victory did gain.

Prophets, they say, are not believed
In their own time and place,
And p'raps we cannot well expect
An exception in this case.

But this one fact of many, that
Foretold by this old man
Was just as I do now relate,
Deny it if you can.

We fear that John's claims to prophecy, rest on too slight a foundation to be taken seriously. We do not find on record that he foretold the aeroplane, which is so familiar to those of a later generation, but it is, perhaps, too much to expect a "prophet" to foretell events a hundred years ahead of his own day.

The rhyme from which these extracts are taken is dated Shoreham, Roast Goose Day, 1849, and is written on the back of an oil painting on wood (in the possession of Mr. Ellman Brown), from which the sketch has been made. Old Moorey was not living in 1849, but the rhyme refers to his daughter Alice, then living, who "tho' no prophetess," was "a living chronicle of all that's past and gone, just as her father could tell of all that was to come!" She was wont to recount stories of several local celebrities, such as Molly Lawn, a reputed witch, "Single-brains," and Phoebe Hessell.

The last-named was certainly a remarkable character and lived many years in Brighton and Shoreham. She served in the Army as a private soldier and was wounded at the battle of Fontenoy, which led her to confess the fact that she had entered

The Carrier.

OPENING OF THE RAILWAY

the Army as a means of getting abroad to search for her lover. George IV. allowed her a pension during the latter part of her life, and she died at Brighton, 12th December, 1821, aged 108.

The spot referred to as "Bo-peep," where John Moorey is said to have had his remarkable vision of the Battle of Trafalgar, "the very day it was fought," was a romantic public house standing under the cliff, half a mile westward of Copperas Gap. It was a noted spot for smuggling. Along the shore near it, the fishermen were often at night, as they asserted, disturbed by the ghost of a Dutchman, crossing and recrossing their track and at such times no fish could be caught.

As early as February, 1825, a "Brighton and Shoreham Railway" was projected, and though much favoured by the land-owners of the district, it was not destined to be carried out; nevertheless it is interesting to notice that the first portion of the London, Brighton, and South Coast Railway Company's system opened for traffic, was that running between Brighton and Shoreham, the event taking place on Monday, May 11th, 1840. A very large number of spectators assembled to watch the departure of the first train for Shoreham, which left Brighton Station about 3 o'clock in the afternoon, to the strains of the Lancers' Band and the cheers of the spectators, to the majority of whom that railway train was a "new sensation."

The trip to Shoreham occupied 11½ minutes only, the return taking a trifle longer. The train continued running throughout the afternoon and the scene down the whole of the line was exceedingly animated, crowds of persons assembling at the different points to witness its passing. "Business" commenced next morning at 8 o'clock from Shoreham, the train returning from Brighton at 9. During the day 1,750 passengers were carried, not a few visiting the Swiss Gardens, where the opening of the Railway was celebrated by a Grand Fete.

The first Time Table issued by the Company advertised six trains each way on week-days. The first left Brighton at 9 a.m., returning from Shoreham at 10 and the last at 7 p.m., returning at 8 p.m. On Sundays there were five trains each way, the first leaving and returning at the same time as on week-days, but the last an hour later. The fares were, First class, 1s., Second, 9d., and Third, 6d. In the coupé of the First class carriages, 1s. 4d. The trains stopped at intermediate stations to take up and set down passengers.

THE STORY OF SHOREHAM

Business went along pleasantly for the remainder of the week, and day after day hundreds embraced the opportunity and novelty of a railway ride. On the Sunday evening, however, a fatal accident occurred. A young man who was incautiously sitting on the tail board of a luggage waggon, which had been temporarily used to accommodate the extra traffic at Shoreham, was, at Southwick, precipitated by a sudden jerk beneath the train and killed on the spot.

The late Mr. John George Bishop, at one time a resident of Shoreham and for many years proprietor of the *Brighton Herald*, in his "A Peep into the Past, or Brighton in the Olden Time," contrasts the conditions of modern railway travelling with those prevailing in 1840. " The Third class carriages were of the poorest description, being little better than cattle trucks. They were wholly uncovered and some had not even the accommodation of seats, the divisions of the sections in each carriage being simply an iron rail. The dust and smoke from the engine were annoying in the extreme, but worse than these was the almost constant descent of fine ashes ! Umbrellas were in frequent requisition to protect the eyes and to avoid the chance of a burn." With a good sou'-wester blowing and a driving rain, even the short journey between Brighton and Shoreham could scarcely have been a pleasant experience. " Later on, covered carriages were introduced, but even these were, at first, without windows ! Such luxuries are modern improvements, while the introduction of cushions in Third class carriages is well within the memory of the present generation."

To extend the Shoreham branch to Worthing it was necessary to carry the railway over the river Adur and this was accomplished by means of a trestle bridge approached by a viaduct. On November 24th, 1845, Worthing received its first railway passengers, and Chichester on June 8th, 1846. The junction from Shoreham to Partridge Green was opened 1st July, and the extension to Horsham 16th September, 1861.

The original trestle bridge over the Adur becoming unsafe, was replaced about a quarter of a century ago, by the present steel bridge designed by Sir John Aird. The supporting cylinders are filled with concrete and some of them find a firm footing 70 feet in the river-bed. With this fact in mind, it is surprising that the former bridge of wood had served its purpose for so many years. The Railway Station has been once rebuilt. Many will recall to mind its predecessor with the old "box-like" waiting room on the down-side, out of which one went up a flight of steps on to the platform.

Trams formerly ran between Shoreham and Hove. The rails were laid and it was opened in the early 'eighties, the cars being drawn by steam-engines. They ran from the Hove Borough boundary by way of New Church Road, through Portslade, Southwick and Kingston, thence along Ham Road and Western Road to Southdown Road. We have said "ran," but it is probable that no self-respecting traction engine ever "snailed" it like the Shoreham steam tram. Moreover, it had a decided propensity for running off the line at every possible opportunity, and few were the occasions when it kept to the rails in turning "Pennifold's Corner," in its painful endeavours to get into Western Road.

The journey was afterwards curtailed to terminate at the end of Ham Road, and eventually, engines being so unsatisfactory, horses took their place. These cars ceased running about eight years ago and the rails have since been removed.

When a traveller, returning after a fifty years' absence in the Australian Colonies, revisited Shoreham in 1901, he found the town "for all practical purposes" much in the same condition as he had known it in the 'forties, "only, perhaps, a trifle more drowsy." In the main street few shops appeared to have been altered, though most of the shop-keepers had long been at rest in the shadow of the glorious old church. He recalled the old familiar names of Gates the butcher, Adams the baker, Battcock the draper, Bradley the grocer, and Hore the chemist. He missed the little general shop where you could buy fruit, coals, cakes, malt liquor, snuff, and hardbake, while the sign outside the shop informed the passer-by :—

> Here he lives, Old uncle Nat,
> Try his oysters fresh and fat;
> Full-roed herrings ready to burst,
> Table beer to quench your thirst.

Corbett, the clerk and sexton of the church, is remembered as "a short squat man with wavy grey hair flowing over his shoulders in silver ripples." A man who could say "Amen" at the end of the prayers with unction and emphasis. Another local celebrity was a man who hawked crabs at 4d. each, and hares

THE STORY OF SHOREHAM

"below their market value." Mr. Gates, Comptroller of Customs, "lived in a house of unbroken flint (St. John's) in a street nearly opposite the Custom House."

"In the winter time there was not much in the way of public amusements, but the big room at the Bridge Inn (Mechen's) was occasionally used by companies of strolling-players." There Herman Vezin once appeared in a piece called "Clari." He was then unknown to the annals of histrionic fame and his costume was of the "make-shift" order.

Tom Sayers, the noted pugilist, sometimes trained at the Royal Sovereign in Middle Street, and was seen about the town with the words, "Champion of England" on his belt.

The celebrated Swiss Gardens, established in 1838 by James Britton Balley, the ship-builder, retained their popularity as a pleasure resort for more than fifty years. The amusements included bowls and archery, a well-appointed theatre, a refreshment room for 1,000 persons, a "magic cave," and an ornamental lake. The ball-room—in its day possibly the finest on the South Coast—had a length of 150 ft. and a breadth of 54 ft. Here a former generation of Shoreham and Brighton people were wont to trip it right merrily, celebrating the successful launch of a new-built ship, or as a suitable wind-up to Regatta Day. The ornamental gardens were tastefully laid out and well kept, and some peacocks added not a little to the beauty of the place. Balloon ascents and firework displays were frequent.

Many people retain pleasant memories of these gardens in what may be termed their "palmy days." This was at the time that they were owned by Mr. Edward Goodchild and admirably managed, and thousands from far and near came to Shoreham for "a day at the gardens." In those days they were also considered a part of the social life of the town, and it was the usual fashion to meet friends and take tea with them, in one of the delightful arbours which were to be found there. The evening performance in the theatre followed and then the dance in the ball-room.

But the pleasures of one generation are not the pleasures of the next. The popularity of this resort began to wane. It became in time the favourite haunt of a somewhat rough element, and it was then considered "not quite correct" to go there. At length the gardens were closed, but occasionally performances were given by local amateurs in the theatre, which was also

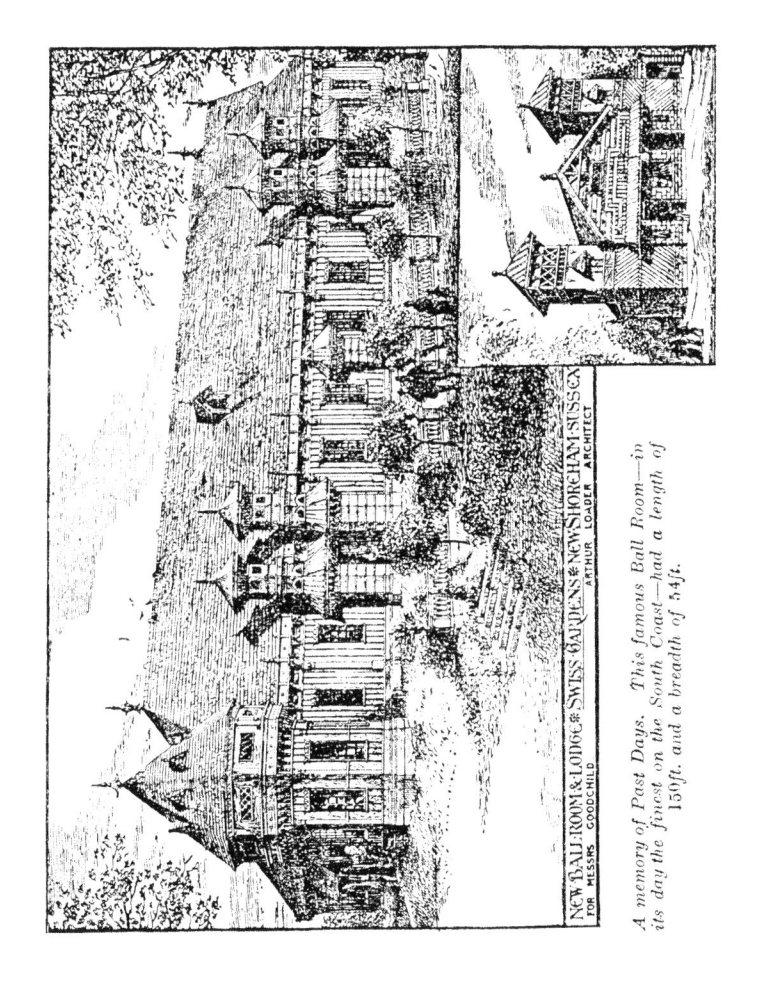

NEW BALL-ROOM & LODGE & SWISS GARDENS & NEW SHOREHAM SUSSEX
FOR MESSRS GOODCHILD   ARTHUR LOADER ARCHITECT

A memory of Past Days. This famous Ball Room—in its day the finest on the South Coast—had a length of 159ft. and a breadth of 54ft.

THE STORY OF SHOREHAM

occasionally opened for concerts and entertainments, such as those given by the "Adur Minstrels," a sometime flourishing company of Shoreham gentlemen, much addicted to the practice of "blacking up," after the manner of the Mowhawk Minstrels. "But they, I hear," says a local poet, "have washed themselves and so have ceased to be."

And then came the days when the gardens were entirely closed to the public. Nature alone held sway there and had her own way with them, and a beautiful way it was, too. Surely, never in former times, when so carefully tended by expert gardeners, had they appeared so lovely. A veritable wild garden. So the place remained until a part was acquired for building the New Council School. This stands nearly on the site of the ball-room, of which, and the entrance to the gardens, we give illustrations reproduced from the late Mr. Arthur Loader's architectural drawings.

The first Shoreham Regatta was held in 1854 and was an annual fixture up to the outbreak of the War, during the continuance of which it remained in abeyance. It was resumed with all its former vitality in 1919. Always an event of great local interest, it was formerly the custom to wind up the day with a ball at the Swiss Gardens. In more recent times, illuminated boats on the river, street processions, and carnivals, have formed a fitting termination to the day's proceedings. The late Mr. John Ellman Brown was the first Honorary Secretary of Shoreham Regatta. It may be mentioned that the same gentleman was an enthusiastic archaeologist and took much interest in the history of the town. He was Vice-Consul to five nations, and for many years, held the office of Clerk to the Local Governing Body, a position now held by his son, Mr. Harold Brown. Altogether the period served in this office by father and son, extends to nearly fifty years.

Guy Fawkes Day was formerly celebrated with much spirit, and sometimes with a certain amount of rowdyism. Years ago the bonfires were lighted in the High Street, and many a tradesman in those days—especially if he had the misfortune to be unpopular —would find his shop minus its shutters, which had been carried off to feed the flames. On one occasion at least, the church-yard gates suffered a like fate, for the "boys" burnt up anything they could lay their hands upon. The celebrations of later years were happily free from this sort of thing, and although much liveliness entered into the proceedings, they were but splendid opportunities for the processions of Bonfire Boys in all manner of fantastic costumes, the rolling of blazing tar barrels, the display of fireworks, and the concluding bonfire on the "Ham." It is a good many years since the "fifth" was properly celebrated in Shoreham.

The "Tipteerers" are never seen in Shoreham in these days. Like many another old and somewhat picturesque custom, it has fallen into disuse and is almost forgotten. The "Tipteerers" flourished at Christmastide. They were usually a party of about six men, dressed in costumes to represent various characters, such as Old Father Christmas, a Noble Captain, St. George (sometimes "King George"), a Turkish Knight, a Valiant Soldier, a Prince Feather-in-hand, and a Doctor. They acted a curious mumming play, which may possibly have had its origin in the miracle play, "St. George and the Dragon," well known in the fourteenth and fifteenth centuries. The practice of "Tipteering" was not, of course, peculiar to this town, but flourished elsewhere in the county, especially in West Sussex, where it is even yet not quite a thing of the past. Some of the actors who were wont to take part in this diversion at Shoreham are still living, but the custom has not been observed in the town for the last forty years or more.

During the afternoon and evening of Boxing Day, Father Christmas would visit the houses of rich and poor. Entering, he addressed the inmates in doggerel rhyme, somewhat after the following fashion :—

"In comes I, Old Father Christmas,
Welcome in or welcome not ;
And I hope that I, Old Father Christmas
Will never be forgot."

He then introduced his characters. "King George" entering, boasted of his prowess and challenged all brave warriors to fight His challenge having been accepted by the Turkish Knight, a vigorous fight ensued between the two champions, in which "King George" was usually victorious, his opponent falling grievously wounded. Sometimes "King George" was defeated, but fighting again, he vanquished his rival. The Doctor was then hastily summoned, who, arriving on the scene, administered a wonderful pill which revived the prostrate foeman.

THE STORY OF SHOREHAM

Topical allusions were often introduced, and an "Indian Mutiny" version was much in favour at Shoreham about the middle of the last century. At the close of the play, the company in turn sang modern ditties, after which the actors were invited to partake of Christmas cheer.

There was formerly at the "Red Lion," Old Shoreham, a custom called "the Bushel," which was observed on New Year's Day. A bushel corn measure decorated with flowers, leaves, and green paper, was filled with beer, which, frothing up, made it appear like a huge cauliflower. From this all comers might drink free. The beer was ladled out with a pint mug and drunk from glasses. There was a regular chairman, and the man who ladled out the liquor was called "the baler," and the latter had the privilege of drinking from the measure itself. How far back this custom dated is uncertain, but it was duly observed on January 1st, 1883, and it was then known to go back to the beginning of the century.

Martin Richard Cobbett, in "Wayfaring Notions," mentions "good Mrs. Cuddington at the little Inn facing Old Shoreham Bridge." He says:—"I always pay that road-side hostelry a visit out of respect for the proprietor and better half; also to show friends the massive wood tables a former village blacksmith used to raise to the ceiling—a low one mind—with his brawny arms. The said arm's muscles must have been strong as iron bands if he performed the feat, as tradition asserts, with a palm under each."

The faint echo of a former custom, is to be heard in the name still sometimes given to the hill, whose steep sides slope to the river valley at Old Shoreham. It was to "Good Friday Hill" on the afternoon of that day, in years gone by, that the school children and others, marched in procession to take part in various games and amusements. Hard-boiled eggs, dyed various colours, such as yellow, violet and pink, were much in evidence at this time and may have been a survival of the "Pace eggs" once so universal at Eastertide. These eggs, and also oranges, were rolled like bowls, down the steep sides of "Good Friday Hill."

In dealing with sport it behoves the present writer to tread warily. He knows little of Football and less of Cricket, but both these games flourish at Shoreham.

By the courtesy of "Leather Hunter," of the *Sussex Daily News*, the copy of the original card of admission to a Cricket Match played at Old Shoreham in the 'fifties, is appended:—

CRICKET AND FOOTBALL

Old Shoreham Cricket Ground.
Gentlemen v. Players of Sussex.
On Thursday and Friday, June 17 and 18, 1858.
For the Benefit of the Players.
Admission Ticket for the Two Days—One Shilling.

Much might be written of present day sport. The Shoreham Cricket Club flourishes under the presidency of Major G. F. Sexton, of "Tipperary." The liberal response of that gentleman to all that concerns local sport and the social life of the town, is greatly appreciated, but above all, his kindly and practical interest on behalf of "demobbed" soldiers is well known. A "Comrades of the Great War" Cricket Club, is in course of formation.

Local Football does not arouse quite the same enthusiasm as in by-gone years,—when some notable matches were played in the Oxen Field.—Possibly because so many now find their way to the Goldstone Ground at Hove. The town numbers among her sons, Albert Edward Longstaff, one of the most clever and popular players in the Brighton and Hove Albion team.

Indoor recreations include a Social Club held at St. Mary's Hall, there is a Beach Club at Bungalow Town, and the Sussex County Aero Club at New Salts. There are three popular Picture Houses, the Coliseum, the Bijou, and the Star.

An Ex-Service Men's Club has recently been erected at Old Shoreham, and was opened on the 19th July, 1921, by His Royal Highness, the Duke of Connaught.

The Masonic Lodge of St. Mary de Haura, holds its meetings at the Town Hall. The Dolphin Lodge, meeting at the Inn of that name from 1766 to 1773, is the earliest record of Freemasonry in the town. The Harmony Lodge of Freemasons established first at Chichester in 1790, was removed to the Fountain Inn, Shoreham, in 1800, and became extinct in 1832. The Burrell Lodge, named after the Provincial Grand Master of Sussex, the late Sir Walter Wyndham Burrell, Bart., M.P. for Shoreham, was consecrated at the Old Town Hall, East Street, Shoreham, in 1879. It was subsequently moved to the Royal Pavilion, Brighton, and still meets there.

CHAPTER XVI.

AVIATION—THE MILITARY CAMP—MEMORIALS TO THE FALLEN.

THE first "flying machine" to arrive in the town attracted a great deal of attention. It was in quite the early days of the science of aviation, and attempts to fly excited the keenest interest.

To Mr. H. H. Piffard, an old Lancing College Boy, belongs the honour of being the first to experiment, in the spring of 1910, with an aeroplane at the Shoreham Aerodrome.

It is a study in evolution to compare the splendid flights and the high altitude reached by the machines of to-day, with the modest achievements of the first "flying machine" at Shoreham.

This was a somewhat timid creature, and was at first familiarly known as the "Mayfly," probably from the fact that she seemed to prefer the safety of terra-firma rather than the uncertainty of an almost un-tried element. If the machine succeeded in "jumping" a brook it was looked upon as a wonderful performance. If such an astonishing feat as a rise of thirty feet into the air was accomplished in safety the excitement was intense and the onlookers waited with bated breath until the machine again alighted without mishap. But the "flying" of those days seemed to consist for the most part of "hopping" round the Aerodrome, and hence she was sometimes known as the "Grasshopper."

But rapid advances were made in the science and we have lived to witness such feats as looping-the-loop, diving, and other tricks and wonders too numerous to mention in detail.

On the 6th March, 1911, Mr. O. C. Morrison made a flight from Hove Lawns to Shoreham in seven minutes, and subsequently circled round Lancing College.

In June of the same year, when the "Flight across Europe" from Paris to London via Brussels took place, the competitors called at Shoreham.

The brothers Eric and Cecil Pashley must be reckoned among the pioneers of British Aviation. When Shoreham Aerodrome came definitely into being they set up a school of their own, where they taught several people, who turned out, ultimately, to be good pilots. They built a bi-plane of their own on the general lines of a Farman, and with it they became excellent, if somewhat

THE MILITARY CAMP

rash pilots. But their rashness consisted in playing tricks in the air which to-day would appear harmless enough, compared with the every-day acrobatics of service pilots during the War.

The Pashley School was going well and looked like becoming a success, when war broke out and the R.F.C. took possession of the Aerodrome and all thereon. The two brothers left Shoreham and eventually Cecil became senior instructor of the Grahame-White School. Eric went to Vickers' School at Joyce Green, where he became an exceedingly clever pilot of Vickers' gun-machines. In 1916 he was given a commission in the R.F.C. and soon turned out to be a first-class pilot. He was killed in action in France on Saturday, March 17th, 1917. During the comparatively short time he was in the R.F.C. he accounted for ten enemy machines and on two occasions rescued photographic machines from superior enemy attacks.

Several distressing and fatal accidents connected with aviation at Shoreham, before and during the War, are painfully fresh in the minds of most of us. In Old Shoreham Churchyard are the graves of gallant and fearless young men, who came from overseas to fight Old England's battle.

The Military Camp requires only a brief notice in these pages. Anything like a detailed account of all that happened during the period of its existence would fill many volumes, and although those years must ever be numbered as the most remarkable that the town has seen, we must confine ourselves to a few reminiscences.

During the second week of September, 1914, it was rumoured that a camp would be formed on Slonk Hill, but it was imagined that such would be similar to the Volunteer camps of previous years. Thus it was that the town was only very mildly interested in the few tents that were already pitched as the week-end approached. The War had only just begun and few people dreamed that it was to last a matter of years.

The startling developments which took place the next day threw all such calculations to the winds ; the camp was not to be the small affair of former peaceful years.

Who can forget that Saturday afternoon, when a train steamed into Shoreham bearing some hundreds of men—part of that great army which will ever be known as Kitchener's Boys. Train after train followed till far into the evening. In drenching rain thousands of men marched by way of Buckingham Road to the camp—a camp in name only, for there, all was in a state of chaos.

THE STORY OF SHOREHAM

Stores had gone astray, provisions were lacking and much hardship was experienced. The resources of the town were taxed to the uttermost for no chance had been given to prepare for this invasion.

The thousands who thronged the streets of Shoreham that night were hungry, cold and wet, but many of the townspeople extended a ready welcome to numbers of the men and gave them shelter for the night.

The following days witnessed the arrival of thousands more, and the daily routine of camp-life began in earnest, and with it there arose something of a holiday-making atmosphere, and our somewhat dull little town took on a new garb, as its streets were thronged with these light-hearted warriors in the making.

Those were the days when battalions of men marching through the High Street and over the Norfolk Bridge to take their morning or afternoon dip, would lustily sing "It's a long way to Tipperary," and "Who's your lady friend ?" or other popular song. Who, remembering what followed a year or two later, can look back on those fair autumn days of 1914 and remain unmoved ? In the eloquent words of Mrs. Humphrey Ward : "Before the inward eye rises the phantom host of these boys, part of that great army which sprang to England's aid in the first year of the War and whose graves lie scattered in an endless series along the Western Front and on the heights of Gallipoli. Without counting the cost for one moment, they came at the call of the Great Mother from near and far—these boys and their officers—boys like themselves, of nineteen or thereabouts—laughing, eager, undaunted, as quick to die as to live, carrying in their hands the fate of England."

Then followed the building of the hutments, during which time the camp was pitched in Buckingham Park and the Oxen Field, which became a tented plain. Meanwhile this immense influx of visitors was accompanied by a great increase in the trade of the town. Many new businesses made their appearance and such establishments as "Dimity Dining Rooms" and "Tasty Tea Rooms," springing up like mushrooms, catered well for the inner man.

During the winter of 1914-15, the soldiers were billeted upon the inhabitants of Worthing, Shoreham, Southwick, Portslade, and Brighton, returning to camp as the 24th Division when the huts were completed.

LETTERS FROM FRANCE

The Division left Shoreham in June, 1915, and marched to the neighbourhood of Blackdown, where they were stationed for some weeks before their final departure for the front.

Then came a time of suspense, the circulation of rumours of disaster to the 24th Division, which had been terribly "cut up," and all too soon came the tidings of this one and that one, who had gone under. Many, too, were reported missing. A sergeant, writing of one with whom he had formed a firm friendship during the period of training at Shoreham, said : "We slept together under a haystack the night before the battle. Our duties necessarily separated us when the fighting commenced and I have not seen or heard anything of him since," and, in a later letter, "I cannot hear anything of C. ; he is officially reported as missing." One of many—alas that it has to be written.

Another wrote of his experiences and related how he helped to "cart a dixie of stew to the trenches," and how, before this was safely accomplished, the firing commenced. "Shells dropped all round us and snipers, too, were at work," but the stew was taken to the trenches and, "while it was being dished out, fellows were strolling along the parapet as though they were walking down Buckingham Lane. Then the order to get out and attack. With full pack on we scrambled up, doubled away, and getting into line, the fellows went forward as though attacking Cissbury Ring or Lancing Clump. Not the slightest heed was paid to the hail of bullets absolutely raining upon us, but one saw the awful reality of it all when our chums fell beside us, either fatally struck or wounded, and only 73 of the 240 who went into action in this particular attack returned."

These letters from "somewhere in France" recall to memory the following lines which appeared in an issue of the London *Daily News* during the War :—

CHANCE MEMORIES.

I can't forget that lane that goes from Steyning to the Ring
In Summer time, and on the Downs how larks and linnets sing
High in the sun, the wind comes off the sea, and oh the air !
I never knew till now that life in old days was so fair.
But now I know it in this filthy rat-infested ditch,
When every shell must kill or spare and God alone knows which ;
And I am made a beast of prey, and this trench is my lair—
My God ! I never knew till now that those days were so fair.
And we assault in half an hour, and—it's a silly thing,
I can't forget the lane that goes from Steyning to the Ring.

PHILIP JOHNSON.

THE STORY OF SHOREHAM

With the arrival of the Derby Recruits the camp became again a scene of busy activity. Then came the Convalescents, both Imperial and Canadian, and part of the camp was taken over by the Canadian Government. Then the town assumed almost the appearance of a city in Scotland, so many of the Canadian soldiers being in the National dress of the Northern Kingdom.

A remarkable service was held in New Shoreham Church at the Jubilee of the Federation of the Dominion of Canada. The General Officer Commanding, attended by his staff, fifty officers and one hundred men, representing various units in camp drawn from all parts of Canada, were present. The Canadian Colours, battle-worn from the front, were borne in the opening procession and the Canadian National Anthem, " O Canada," sung by a congregation which overflowed to the Churchyard.

Their Majesties, King George and Queen Mary, visited Shoreham on the 3rd November, 1916. Though purely a military visit, on the arrival of the Royal train, a considerable number of the inhabitants of the town and neighbourhood, gave the King and Queen a hearty welcome as they entered a motor car and sped along Buckingham Road. The whole distance from the station to the camp was lined on either side by Canadian soldiers, standing at attention. At the Triangle Plantation, close to the entrance to Buckingham Park, the Royal car stopped and the Colonel in Command of the Canadian troops was presented to their Majesties. The King and Queen alighted at the entrance to the Steyning Union and visited part of the Infirmary reserved as a Military Hospital. The Royal Standard was flying at the camp and their Majesties walked up the hill to the Headquarters, from whence they watched a detachment of men go through physical exercises to the music of a band and in pouring rain. The weather left much to be desired. An inspection was made of the arrangements for the men's recreation, of the " Welcome Hut " and the Camp Church. The Queen took shelter in one of the Institute Rooms with her lady-in-waiting and attendants. The Royal visit terminated about 1.15.

His Majesty the King again visited Shoreham Camp 26th March, 1918. It was at a time when the outlook grew darker and ever darker. The submarines daily added to the awful toll of sunken ships. But " 'tis darkest before the dawn," and dawn came with that grey November morning when the bells

THEY DIED FOR ENGLAND

rang out their glad tidings of the Armistice. It seemed the fair promise of a New Era, the dawn of which, alas, is not yet.

But in Shoreham, as elsewhere, there was many a glad homecoming. The happy re-union of wife and husband, parents and sons, alas there were many desolate homes, in which there could be no rejoicing. Homes from whence lads in all the freshness and beauty of youth, or men of riper years, had gone forth to that tremendous struggle, and to which husband, father, son or brother returned not again.

> They are a part of England's splendid story,
> To fight for her, went forth, their all to give ;
> And on the fields of war, shell-torn and gory,
> Paid with their lives, the price, that she might live.
>
> They did not heed the joyful acclamation
> Nor hear the cheering when the fight was done ;
> No welcome home, no loving salutation ;
> Their lives had ended, ere their cause had won.
>
> Shoreham will hold their names in sacred keeping
> And generations yet unborn shall read ;
> They fought for Freedom, not for glory seeking
> And died for England in her hour of need.
>
> A. F. W. EADE.

The names of the men of Shoreham-by-Sea who laid down their lives in the Great War :—

THE MEMORIAL IN THE CHURCH OF ST. MARY.

Oswald F. G. Ball, 2nd Lieut. – George Banfield, Stoker – Albert Barnes, Pte. – Alfred E. Bingham, Gunr. – Frank W. Bish, Pte. – Herbert G. Bishop, Pte. – Benjamin R. Black, Pte. – Ernest Bunton, Lce.-Cpl. – Frederick Burstow, Cyclist – Cyril C. Carley, Pte. – A. Wesley Chambers, Sgt. – Henry V. Christmas, Signaller – Norris W. Clevett, Lce.-Cpl. – Victor J. H. Coles, Pte. – Thomas A. Coleman, Pte. – Cecil H. S. Collis, Signaller – George H. Cooke, Pte. – L. Davis – Frederick Dearing, 1st A.M. – Charles A. T. Dorey, Sgt. – Charles S. Dorey, Rfle. – Charles Dyer, Sapper – Percy Earthey, Pte. – Thomas F. R. English, Pte. – Henry E. Fairs, Lce.-Cpl. – George F. Felton, Pte. – John E. Gasston, 1st class Stoker – George W. Gearing, Leading Seaman – Frank L. Goodchild, Pte. – Bertram G. Green, Pte. – Douglas W. Green, Pte. – Brooking A. J. Harrison, Lce.-Cpl. – Garland B. Harrison, Pte. – George T. Hart, Pte. – James Henson, Lce.-Cpl. – Walter J. Hitchman, Sgt. – Albert V. A. Hooker, Rifleman – Gordon E. Hughes, Sgt. – Joseph Hunter, Pioneer –

THE STORY OF SHOREHAM

Cavendish Jarrett, Lce.-Cpl. – Jesse H. Kennard, Leading Seaman – William E. Kimmens, Pte. – F. Kingshott, Pte. – John E. Knight, Pte. – Ernest H. Knight, Pte. – Fred A. Laker, Sgt. – Albert Lee, Pte. – Albert Lind, Seaman – Charles N. Lind, 1st class Stoker – Thomas Lind, Pte. – Thomas C. Lind, Rifleman – William J. Lind, Pte. – Albert H. Maple, Pte. – Arthur Meachen, Pte. – Charles E. Merrix, Pte. – Charles H. R. Merrix, Pte. – James F. Mills, Pte. – James Moore, Gunr. – Ernest Morphew, Pte. – William G. Oliver, Pte. – William J. Page, Pte. – Wallice P. Parsons, Pte. – George H. Patching, Driver – William R. Peacock, Captain – William C. Player, Pte. – Herbert H. Portlock, Pte. – Percival Portlock, Lce.-Cpl. – John A. Puttock, Pte. – Charles G. Rapley, Cpl. – James A. Rouse, Pte. – William H. Rowe, Pte. – Percy Sampson, Pte. – Joseph Saunders, Farrier Q.M.S. – George A. R. Scott, Lce.-Cpl. – W. Scott, Pte. – Henry E. Sheaff, Gunr. – Frederick Simmonds, Pte. – Fred A. Simmonds, Pte. – Frederick Slater, Pte. – Charles R. Smart, Pte. – Alfred G. Snook, Gunr. – Harold Standen, Pte. – Alfred H. Standing, Pte. – Charles A. Still, Lce.-Cpl. – John Stoneham, Lce.-Cpl. – Philip Stoneham, Sgt. – Arthur R. Stoner, Chief Engineer – John H. Tanner, Lieut. – Reginald J. C. Tansley, Sgt. – David B. Taylor, Pte. – Charles S. Turrell, Pte. – Frank F. Turrell, Pte. – Fred Upton, Pte. – John J. Welch, Leading Stoker – Edward Welch, Bomb. – Charles Welch, Seaman – William A. Weller, Pte. – Douglas G. White, Pte. – Leonard G. White, Pte. – Arthur T. Willins, Pte. – Wallace E. Wimble, Sapper – Robert E. Winter, Pte. – John H. Woods, Sapper – Ernest W. Young, Pte.

THE MEMORIAL IN THE CHURCH OF ST. JULIAN, KINGSTON.

William V. Atherfold – Arthur H. Ayling – Trevor Howard Beves – Charles Binstead – Harry Corke – Henry E. Fewtrell – Gilbert Grune – Richard Howell – Victor Mercer – Valentine B. Oldhams – William Plummer – Thomas V. Skinner – George W. Strevens – Christopher Upton – Rowland Williams.

THE MEMORIAL AT THE CHURCH OF THE GOOD SHEPHERD.

Frank W. J. Harvey, Capt. – Basil Blogg, Major – Eric Oddling, Lieut. – Clement Smith, Cpl. – Percy Faulkner, Pte. – Ernest Squires, Pte. – William Nettlingham, Pte. – J. N. D. Keys, Capt. – Patrick Harter, Lieut. – Humphrey H. Grundtvig, Lieut. – Lionel Winnington Forde, Lieut. – Leonard R. Burrows, Lieut.

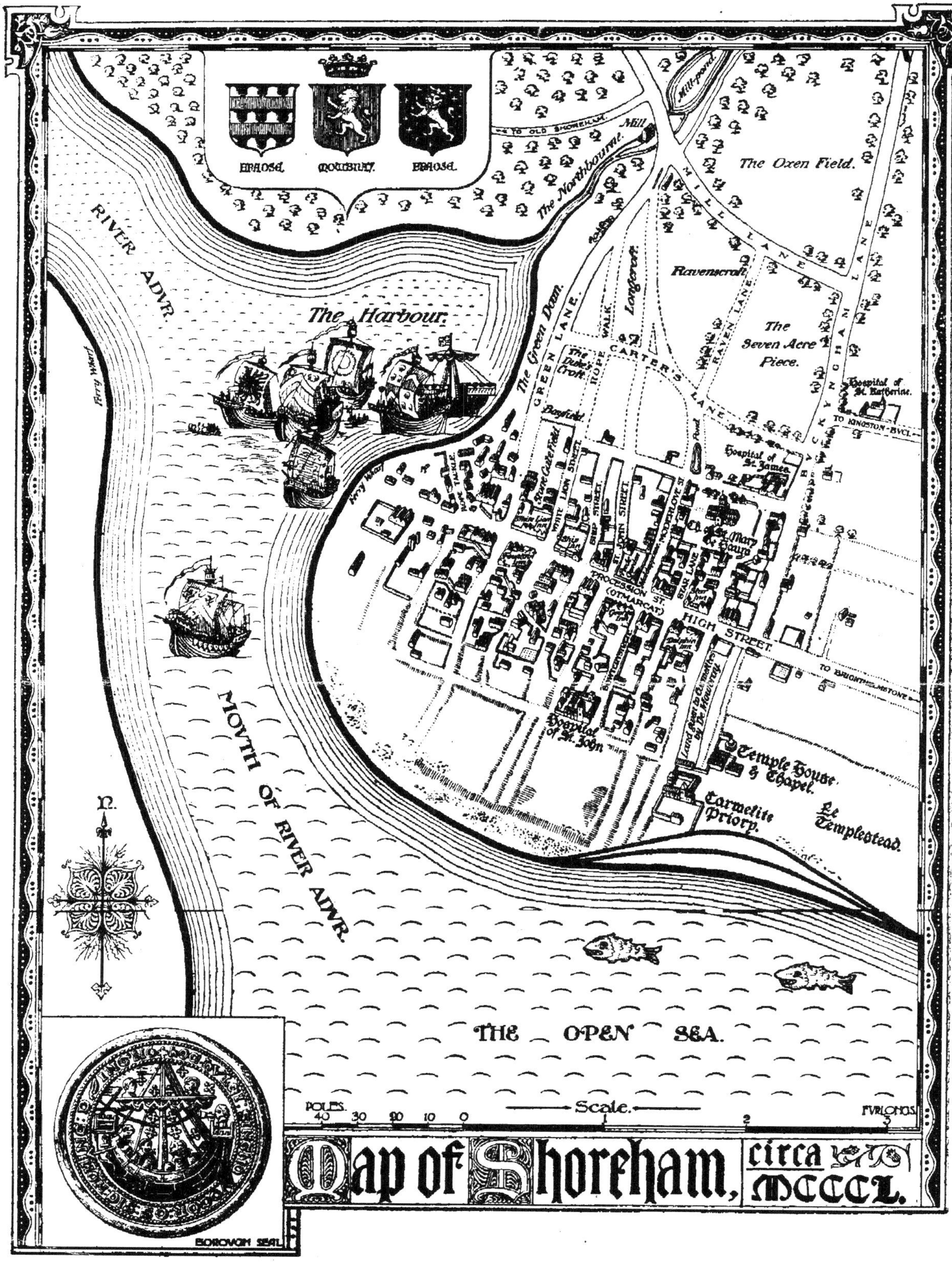
Map of Shoreham, circa MCCCL.
The Oxen Field.
The Seven Acre Piece.
Ravenscroft
Longcroft
The Duke's Croft
Bayfield
Stone Gate Field
Mill-pond
Mill
The Northbourne
The Green Dam.
GREEN LANE
ROPE WALK
CARTER'S LANE
RAVEN LANE
MILL LANE
KYNGHAM LANE
Hospital of St. Katherine.
TO KINGSTON-BVCI.
Hospital of St. James.
Pond
St. Mary de Haura
STAR LANE
MODERLOVE ST
ST. JOHN STREET
SHIP STREET
WHITE LION STREET
ROPE TACKLE
PROCESSION ST.
(OTMARCAT)
HIGH STREET.
TO BRIGHTHELMSTONE
Hospital of St. John
Land given to Carmelites by De Mowbray
Temple House & Chapel.
Carmelite Priory.
Le Templestead.
Ferry Wharf
The Harbour.
RIVER ADVR.
MOVTH OF RIVER ADVR.
THE OPEN SEA.
BRAOSE
MOWBRAY
BRAOSE
N.
Scale.
POLES 40 30 20 10 0
1 2
FVRLONGS 3
BOROVGH SEAL

INDEX

Aaron the Jew, 114-116
Abberbury, Richard de, 37
—— John de, 38
Absolon, Laurence, 112
Adberton, Edmund de, 103-5
Aethelwealh, King, 170
Adam, Thomas, 96
Adams, Rev. H. C., 198-9, 202
Adelaide, Queen, 179
Adrian, IV., 164
Adur Lodge, 39, 67
—— River, 5, 6, 12, 25, 81, 83, 88, 133, 157, 160, 205
—— Valley, 1, 2, 5, 9, 35, 42, 202
Adurni, Portus, 5, 6
Aerodrome, 258
Agnes de Veteri, Shoreham, 44
Aird, Sir John, 250
Alan the Blowere, 34
Alan the Younger, 118
Alcock, Mr., 131
Alder, 5
Aldridge, John, 212-3, 237
Aldrington, 5, 32, 33 129, 161
Aldersey, Abraham, 193
Alexander de Fortune, 118
Alford, Edward, 138
—— John, 222
Alfred, King, 10
Alisaundre, Robert, 121
Alleyn, Henry, 108
Alleyne, Prior, 16
Ambberbye, Thos., 36
Anchor Bottom, 44
Anderida, 6
Androeni, Peter, 119
Anne, Queen, 141
Annington, Charles, 77
Annyngdon, Ralph de, 49
Apineto, Berenger de, 84
—— Viel, 84
Apps, Joan, 135
Aquilon, Robert, 102
Arnold the Draper, 103
Arthur, Duke of Brittany, 122
Arthur, Prince, 117, 182
Arun, 25, 160
Arundel, 41, 225
Arundel, Earl of, 40
—— Nich., 129
—— Richard, E. of, 113
—— Thomas, E. of, 70, 74
—— John de, 38
—— John Bishop of Chichester, 16
—— Sir John, 70
—— William of, 83
Ashman and Turner, 155
Astodyllos, Diego de, 129
Aston, John, 152
Atte Gate, John, 127
Atte Hale, Phillip, 112
Attehalle, Thomas, 128
Atte Helde, William, 87

Atte Hurn, Richard, 112
Atte Hyde, Isabel, 51, 88
—— John, 51, 88
Atte Vanne, Thomas, 95
Atte Wode, Adam, 38
Atrebates, 4, 5
Audele, Hugh de, 37, 38,
Aune, William de, 118
Austen, Jane, 65
Aviation, 258-9
Avis, John, 191
—— Repentance 191
—— Robert 191
—— Sara, 191
—— Thomas, 191
—— William, 131, 191
Awood, Agnes, 171
—— Richard, 171
Ayling's, 75
Azor, 35

Babylon, 96
Bagge, Philip, 124
Bailiff, Walter, 207
Baker, John, 41, 212
—— Ralph le, 108
—— Robert le, 98
Bak, Simon, 124
Baldefare, Hugo, 110
Baldwin, Archbishop, 116
Balley, J. B., 156, 252
Bank House, 77
Barbe, Ellis, 121
—— Segwin, 121
Barbour, Richard le, 98
Barlynglyde, Nicholas, 111
Baron's Croft, 78
—— War, 120
Barrett, Nicholas, 151
Battle Abbey, 82
Baudefar, Isabel, 47
—— Joan, 47, 110-11
—— John, 47-48, 110-11
—— Richard, 44, 48
—— William, 47-48, 103-5
Bavent, Adam, 50, 56,
—— Roger, 50
Bayfield, 78
Beach Club, 257
Beauchamp, John, 83, 106
—— Matilda, 83
—— Roger, 207
Beaufz, Ralph, 89
—— Letitia, 89
Bedenye, 16
Beeding, 121
Beeding, Bostal, 62, 133
—— Bridge, 17
—— Hill, 7
—— Priory, 13
—— River, 5
Beedinges, John de, 103
Beeston, Hugh, 219

265

INDEX

Beicher, Godfrey le, 110
Bellingham, Ann, 53, 55
—— Edward, 52, 53, 55
—— Sir Edward, 53
—— Elizabeth, 52, 53, 55
—— Francis, 56
—— Sir Henry, 52
—— Jane 52, 56
—— Joan, 52
—— John, 53-55, 56
—— Mary, 53, 55, 56
—— Ralph, 52, 53
—— Richard, 52, 53, 55, 56
—— Sir Robert, 52
—— Thomas, 52, 53, 56
Benet, Agnes, 196
—— John, 196
Benjamin, Richard, 95-96
Bernard, John, 106, 126, 207
—— William, 63, 106
Bernehus, Agnes, 91
—— William, 91
Best, Thomas le, 108
Biddulph, Rev. Z. H., 198, 201, 214
Bishopp, Sir Cecil, 197-213-4, 237-8
Bisshop, Dionysia, 84
—— William, 84
Bishop, J. G., 250
Blake, William le, 112
Blaker, Ann, 65
—— Dorothy, 64, 65
—— Edward, M.P., 64, 65, 223, 226
—— Edward, senr., 64, 223
—— John le, 87
—— Susannah, 64
—— William, 65
Blechington, Robert de, 47, 48, 49, 195
—— Henry de, 108
Blisset, Anna, 177
Bohun, James de, 70
—— Joan de, 70
—— John de, 70
Bockyngham, Richard de, 63
—— Robert de, 63
Bolney, John, 89
Bolonia, Siward de, 84
Bond, Young, 127
Bonner, Richard, 200
Booth, General, 206
"Bo-Peep," 249
Borlee, John, 88, 89, 90
Borughersh, Isabel, 63
—— William, 63
Botiler, John le, 98
Botolphs, 5, 7, 9, 13
Bourbon, Duke of, 128
Bourne, Henry le, 105
Bowyer, Jane, 56
—— Thomas, 56
Bradbrege, John, 127
Bramber, 4, 5, 12, 13, 119, 121, 131, 133, 154
—— Bridge, 15-16, 30, 41, 62
—— Castle, 69-70, 103
—— Constable of, 111, 118
—— Rape, 2, 12, 35, 117
—— Water, 5, 16
Brand, Henry Bouverie, 234
Brand, Thomas, 233-4
Brantyngham, Thomas, 196

Brasur, Gervase le, 98
Brazour, German le, 98
Brembre, Thomas de, 196
Brench, Nicholas. 103
Brewer, German le, 98
Brewose, John de, 195
Bridger, Colville, 57, 66
—— Lieut.-Col., 67
—— Family, 63, 66, 67, 167
Bridge Inn, 252
Brighton, 34, 129, 130
Broadwater, 22, 41
Brodnax, Thomas, 66
Brom, Thomas de, 92
Bromlee, John, 89
Browne, George, 146
Brown, John E., 155, 254,
—— H., 254
Brus, Robert, le, 122
Brydham, Thomas, 88, 200
Brykles, William, 125
Buckingham, Duke of, 136-7
Buckingham, 63
—— Farm, 64
—— House, 62, 66, 67
—— Little, 29, 34, 44, 47, 67
—— Park, 29, 34, 260, 262
Buckyngham, John de, 63
—— Richard de, 63
Bulter, John le, 106
Bungalow Town, 25, 28, 79-81
Burgess, Isabel, 94
—— John, 128
—— Thomas, 151
—— Walter, 94
Burrell, Sir Charles M., 214, 240, 241-2
—— Sir Charles R., 243
—— Sir Percy, 241-3
—— Sir Walter, W., 241, 242-3, 257
—— Sir William, 57, 241
Burstall, Meadow, 88
Burton, Dr. (quoted), 41, 209
Butcher, John, 194
Butler, James, 212-3
—— Capt. John, 144
—— Robert (note), 144
Butts, 42

Cadwaladyr, 182
Caesar, 1-4
Calais, 100
—— Siege of, 124
Calceto Priory, 83
Caldwell, Gregory, 103
Camden (quoted), 23
Camp, Military, 259-62
Canal, 161
Canterbury, 121
—— Archbishop, 203
Cantrell, 129
—— William, 56
Carmelite Friars, 51
—— Priory, 25, 26, 27, 69, 86-88
Carrickfergus, 123
Cartere, Juliana, 95
—— Reginald, 95, 106-108
—— Richard, 95
Carver, Derick, 135
—— Mary, 135
—— Richard, 134-5

INDEX

Carver & Co., 154
Cave, Sir Stephen, 242-3
Castell, William, 150
Challen, John, 213
Chamberlayne, Francis, 232
—— Travies, 232
Chamond, Robert de, 103
—— William de, 99, 103
Champneys, Bert, 122
Chanceleur, Robert le, 111-12
Chanctonbury, 6-7, 130
Chantry of St. Mary, 97, 187-9
—— Lands, 189
Chapelier, Isabel, 109-10
Chapman, James, 71
Charles, Duke of Burgundy, 128
—— Duke of Norfolk, 42
—— Earl of Surrey, 42
—— Prince of Wales, 40
—— I., 171, 172
—— II., 131-135, 224, 227-8
Chatfield, Robert, 151
Chaunterell, William, 100-1
Cheverell, John, 96
Chichester, 9, 100, 121, 250
—— John, Bishop of, 16
Christian Society, 210-11
Cissa, 7, 9,
Cissbury, 1-4, 130
Clark, W., Tierney, 75
Clayton & Hyde, 75
Clearke, Thomas, 149
Clubb's Hall, 78
Clunas, Margaret, 193
Cobbett, Martin, R. (quoted), 256
Coby, Cobye, Henry, 96
—— Hugh, 52
—— Isabel, 51
—— John, 51
—— Lettys, 52
—— Thomas, 52
Cocket, 99-100
Cockeroost, 34, 67
Coggeshall, Richard de, 119
Cokeham, Manor of, 94
Cole, Agnes, 111-12
—— Robert, 111-12
Coleman, Robert, 95
Coles, Christopher, 139
Colet, John, 112
Collins, William, 151
Commius, 4
Comyn, Thomas, 108
Coney, William, 152
Connaught, H.R.H. The Duke of, 257
Cooke, Capt., 181
Cooke, A. S., 60
Cookson, John, 95
Copperas Gap, 249
Corbett, 251
Corner, John atte, 97
—— Roger atte, 97
Cornish, Sir Sam, 210-11, 236
Cornmarket, 95
Court Farm, 40
Covert, Sir John, 87
—— John, 217
—— Margaret, 87, 89
—— Richard, 55, 218
Cowfold, 215

Cowper, John, 16-17
Coxtyll, Thomas, 108
Crabwych, Simon, 87
Crane, John, 131
Crawle, John, 89
Crawt, the, 44
Crecy, 124
Cricket, 256-7
Cromwell, Oliver, 186
—— Thomas, 186
Crooked Moon, 44
Cross, George, 245-6
—— Leonard, 136
Crouchpreste, John le, 108
Crown and Anchor, 74
Croydon, 6
Cuckfield Park, 230-1
Cuddington, Mrs., 256
Cupola House, 77
Curteis, William, 128
Custom Houses, 143, 145-6
Cust, Peregrine, 236-7
Cuthman, St., 9-10, 12, 15
—— Port of, 10
Cymen, 7
Cymensora, 7

Dalyngrygg, Walter, 38
D'Annebault, 129-30
Dawtre, William, 39
Deane, Sir Anthony, 224-7
De Braose, Beatrix, 56
—— Joan, 56
—— John, 15, 72
—— Peter, 50, 56
—— Sir Peter, 56
—— Philip, 15, 30, 82, 164, 181, 185
—— William, 12, 35, 50, 69-70, 72, 82, 86, 94, 99, 102-3, 117, 164, 181-3, 185
Defoe, Daniel (quoted), 143
De la Folde, William, 49
Despenser, Hugh, 69, 100
Deth, Ralph, 90
Delve, Joan, 53
—— John, 96
Devil's Dyke, 6
Dix, 129
—— William, 56
Dolphin Inn, 76
Domesday Book, 35, 50
Double, Ralph, 88, 200
Douglas, Andrew, 152
—— Stair, 155
Drake, John, 123
Dyer & Son, 156
Dymocke, Thomas, 95
Dytton, Nicholas, 99, 102, 103

East India Co., 147, 148
Edburton, 199
Edmund, E. of Cornwall, 36, 37, 49, 195
Edulnebregg, John de, 110
Edward the Confessor, 12, 15, 35, 50
Edward I., 37, 100, 121
—— II., 70, 85, 94, 121-122
—— III., 50, 70, 100, 124, 127
—— VI., 53
—— VII., 181
Edwards, Brown & Olliver, 156

267

INDEX

Edwards, John, 155-6, 195
—— Tim, 154,
—— Thomas, 208
Eleanor of Provence, 120
Elgar, Sidcrik, 176
—— Mary, 176
Elizabeth, Queen, 39, 171
Ella, 7, 9
Ellerton, John de, 125
Elliott, Edward, 1st Lord, 66
Ellis, Thomas, 151
Elliston, Catherine, 66
—— Edward, 66
Ely, Guy de, 106
English, 155-6
Eppilos, 4
Erringham, Celea de, 50
—— John de, 50
—— Braose, 55, 56
—— Chapel at, 57-60
—— Manor, 35, 195
—— New, 61
—— Old, 50-60, 82
—— Shaw, 50
—— Walstead, 53, 55, 56
Esther Waters (novel), 62
Ethelwulph, King, 10
Eugenius III., 164
Evelyn, 225

Fagge, Elizabeth, 227
—— John, 224
—— Sir Robert, 227
Fairs, 72, 75, 117
Farley, Walter, 90
—— John, 90
—— Thomas, 90
Fawler, Capt. John, 176-177, 192, 201
—— John, 177
—— Mary (2), 176, 177, 192, 201
—— Thomas, 177
Fécamp, Abbey of, 12, 125
—— Abbot of, 12, 15, 30, 82, 127
Fenner, Thomas, 55, 147
Ferry, at New Shoreham, 22, 91-93
—— Old Shoreham, 40-43
—— to Beach, 81, 91
Ferur, John le, 87
—— William le, 98
Filde, Thomas, 96
Findon, 41, 111
Fishere, Roger le, 111
Fleetwood, Lieut.-Gen., 232
Fletcher, Sir Henry, 72
Florent, Abbey of, 13, 88
—— Abbot, 84, 85
Florentius, 49, 195
Football, 256-7
Foresta, Guido de, 85
Forty, Richard, 141
Foster, William, 146
Fountain Inn, 32, 76, 148, 178, 214, 245
Fowkes, John, 197
Franckelin, John le, 103
Frederick, Charles, 234
—— John, 233
—— Thomas, 233
Fredri, 50
Freland, Thomas, 191
—— Capt. William, 136

Freeman, Clement, 150
Frewyn, William, 103
Fuller, Capt., 131
Furbisher, Richard, 147
Fynian, David, 108
—— Thomas, 108, 207

Gage, James, 53
—— Sir John, 53, 64
Garston, Thomas, 96
Gascoigne, John, 127
Gate, John, 127
Gates, Clara, 79
—— Thomas, 79
—— T. B., 71
Gates, Mr., 252
Gatesden, John de, 92
Gaynesford, Nicholas, 53
Geere, Eleanor, 175
—— Elizabeth, 175
—— Richard, 175
George Inn (Brighton), 132, 133
George IV., 249
—— V., 181, 262
Germayne, Roger, 108
Gibbet Barn, 178
Gilbert, Bishop, 202
Gladstone, Mr., 198
Gloucester, Walter de, 36
Glyd, Richard, 75
Godwin, Earl, 12
Goldismark, Reg., 98
Goldsmith, William le, 98, 105
Gonshill, Elizabeth, 70
—— Sir Robert, 70
Goodchild, Edward, 252
Goode, Rev. J. E., 205
Good Friday Hill, 44, 256
Goring, Charles, 143, 212-3, 240
—— Sir C. F., 75
—— Capt., 226,
—— Family, 239-40, 41
—— George, 55
—— Sir Harry, 213-14
—— Sir Henry, 239
—— Henry, 64
—— Henry Dent, 239-40
Goringe, John de, 105-6
Gould, Cicely, 191
—— Jane, 191
—— Joan, 191
—— John, 232
—— John (jun.), 233
—— Margery, 191
—— Nathaniel, 208-9
—— Sir Nathaniel, 74, 232
—— Richard, 191
—— Sara, 191
Gower, Harry, 112
Grammar School, 78
Gras, William le, 122
Graseden, Richard, 137
Graunger, Ralph, 123
Gravesend, John, 128
Green Dam, 30
Green Lane, 29-30
Groonde, Ralph le, 108
Guldeford, Henry de, 92
Guy Fawkes Day, 254-5
Gyffard, Richard, 136-7

INDEX

Gyselham, William de, 102

Haclut, Richard, 69
Haddock, Sir Richard, 227, 228
Hagia, Bernard de, 83
Haleghton, Robert de, 111
Hall, Robert, 65
—— Dorothy, 65
Hallett, Thomas, 200
Ham Field, 34
Hamilton & Co., 154
Hammond, Anthony, 231
Hangleton, 34
Harbour, Ancient, 28-30
—— Modern, 159-63
Harcourt, Agnes, 56
—— William, 56
Harfill, William, 195
Harold, King, 12
Harper, W. H., 78
Harrald, Rev. J. H., 205
Harrys, John, 52
Hartopp, Sir John, 232
Haseline, 82
Hastings, Philip de, 84
—— Ralph, 84
—— Richard, 84
Hatch, Thomas, 197
Hayler's Mill, 201
Hayman, 155
Head, Henry, 67
Hemeri, John, 95
Henry de Sco. Walerico, 44
Henry I., 167
—— II., 116, 181
—— III., 120, 170, 171
—— IV., 39
—— V., 38, 128, 189
—— VI., 38-39
—— VII., 31
—— Prince of Wales, 38
Herrings, Herryngs, Richard, 195
—— Robert, 87
Herryngham (Hardham) Priory, 94
Hessell, Phoebe, 178, 248-9
"Hie Cakge," 90
Hobeday, Henry, 110
Hobelit (German), Germanus, 100, 106, 108
Holand, John de, 38
Holbourne, James, 154
Holmare, Owen, 189-90
Hooper family, 72, 192-3
Hooper, George Henry, 171, 192-3
—— James, 192
—— John, 177, 192
—— J. B., 192
—— Robert, 176, 192
—— Robert, Poole, 193
—— Thomas Poole, 192, 201
Hoore, Thomas, 128
Horsham, 19, 213
Horsley, Gilbert, 129
Horton, Adam de, 48
—— William de, 48
Hospitallers (see Knight's Hospitallers)
Howard, Lord Edward, 240
—— Henry, 214
—— Lord William, 74
Howell, Edward, 178
Huklesmouth, 19, 92

Hungerford, Sir Edward, 228-9
Hunt, John, 96
Hyda, Roger de, 91-92
Hyde, Joan de la, 92
—— Walter, 92

Ifeld, Philip de, 106
Irish, William le, 105
Iryngham (see Erringham)
Isabel, Prioress of Ruspar, 63
Isemonger, Arnald le, 103
—— Ernald le, 98
Ivory, John, 106

Jackson, Elizabeth, 191
—— Richard, 191
—— Robert, 191
—— Thomas, 191
James I., 74, 171
—— II., 141, 227
—— Wiilliam, 210
Jay, Richard, 89, 90
Jenan ap Rhiryd, 182
Joan, Princess of Wales, 38
Jocelin, 195
John, Duke of Norfolk, 15
—— King, 35, 36, 91, 117-119, 182
—— Prince, 116
Johnson, Cornelius, 128
Jones, Inigo, 149, 220-221
Jordan, 84
Jordan, Peter, 98
Judde, John, 108, 111
Juxon, John, 56
—— Sir William, 56

Katharine the Fair, 38
Kent, Thomas de, 199
Kilvington, Henry Medley, 193
Killingworth, John, 174
—— Thomas, 151
King, Edward, 83
King's Arms Inn, 76, 201, 208
—— Barns, 12
—— Head Inn, 76, 214
King Charles' Cottage, 133
King, Matthew le, 108
Kingston Church, 33, 34
Kingston-Bowsey (Kington-by-Sea), 32, 65, 143, 146
Kingswoode, John, 87
Kitchener's Boys, 259-61
Knauc, John de la, 87
Knepp Castle, 254
Knights Hospitallers, 26, 83-5
—— Templars, 83-6, 88
Kynor, 7

Lacey, Walter de, 118
Laines, 44
Lancing, 22, 41, 142, 170
Lancing Clump, 6
—— College, 202-3, 259
—— Downs, 2, 5, 177
Larchier, Thomas, 86
Lawrence, 131
—— Edward, 141
Lawn, Molly, 248
Laxman, William, 88
Leake, Andrew, 151

269

INDEX

"Leather Hunter," 256
Ledham Quarter, 189
Leedes, Bridget, 220
—— Sir John, 131, 220
—— Thomas, 220
Le Millhouse, 189
Lenchlade, William, 127
Lennox, Lord Alexander, 211
Leonibus, Petrus de, 117
Lewes, 6, 34
—— Prior of, 19, 91-2
—— John, 55
Lewis of France, 119
Lewkenor, Edward, 64
—— Sir Edward, 219
—— Margaret, 189
—— Richard, 64
—— Sir Richard, 217
—— Lady Susan, 219
Lewsley, Thomas, 174
Lichpole, A. de, 92
Light House, 161
Lincoln, 114-116
Lindon, Robert, 88
Lisle, Admiral John, 129-30
Little, Bickingham, 34, 44, 47, 67
Lladloes, 77
Lloyd, Sir James, 75
—— Richard, 209
Loader, Arthur, 254
Local Government, 71-2
Loder, Sir E. G., 244
—— G. W. E., 244
—— Sir Robert, 244
London Bridge, 6
Longcroft, 78, 191
Longstaff, A. E., 257
Lote, John, 85
—— Matilda, 85, 86
Loudeneys, Robert, 123
Louis XIV., 226
Lucas, E. V., 158
Luffard, Humbald, 118
Luttrell (quoted), 231

Mabbot, Thomas, 152
Magdalen College, 16, 88, 165
Mahun, Isabel, 111
—— John, 111
Mall Robbery, 178
"Malappynnys," "Malduppynne" (see Marlipins)
Malt House Lane, 42
Manning, Cardinal, 198
Mannyngfield, Simon, 127
Manor House, 145
Mansiot, Rich. de, 103
Mardyke Bank, 31
Margaret, Countess of Cornwall, 37, 38
Markets, 72-74
Market Houses, 74
—— Charter, 74
—— Place, 74, 95, 96
"Marlipins," 94-97
Marlott (see Merlott)
Marshall, Henry, 89
Martin, Edward, 201
Martyn, John, 95
Mary, Queen, 262
Mason, Rachel, 175

Masonic Lodges, 257
Maude, Rev. Joseph,
—— Mary Fawler, 193
—— de Temple, 84
—— de Valerie, 183
Mayhewe, John, 127
May & Thwaites, 157
—— (Brodnax), Thomas, 66
May, W., 156
Meads, 28, 29
Mercer, Ed., 191
Merlott, William, 174, 222
Mersh, John, 90
—— William, 90
Mervyn, Sir Henry, 137
Middleton, George, Vis., 234-5
—— Henry, 152
Military Barracks, 194
—— Camp, 259-62
Mill Hill, 44
—— Lane, 33, 34, 44, 78
Minter, Robert, the, 83
"Moderlove Strete," 95-96-97
Moigne, William, 69
Monk, Barbara, 65-66
—— Hannah, 65-66
—— Jane, 65-66
—— John, 65
—— Susannah, 65
—— William, 65
Monmouth, Duke of, 226
Montague, F., 213
Montfort, Simon de, 120
Moore, Sir Ralph, 77
Moorey, John, 246-9
—— Alice, 248
More, John, 149
Morley, John, 219
Morrison, O. C., 258
Mossy Bottom, 62
Mowbray family, 70
—— Alina, 69-70
—— John, Duke of Norfolk, 70
—— Sir John, 25, 26, 51, 69, 73, 86, 87, 100
—— Thomas, Duke of Norfolk, 70
Mounier, Adam le, 110
Mourant, Thomas, 87, 125
Mozley, Rev. James, B., 198
Muggridge, Widow, 77
Mulsham, Gilbert de, 195
Must, John, Richard, Stephen, 108
Mutuantonis, 6
Mutenir, Robert le, 118
Mylles, Thomas, 189, 200
"Mystery" Ships, 158

New Barns Lane, 78
New Erringham, 61-2
New Salts, 257
—— Shoreham High Constable, 71, 75
—— Local Government, 71
—— Manor, 69-71
—— Town Crier, 71
—— Town Hall, 72
—— Urban District, 72
Nicholas, 89
—— IV., 164
—— de Bedinges, 87, 89
—— Edward, 136-138
—— Sir Edward, 149

270

INDEX

Niger, Robert, 119
Norfolk Bridge, 22, 75, 81
Norfolk, Duke of, 71, 75
Northbourne Stream, 28, 29, 30, 189
Northou, Christine, 199
—— Olyve, 199
—— William, 106, 199
Norton, Sir Fletcher, 211
—— Henry, 38
—— J. B., 146
Nyman, 51

O'Hara, Capt. John, 176-7
—— Susan, 176-7
O'Hara, John, 68
Old Erringham, 50-60
Old George Inn, 76, 176
Oter, Robert, 34
"Otmarcat" (Oat-market), 95
Old St. Paul's, 149-50
Old Shipyard, 76, 156
Old Shoreham Bridge, 15, 34, 42, 177
—— Church, 164,-177
—— Ferry, 39-42
—— Manor, 35-42
—— Ruspar, 63
Ongley, Samuel, 232-3
Ormonde, Earl of, 224
Ouse River, 6, 25
"Owlers," 101
Oxenbridge, Robert, 19
Oxen Field, 257, 260
Oyster Fishery, 161-2

Page, Gregory, 209
—— Sir Gregory, 231-2
Panethorne, Hugh, 108
—— John, 108
—— William, 108
Parliamentary History, 207-244
Parrant, Henry, 136
Parsons, John, 191
Pashley, Cecil and Eric, 258-9
Paston, Robert, 153
Pastoreaux Invasion, 120
Paterlyng, Thomas, 126
Payne, Captain Charles, 155
Paynell, John, 94
—— Margaret, 92
—— Matilda, 94
—— William, 92, 94
Paxton, Wentworth, 153
Paynter, Thomas, 136
Peachey, John, 213, 237
Peacock Hill, 171
Pearson, Thomas, 62
Peleter, John le, 98
Pelham, Ernest, 155
Pende, 22, 124, 127-128
Penney, R. H., 158
Pennington, Capt., John, 149
Penton, 178
Pepys, Samuel, 224-6
Perchyng, J. de, 108
Percur, Richard le, 98
Perry, John, 193, 209
Peshale, Richard de, 106
Pevense, Alexander, 34
—— John de, 106
Pevensey Castle, 111

Peverell, Andrew, 89
Philip, King of France, 116
Piepowder, Court of, 74
Pitfard, H. H., 258
Pilcher, Godfrey le, 98
Piracy, 121, 122, 125-126, 127, 128
Plumby, Robert, 150
Plunkett, Capt. Thomas, 172
Polstede, Henry, 189
Pontoyse, Thomas, 207
Poole family, 171-77
—— Eleanor, 176, 177
—— Elizabeth (2), 175, 176
—— Ellen, (Hellen), 174, 175, 176
—— "Faint-not," 174
—— Faith, 174
—— Fanny, 174
—— John (2), 175, 176
—— Lodovick, 176
—— Mary (Fawler), 176
—— Rachel, 175
—— Richard (2), 171-76
—— Thomas (3), 171, 172, 174, 175, 176, 177, 194
—— Susan (O'Hara), 176, 177
—— William, 175, 176
Portslade, 6
Portus, Adurni, 5, 6
Pottere, John le, 95, 98
Pownall, Philemon, 154
Poynings, Lord de, 63
—— Sir Michael, 88
—— Robert, 128
Praty, Bishop, 16
"Prede," 95, 97
Preston, 7
Priestman, Capt. Henry, 229-30
Privateering, 136-141
"Procession Strete," 95-96
Puffare, Puffer, Robert, 106, 207
Pulborough, 225
Purfote, John, 128
Puuling, John, 210
Pynson, Alexander, 127

Quartermain, William, 223-4

Railway, 249-50
Randolph, Isabel, 19
Ranger, W., 75
Ravenscroft, 78, 194
Rede, Bishop Robert, 88
Red Lion Inn, 67, 178, 179, 256
Regatta, 254
Reginald of Cornhill, 118
—— the Smith, 98
Regni Tribe, 4, 5
Regnum, 4, 6, 9
Religious Houses, 82-90
Renham, Thomas de, 199
Richard, Earl of Arundel, 113
—— Earl of Cornwall, 36
—— I., 116, 117, 182
—— II., 38
Rizpah, 179
Roberts, Bartholomew, 178
—— Capt., 179-81
—— Hugh, 77, 155, 210-11
—— John, 146
—— John O., 146

271

INDEX

Roberts, Richard, 177
Robbyn, John, 128
Robyn, Thomas, 124
Rocelin de Fos, 85
Rolle, Richard, 96
Rooke, James, 178
Ropewalk, 155-6
Ross, Alexander, 193
—— John, 193
Royal George Inn, 214
" Royal Oak " (Drama), 132
Rumbold, Thomas, 210-237
Ruspar, Manor of, 63
—— Priory, 63
—— Prioress, 63
Russell, John, 129
Rye, 131
Ryman, Elizabeth, 38-39
—— William, 38
Rymund, Adam, 50
Ryver, Arnald de, 100

St. Alban's Abbey, 114
St. Avory, Michael, 141
St. Cuthman, 9, 10, 12, 15
——Port of, 10, 30
St. Florent, Abbey of, 84, 88, 164
St. James, Hospital of, 89-90
—— Croft, 90
St. John's Common, 6
St. John Street, 85-86, 97
St. Lo, Ed, 153
St. Katherine, Hospital of, 89-90
St. Mary (de Haura), 15, 164, 168, 171, 181-194
St. Mary's Cottage, 185
—— Hall, 72, 257
—— Hospital, Chichester, 83
St. Nicholas, Bramber, 13, 15, 164, 168
—— Brighton, 169
—— of Myra, 168-9, 171, 203
—— Old Shoreham, 13, 15, 35, 164-171
—— Portslade, 169
St. Paul's, Cathedral of, 149
St. Peter de Veteriponte, 13, 15
—— Sele, 13, 15
St. Peter's (R.C.) Church, 206
—— Richard, 168, 170-1
St. Saviour's College, 202
—— Hall, 202
—— Hospital, 89
St. Wilfrid, 9, 168-70
Sable Island, 157
Saddlescombe, 6, 84, 85
Sancta Fide, Ralph de, 126
Sanctiary, 109-12
Salisbury, Lord, 177
Saltings, 39
Sansom, John, 141
Saracenus, 185
Saunders, George, 151
Sayers, Tom, 252
Scherington, Simon, 149
Schools, 78-79
Schooner Inn, 214
Scot, Cicely, 44
—— Thomas, 44
Scras, Tuppyn, 136, 223
—— Capt., William, 136, 137-8
Scullie, John, 127

Scurvy Bank, 31
Seaford, 25, 129
Sele, Prior of, 16, 63
—— Priory of, 13, 15, 16, 72, 82, 88, 89, 164, -5, 185, 195
Selina, Countess of Huntingdon, 146
Sessylt ap Dynswald, 182
Serle, Maud, 94
—— Richard, 87, 94
Sergison, Charles, 230-1
Seven Acres, 78
Seville, 121
Seymour, Sir Thomas, 53, 71
Sexton, G. F., 257
Sharpe, John, 95
Shelder, John, 189
Shelley, Sir John, 212-3, 237
—— Sir Timothy, 238-9
—— George, 53
—— John, 53
—— Margaret, 56
—— Richard, 53
Sherman, Stephen, 112
Shipbuilding, 147-158
Shipley, 84
Shipwrights' Arms, 32, 148
Ship Inn, 76, 201

SHIPS—
Alysetta, 123
Ann and Sarah, 149
Antelope, 229
Arbutus, 229
Arundel, 152
Athol, 162
Bark Fenner, 147
Barthelemewe, 127
Bartholomew, 191
Blackwell, 152
Blessing, of Dover, 149
Bonaventure, 129
Brighton Queen, 163
Britannia, 157
Charles, 149
Comte de Hunebourg, 155
Confident, 149
Conflagration, 155
Content, 149
Courier, 155
Greteshade, 158
Cretestream, 158
Cretestyle, 158
Cretewheel, 158
Crystofre, of Gypswold 127
Discovery, 172
Dispatch, 154
Dolphin, 136, 138
Dover, 150-1, 152
Drake, 173
Duc de Broglie, 154
Dunwich, 152, 153
Esperance, 151
Falcon, 152
Favourite, 154
Feversham, 153
Fortune, 136
Fowey, 153
Fox, 151
Francis, 151
Francis, of Bordeaux, 173

INDEX

Garland, 149
Gosport, 153
Grouzard, 154
Hampton Court, 229
Hastings, 152
Heros, 155
Hopewell, 151
Hound, 154
Hound (Rev. Cutter), 144
Indeavour, 149
Joan Bonaventure, 149
John Miles, 162
Joseph, of London, 149
Kingston, 159
La Feroa, 151
La George, 125
La Jonette, 123
La Laurence, 124
La Margarete, 122-127
La Messager, 123
La Nicholas, 124
L'Egalite, 155
L'Hirondelle, 155
Lark, 229
Lion (2), 137, 151
Ludlow Castle, 153
Lynn, 153
Magnanime, 236
Margaret Speedwell, 147
Mary, 191
Mary and John, 149
Matthew, 155
" Mystery " Ships, 158
Newport, 153
Nimble, Cutter, 143
Orford, 153
Pendennis, 152
Penzance, 152
Peter, 136, 171
Peter, of Conquet, 138
—— of Dunkirk, 136-7
Pheasant, 155
Pomona, 143
Republicain, 155
Reserve, 229
Revenge, 151
Richard and Thomas, 174
Richmond, 229
Rose of Conquet, 138
Royal James, 227-8
St. John of Dieppe, 139-141
—— St. Joseph, 155
St. Mary, of Bayonne, 121
—— of Shoreham, 121
St. Marie, of Shoreham, 123
—— of Winchelsea, 122
St. Michael, 138
St. Peter, 136
Sanspareil, 155
San Salvador, 152
Scorpion, 155
Seaford, 154
Sea Horse, 137, 171
Shoreham, 151
Sorlings, 152
Stork, 154
Spy, 155
Swan, 229
Tenth Lion's Whelp, 149
Terrible, 152

Thomas Bonaventure, 149
Thomas & John, 149
Trench-le-Mer, 117
Trinity, 128
Tropard, 155
Valeur, 155
Vauban, 151
Vesuvius, 152
Victoire, 155
Volland, 152
Vulcan, 155
" William Restall " Lifeboat, 159

Shirley, Barbara, 219
—— Elizabeth, 218
—— Francis, 218-19
—— Joan, 53
—— Ralph, 52
—— Sir Thomas, 55, 56, 218
—— Thomas, 192
Shoeburyness, 122
Shoreham Gap, 142
—— Half-penny, 75
—— Marsh, 39
—— River, 5
—— Shoreham Shilling, 75
Shovell, Clowdesley, 150-1
Shuttleworth's Yard, 158
Simon de Montford, 120
—— de Ponte, 110
Simon of Tarring, 170
" Single Brains," 248
Slonk Hill, 7, 34, 259
Smirke, Sidney, 146
Smith, Capt. Cornelius, 193
—— Francis, 197
Smuggling, 60, 78, 141-5, 249
Snellyng, William, 125
Sompting, 9, 41, 170
Sompting Peverell, 56
Sopere, John le, 98
Sonde, Pauline, 51
—— Richard, 51
Sore, 5
Sourale, Hamo, 98
Souter, Simon le, 98
Southwick, 32, 90, 161
" Sowterystrete," 97-98
Sparham, Stephen de, 119
Springett, Sir Herbert, 56, 223, 224
—— Mary, 56
—— Sir Thomas, 56, 223
Spurgeon, Rev. C. H., 205
Stane Street, 6
Stapleton, Richard, 88
Stapley, Anthony, 221-2
Star Inn, 42, 76, 159, 160, 209-10, 245-246
Star Lane Chapel, 205
Stacy, Ralph, 106
Starry Clover, 177
Steam Packets, 162
—— Tram, 251
Stempe, John, 95
Stephenson, John, 178
Stevens, William, 77
Steward, Charles Edward, 201
—— John Mainwaring (Bishop), 201
Steyning, 5, 10, 12, 30, 130, 131, 135, 141, 154
Stock, William de la, 63

273

INDEX

Stone & Bartlett, 154
Stonegate, 30, 78
Stone, the, 215
Stone House, 78, 215
Stow, Thomas, 81
Stretton, Roger de, 19
Stringer, Stephen, 65
Suffolk, Thomas, Earl of, 74
Sugden, E. B., 214
Surrey, Earl of, 53, 213
Sussex Pad, 42, 142, 245
Swainson, Robert, 149
Swele, John, 108
Swinburne (quoted), 186
Swiss Gardens, 28, 29, 156, 249, 252-4
Sysson, Richard, 197,200

Tabler, Robert, 98
—— Thomas, 98
Tarmount, 27
Tarring, 130, 170
Tate, Thomas, 195
Tattersall, Capt., 133
Taverner, Elias, 106
—— Nicholas, 106
Taylor, S. Gregory, 78
Taylur, Nicholas, 48-49, 98
—— Maud, 48, 49
Templars (see Knights Templars)
Temple, Capt., James, 131
Temple, the, 85, 86-87
Templestead, 87
Tester, William, 103
Thaccher, Thomas, 96
Thomas, James, 128
Three Houses, 78
Thunders Barrow, 7
Tincommius, 4, 5
Tilstone, Joseph, 155
—— Thomas, 155
Tipteerers, 255-6
Tower, Rev. C. M. A. 194, 202
Town Hall, 177
Tramway, 251
Tranckmore, John, 149
—— Nicholas, 149
—— Robert, 32, 148-9, 192
Tregol, Robert, 48
Trenchmere, Alan, 84, 117,
—— Simon, 87
—— William, 84
Trenchnote, William, 83
—— Trinity House Certifs., 148-9
Trower, Thomas, 96
Tufton, Cecil, 56
Tunstall, Nicholas, 100
—— Sir Richard, 52
Tutting, Richard de, 103
Tyndale, Rev. E. F. G., 201
Tyrrell, Admiral, 130

Ulnare, the Clerk, 185
Urban District, 72
Urban III., 164
Urlin, John, 41

Van Ghent, 227

Veel, Hawlse, 94
——Robert, 94
Verica, 4, 5
Vezin, Herman, 252
Vicars of Old and New Shoreham, 195-202
Victoria, Queen, 181
Vyvian, William, 100, 106, 122, 123

Wade, Mr. 143
Wakehurst, Richard, 19.
Walkstede, Walter, 51
Waller, Sir William, 221
Walsteedes, 56
Wappingthorne, 131, 239
Warminghurst, 82, 127
Water Mills, 29, 33, 44, 46, 47
Waynflete John, 128
Waynefleet, Bishop, 16, 88
Wayte, Amicia de, 88
Wells, Walter de, 117
Wenceling, 7
West Blatchington, 7, 136
West Richard, de la Warr, 128
—— Thomas, de la Warr, 64, 71
—— William, Lord de la Warr, 56
West, Walter, 192
Western, Thomas, 155
Weston, Thomas de, 106-8, 121
Wheeler, William, 198, 201, 206
Whitaker, Edward, 151
White Lion Street, 76
—— Inn, 76
Wicker, Mr., 209
—— John, 231
Wilfrid, St., 9, 168-70
Willshire, Joan, 52
William of Arundel, 83
—— the Conqueror, 12, 82, 164
William III. and Mary, 191
William, Prince of Orange, 150
William IV., 179-80
Williams, Sir William Peere, 159, 235-6
—— Rice, 201
Willoughby, Capt., Fraser, 150
Wilmot, Lord, 133
Wilson, Henry, 189
—— Owen, 189
Windmills, 44, 46, 47
Winterton, Earl, 81
Winton, Fanny, 42
Wiston, William de, 56
Wodemer, John, 105-6
Wody, John, 19
Woodard, Rev. Nathaniel, 202-3
Wood, John, 141
—— Robert, 197, 200
Wool Cocket, 99, 101
Wool Export, 99-101
Worthing, 7. 250
Woxebrugg, Walter, 207
Wyka, Roger de, 84
Wylughby, Richard de, 106
Wyndham, Charles William, 213-4
Wynton, William de, 111

Young, Agnes, 108 John le, 108

COUNTRY BOOKS

Country Books is a small independent publisher producing reprints of scarce and out-of-print classics on Sussex.

BLACK'S 1861 GUIDE TO SUSSEX Incorporating 1859 Breads's guide to Worthing and a description of the Miller's Tomb on Highdown Hill

Facsimile of the South-Eastern Counties of England series and comprises 184 pages. There is a folding map of the county and steel engravings of the chain pier at Brighton, Hastings and Chichester Cathedral. Major towns are covered as well as the smaller villages.
Paperback 210 x 148mm 276 pages Engravings and folding map
2000 Country Books ISBN 1 898941 21 1 Price **£8.95**

SHEPHERDS OF SUSSEX by Barclay Wills

Written as the last shepherds were disappearing from the rural scene, with notes on Michael Bland, John Dudeney, etc. Foreword by the Duke of Norfolk. The hill shepherd; lure of the shepherd's work; a character study of Sussex shepherds; shepherds of bygone days; the shepherd's possessions; crooks & bells; shearing; sheep washing, marking & watering; dew-ponds; Sussex sheep; the crow-scarer, etc. A facsimile of the first edition published c1933 by Skeffington.
185 x 125mm 280 pages 28 B&W photos
2001 Country Books Hardback ISBN 1 898941 60 2 Price **£20.00**
Paperback ISBN 1 898941 67 X Price **£8.95**

SMUGGLING AND SMUGGLERS IN SUSSEX by 'A gentleman of Chichester'

The inhuman and unparalleled murders of Mr William Galley, a customs house officer, and Mr Daniel Chater, a shoemaker, fourteen notorious smugglers, with the trials and execution of seven of the criminals at Chichester 1748-9. Trials of John Mills and Henry Sheerman; and the trials at large of Thomas Kingsmill for breaking open the Custom House at Poole; also an article on 'Smuggling in Sussex' by William Durrant Cooper, Esq.
Hardback 185 x 125mm 280 pages Engravings
2001 Country Books ISBN 1 898941 61 0 Price **£20.00**

THE HISTORY AND ANTIQUITIES OF HORSHAM by Howard Dudley

This is a facsimile of one of the rarest topographical books on Sussex, first published in 1836 by a sixteen-year-old schoolboy.
Illustrated with lithographs and wood engravings, the book covers the market town of Horsham and the surrounding villages of Rusper, Warnham, Roffy, Nuthurst, Itchingfield, Slinfold and Rudgwick.
The contents include: the parish church, the county gaol, the Independent's chapel, the Wesleyan chapel, Collier's School, the National School, the Royal British Schools, the great houses and estates, the dragon in St Leonard's Forest, a list of Horsham inns, details of coaches, plants found in the area, fossils, population, roads, Horsham fairs, etc.
Published in paperback size: 190 x 125mm 112 pages
2001 Country Books ISBN 1 898941 72 6 Price: **£9.50**

A DICTIONARY OF THE SUSSEX DIALECT by Rev WD PARISH
The dictionary was first published in 1875 by the vicar of Selmeston, the Rev WD Parish. He also recorded provincialisms in use in the county at that time. This new edition is augmented by further pieces on the Sussex dialect, traditional recipes, and a mumming play from West Wittering from the writings of EV Lucas, who died in 1938. Illustrated throughout with line drawings of Sussex views made in the late 19th and early 20th centuries by Frederick L Griggs, ARA.
Paperback 220 x 150mm) portrait 192 pages 70 line drawings
2001 Country Books ISBN 1 898941 68 8 Price **£7.50**

THEY WROTE ABOUT SUSSEX
A Collection of Biographical Sketches by Richard Knowles
This volume provides biographical sketches of the authors of these works, highlighting how they were connected with the county. Some of the writers were, as one might expect, born and bred in Sussex, but some came to the county as children, some came later in life and one was only ever a visitor. Some were concerned to record a local way of life that was disappearing and some sought to uncover the past, while others simply celebrated their emotional attachment to the county by trying to explain what made it so special for them.
Paperback 210 x 148mm 126 pages with line illustrations by the author
2003 Country Books ISBN 1 898941 81 5 Price **£7.95**

SUSSEX IN FICTION A Collection of Biographical Sketches by Richard Knowles
The number of novels that are at least partly set in the county continues to rise, but in most cases the local background is purely incidental to the narrative. The objective in researching this book has been to identify those for which Sussex settings have some real relevance. He also seeks to say something about the authors and how they were connected with the county. The only Sussex novelists that can truly described as 'regional' are Tickner Edwardes and Sheila Kaye-Smith and it is interesting to note that both were compared with Thomas Hardy in their day.
Paperback 210 x 148mm 196 pages with line illustrations by the author
2003 Country Books ISBN 1 898941 82 3 Price **£8.95**

HANGED FOR A SHEEP: BYGONE CRIME IN SUSSEX by Dick Richardson
This book surveys crime and the treatment of criminals in bygone Sussex, illustrated with extracts from late 18th century copies of the Sussex Weekly Advertiser, the county's first weekly newspaper.. "You may as well be hanged for a sheep as a lamb."The saying dates back to the days when sheeep-stealing was punishable by death. For stealing a lamb you would be "hanged by the neck until you were dead." The same punishment was meted out for stealing a sheep, so you ran no greater risk for stealing the more valuable article. (This law was repealed in 1828.)
CONTENTS: CONFIDENCE TRICKSTERS · DUELS · FOOTPADS AND HIGHWAYMAN · KEEPING LAW AND ORDER PRISONS · PUNISHMENTS SERIOUS CRIME · SMUGGLERS · THEFT ·
INDEX OF SURNAMES · INDEX OF PLACE-NAMES
Paperback size: 210 x 148mm 80 pages. Engravings, woodcuts and photographs.
2003 County Books ISBN 1 898941 85 8 Price **£6.95**

OUR SUSSEX PARISH by Thomas Geering
Arthur Beckett declared that *Our Parish* by Thomas Geering was his favourite Sussex book, first published in 1884. Thomas Geering was born in Hailsham in 1813 and lived his whole life in the town. His father, also Thomas Geering, came from Alfriston where he had begun his working life as a shepherd's boy and a ploughboy before becoming a shoemaker. In November 1812 he married Elizabeth Holman, the eldest daughter of a yeoman of Hellingly, in the Ebenezer Chapel at Alfriston and in the following year they moved to Hailsham. Most of the pieces that make up this book first appeared in the columns of a country newspaper. *The Old Sussex Bookseller,* has never appeared in book form and was first printed in the *Sussex County Magazine* 1927. 16 photographs.
Paperback size: 210 x 148mm 232 pages
2003 Country Books ISBN 1 898941 83 1 Price: **£9.95**

THE HISTORY OF DITCHLING IN THE COUNTY OF SUSSEX
by Henry Cheale, Jun.
Facsimile of the first edition of 1901. An invaluable document for those searching their family tree. Alfred the Great and Catherine of Aragon both owned manors in the village. On the basis of this, the author believed that the king spent much time here and that "Wings Place" or the "Old House" is a fragment of a palace built by Queen Catherine! Ignoring these flights of fancy, the book is otherwise thoroughly researched. Contents include: Ancient Ditchling and the manors, Ditchling Park, old inhabitants, miscellaneous notes, St Margaret's Church, rectors and vicars, monumental inscriptions and memorials, the Meeting House, the 'Jernal' of a Ditchling man, and the neighbourhood. Subsidy rolls 1378-9 for Ditchling, Strete Hundred 1549, Ditchling 1562, 1600, 1623, Ditchling wills at Lewes 1541-1640, Ditchling administrators 1578-1640, Ditchling Churchwardens 1638-1750. The appendices include: family trees of the Chatfield family, the Attrees of Wivelsfield and the Pooles.
Paperback 183 x 125mm 184 pages. 12 illustrations by Arthur B Packham.
2004 Country Books ISBN 1 898941 89 0 Price: **£9.95**

THE MISTRESS OF STANTONS FARM by Marcus Woodward
First published 1938. Sussanah Hooker was born in 1814 at Smallfield Place, Surrey. She married Mr Stacey of Stantons and ruled her household at East Chiltington with a rod of iron. She died in 1893 and is buried at Westmeston in East Sussex. There is an introduction by Arthur Beckett. Contents include: Receipts for Food for the Poor, Life at the Farm, Directions to Servants, Ornaments for Grand Entertainments, The Doctor, The Squire, The Parson, Grandma, the Sorceror, Pickles, Preserves and Candies, Grandma's Herb Garden, Vegetables and Herbs, Rural Worthies, Cullis, Sauces and Eggs, Grandma holds her Court, Distilling Cordial Waters, The Good Things of Sussex, Puddings and Savouries, etc., Wine-Making Day, Home-made wines, Punches, etc., A Tale of a Wash-Tub, Family Receipts, Baking Day, Baked Puddings, etc., The Household Gods, Necessary Knowledge, Christmas Gambols, Creams and Syllabubs, The Sign of the Old Thatch, Buns, Black Caps, and Snow Balls, etc.
Paperback 210 x 148mm 187 pages. Black and white photosgraphs
2004 Country Books ISBN 1 898941 88 2 Price: **£9.95**

RECOLLECTIONS OF A SUSSEX PARSON by Rev. Edward Boys Ellman
First published 1912. Edward Boys Ellman was born in 1815 and was rector of Berwick, East Sussex, for sixty years. A keen observer of life and people, this is a fascinating portrait of life in a small village in the 19th century. Among other humourous incidents is the installation of the barrel organ in the church – that insisted on playing secular tunes, and the lady in Lewes, who asked the shopkeeper to trim a yard off the bottom of a dress while she saved up for it! He died on 22nd February 1906. Index of surnames and place-names.
Paperback 210 x 148mm 269 pages. Photographs and line drawings.
2004 Country Books ISBN 1 898941 87 4 Price: **£9.95**

A SOUTHDOWN FARM IN THE 1860's by Maude Robinson of Saddlescombe
Maude Robinson was born in May 1859 at Saddlescombe where her father, Martin Robinson, had a 900-acre farm. Her childhood was idyllic and she wrote an account of it that appeared in the *Sussex County Magazine* in 1935. *A South Down Farm in the Sixties* was issued by J.M. Dent in 1938. The book provides many interesting insights into agricultural practices she also explains what home life was like on a farm in such a secluded situation. In 1872 Maude Robinson went to a private boarding school at Lewes. The school regime was Spartan but the mistresses were kindly and a good education was provided. One by one the older Robinson children moved away from Saddlescombe until, after the death of her parents, only Ernest, who ran the farm, and Maude remained. Both of them loved the downland and took an interest in its wildlife.
Paperback 210 x 148mm 82 pages 19 photos
2004 Country Books ISBN 1 898941 93 9 Price **£8.50**

Titles for Spring 2005
THE COUNTRYMAN'S JEWEL: DAYS IN THE LIFE OF A SIXTEENTH CENTURY SUSSEX SQUIRE Edited by Marcus Woodward
Facsimile of the first edition of 1934. The life of Leonard Mascall of Plumpton Place.
Paperback 210 x 148mm 330 pages
2005 Country Books ISBN 1 898941 97 1 Price **£14.50**

SUSSEX FOLK AND SUSSEX WAYS by Rev John Coker Egerton
Taekn from the 1923 edition with a foreword by Seila Kaye-Smith. First published 1884, the author was rector of Burwash in the 19th century. 8 photos.
Paperback 210 x 148mm 192 pages
2005 Country Books ISBN 1 89894198 X Price **£9.95**

THE STORY OF SHOREHAM by Henry Cheal
Facsimile of the first edition of 1921.
Paperback 200 x 138mm 286 pages
2005 Country Books ISBN 1 898941 96 3 Price **£14.50**

THE SUSSEX RECIPE BOOK Edited by Dick Richardson
Recipes from a medieval manuscript from Arundel Castle, Susannah Stacey of East Chiltington and other 19th century sources. Engravings.
Paperback 210 x 148mm
2005 Country Books ISBN 1 898941 99 8 Price **£9.95**